The Role of Civilian Police in Peacekeeping: 1999–2007

by Garth den Heyer

P POLICE FOUNDATION

Washington, DC

For information about using Police Foundation copyrighted material, please visit http://www.policefoundation.org/content/copyright-information.

Police Foundation
1201 Connecticut Avenue NW
Washington, DC 20036-2636
(202) 833-1460
(202) 659-9149 fax
pfinfo@policefoundation.org
www.policefoundation.org

ISBN 978-1-884614-09-5 (paper)
ISBN 978-1-884614-13-2 (mobi)
ISBN 978-1-884614-15-6 (epub)

Library of Congress Control Number: 2012947130

This research was funded by the United States Institute of Peace grant number USIP-074-09F. The opinions, findings, and conclusions or recommendations expressed in this publication are those of the author(s) and do not necessarily reflect the views of the United States Institute of Peace.

The Role of Civilian Police in Peacekeeping: 1999–2007 is available at www.policefoundation.org.

COVER PHOTOS: Courtesy of the United Nations by photographers (in descending photo order) Marco Dormino, Marco Dormino, Fred Noy, Martine Perret, Martine Perret, and Logan Abassi. BACK COVER: Fred Noy.

For Neville Bradbury Matthews (1952–2011)

Contents

Figures

Maps

Tables

Contents

Foreword

The role of police officers in peacekeeping missions has expanded considerably since their inclusion in the first United Nations mission to the Congo in July 1960. The role of the police in that deployment was to assist the Congo government in maintaining law and order while the Belgian military withdrew from the country.

Since that mission, the role of police has evolved—in unison with the evolution of peacekeeping—from one of monitoring the democratic election process to one of providing law enforcement services and of assisting with reform and reorganization of police services in post-conflict countries. Two of the biggest changes for police in peacekeeping occurred in the late 1990s with the advent of executive policing, which involved international police being responsible for local policing and for undertaking capacity development of indigenous police services.

Coinciding with those changes, academics and practitioners have confirmed that the post-conflict role of police is of great importance and that police are necessary to provide the fundamentals for nation building. In parallel, the complexity of peacekeeping missions has changed the role that police play from one of mentoring the post-conflict nation's police service to one of (a) developing institutional police capacity, (b) supporting reform, and (c) restructuring and rebuilding local police (Hills, 2009; Murtaugh, 2010). The United Nations and the European Union have had to ensure that they had the administrative, strategic, and political structures in place to plan, de-

ploy, support, and manage large comprehensive missions that comprise both police and military goals and objectives that address such changes.

The United Nations recognized the change in the police peacekeeping environment when it created a police adviser position in the mid-1990s. The position included responsibility for advising the Department of Peacekeeping Operations about police-related matters. The significance of the police adviser was increased further on May 15, 2000, with the establishment of the Civilian Police Unit within the Department's Military and Civilian Police Division.

The Civilian Police Unit's core functions included the following:

- Prepare plans for the police components of field missions, monitor their implementation, and revise them as necessary.
- Develop civilian police guidelines and standing operating procedures for field missions.
- Establish a liaison with member states in regard to (a) the identification and deployment of civilian police officers to field missions, (b) the operational requirements of the mission, and (c) the related personnel and administrative issues.

As a result of the change in emphasis and the complexity of missions, the existing institutional framework is now being tested. More than 12,500 United Nations police now exist who are from more than 90 countries and are deployed on 17 different field missions. New ways of thinking about how police are deployed, what their role is during deployment, how they undertake their duties, and how their performance is measured is needed because of the scale and comprehensiveness of modern missions.

The first step in understanding how to best assist post-conflict nations in the rule of law context is to understand the role of police in peacekeeping. The second step is to ensure that the service the police are delivering is meeting the requirements of the local government. The final step is identifying police officers who have the appropriate level of skill for the mission and then ensuring that they understand what their role in the mission is, how the mission is to be achieved, and how their performance will be measured.

The findings from this study may assist police planners, practitioners, and researchers who are part of a widening audience that has an interest in the role of police in post-conflict or underdeveloped nations. The study fills a vacuum in previous research about how peacekeeping missions were planned, managed, and evaluated from the police perspective, and it takes the findings from 23 peacekeeping missions and develops a dynamic new police peacekeeping model that may be used in such situations.

The proposed model is comprehensive but simple and easily understood. It is hoped that this research and the subsequent model provide mission leaders with the tools to implement policies and programs that will effectively reform police agencies in post-conflict nations.

— *Jim Bueermann*
President
Police Foundation

Acknowledgments

The idea for the research leading to this book was triggered by my involvement for a number of years in the deployment of police officers to post-conflict or transitioning nations and by my own experiences "on the ground."

I am indebted to the United States Institute of Peace for funding this project.

The development of this book benefited greatly from the support and comments received from the research quality assurance panel: David Bayley, Chris Cooper, Alice Hills, and Stephen Mastrofski.

I appreciate the support and encouragement of the Police Foundation, especially former President Hubert Williams, current President Jim Bueermann, and Karen Amendola. I am grateful to my Police Foundation colleagues, including Earl Hamilton and David Klinger who provided helpful comments on an earlier draft of this report, and to Mary Malina who oversaw its production. Finally, I would like to thank my wife, Vicki, for her support.

This book is dedicated to Neville Bradbury Matthews (1952–2011) and to the 93 police officers killed on the 23 missions that have been included in this research.

— *Garth den Heyer*

Abbreviations and Acronyms

ACC . . . . ad hoc Coordination Cell (Darfur)
ACPO . . . . anti-corruption prosecutor's office
AFDL . . . . Alliance of the Democratic Forces
for the Liberation of Congo-Zaire
ANP . . . . Afghanistan Nation Police
AU . . . . African Union
AUMIS . . . . African Union Mission in Sudan

BINUB . . . Bureau Intégré des Nations Unies au Burundi
BNP . . . . Burundi National Police
BPU . . . . border patrol unit

CARDS . . . . Community Assistance for Reconstruction,
Development, and Stabilisation
CATs . . . . contract assurance teams
CCSSP . . . . Commonwealth Community Safety
and Security Project
CIVPOL . . . . civilian police (part of AUMIS)
CMC . . . . crisis management concept
CNDD–FDD . . . . National Council for Defense of
Democracy–Forces for the Defense
of Democracy
CNP . . . . Congolese National Police
COP . . . . community-oriented policing
CPA . . . . Accra Comprehensive Peace Agreement
CPAK . . . . Comprehensive Peace Agreement

CPDTF . . . . Commonwealth Police Development
Task Force for Sierra Leone
CSRP . . . . police reform monitoring committee

DDR . . . . disarmament, demobilization,
and re-integration
DRC . . . . Democratic Republic of the Congo

ECOMIL . . . . ECOWAS-led mission in Liberia
ECOMOG . . . . Military Observer Group of the
Economic Community of West African States
ECOWAS . . . . Economic Community of
West African States
EDP . . . . externally displaced persons
ESDP . . . . European Security and Defence Policy
ETPS . . . . East Timor Police Service
EU . . . . European Union
EU AMIS . . . . European Union Support to the
African Union Mission to Sudan and Darfur
EU COPPS . . . . European Union
Co-ordinating Office for Palestinian Police Support
EUPAT . . . . European Union Police Advisory
Team in the Former Yugoslav Republic of Macedonia
EUPM . . . . European Union Police Mission to
Bosnia and Herzegovina
EUPOL Afghanistan . . . . European Union Police
Mission to Afghanistan

EUPOL COPPS ....European Union Police Co-ordinating Office for Palestinian Police Support

EUPOL Kinshasa .... European Union Police Mission in Kinshasa

EUPOL Proxima...... European Union Police Mission to the Former Yugoslav Republic of Macedonia

EUPOL RD Congo ... European Union Police Mission in the Democratic Republic of the Congo

EUSEC RD Congo .....European Union Advisory and Assistance Mission for Security Reform in the DRC

F/FDTL ....Portuguese initials for Timor-Leste Defense Force

FANCI..... Forces Armées Nationales de Côte d'Ivoire

FARDC .... Forces Armées de la République Démocratique du Congo

FDLR.......... Forces for the Democratic Liberation of Rwanda

FPU.............................. formed police units

FYROM...... Former Yugoslav Republic of Macedonia

GFAP ....General Framework Agreement for Peace in Bosnia and Herzegovina

HNP .... Haitian National Police

HNPDP.... Haitian National Police Development Plan

ICFSRT .... Interim Co-operation Framework Sectoral Round Table on police

ICITAP .... International Criminal Investigative Training Assistance Program (U.S. DOJ)

IDP..................... internally displaced persons

IFOR .... implementation force

IGAD ....Inter-Governmental Authority on Development

INPFL .... Independent National Patriotic Front of Liberia

INTERFET .... United Nations International Force for East Timor

Interpol .... International Criminal Police Organization

IPCB ....International Police Co-ordination Board

IPU........................... integrated police unit

IPTF ....international police task force

ISAF........... international security assistance force

JEUAM .... Joint Council–Commission European Assessment Mission

JIAS........... Joint Interim Administrative Structure

JMAC ....Joint Mission Analysis Cell

KFOR .... Kosovo Force

KLA .... Kosovo Liberation Army

KPC .... Kosovo Protection Corps

KPS...........................Kosovo Police Service

LIC .... Local Implementation Component Project

LNP ....Liberian National Police

LPS ....Liberian Police Service

LURD.....Liberians for Reconciliation and Democracy

MICAH .... International Civilian Support Mission in Haiti

MIF .... Multinational Interim Force

MINUCI .....United Nations Mission in Côte d'Ivoire

MIPONUH .... United Nations Police Mission in Haiti

MINUSTAH ....United Nations Stabilization Mission in Haiti

MJP .... Movement for Justice and Peace

MODEL ....Movement for Democracy in Liberia

MONUC.....................United Nations Mission in the Democratic Republic of the Congo (Mission de l'Organisation des Nations Unies en République démocratique du Congo)

MONUSCO............. United Nations Organization Stabilization Mission in the Democratic Republic of Congo

MoS .... ministry of security

MoU................. memorandum of understanding

MPCI .... Patriotic Movement of Côte d'Ivoire

MPIGO .... Ivorian Popular Movement of the Great West

NATO .... North Atlantic Treaty Organization

NCPPM....... new civilian police peacekeeping model

NPFL .... National Patriotic Front of Liberia

NPRC........... National Provisional Ruling Council

NPSDP ... National Police Strategic Development Plan

OAS ....Organization of American States

OIG .... Office of the Inspector General

ONUB . . . . United Nations Operation in Burundi

ONUVEH . . . . .United Nations Observer Group for the Verification of the Elections in Haiti

OSCE . . . . .Organisation for Security and Co-operation in Europe

PATs . . . . .police assessment teams

PCP. . . . . .Palestinian Civil Police

PCPDP . . . . Palestinian Civil Police Development Programme 2005–2008

PDC . . . . police development committee

PDP . . . . predeployment planning

PIPs . . . . program implementation plans

PNTL. . . . . .Portuguese initials for Timorese National Police

POP . . . . Public Order Police

PoRP. . . . . .specific police reform program

PRP. . . . . indigenous police reform plan

PRTs . . . . .provincial reconstruction teams

PSB . . . . .police steering board

PSCs . . . . public security centers

PSCO . . . . .Programme Steering Committee

RAMSI. . . . . .Regional Assistance Mission to Solomon Islands

RoRP . . . . indigenous police reform program

RUF . . . . Revolutionary United Front

SAP . . . . stability and association process

SBS . . . . state border service

SFOR . . . . .stabilization force

SIP. . . . . strategic implementation plan

SIPA . . . . state investigation and protection agency

SLPF . . . . Sierra Leone Police Force

SMART . . . . Support, Monitoring, Advising, Reporting, and Training

SOPs . . . . .standard operating procedures

SPLM/A . . . . Sudan People's Liberation Movement/Army

SSD . . . . Special Security Division

SSR . . . . security sector reform

SSPS . . . . .Southern Sudan Police Service

STOP . . . . special trafficking operations program

TLPS . . . . Timor-Leste Police Service

UN . . . . United Nations

UNAMET . . . . . United Nations Mission in East Timor

UNAMID . . . . United Nations and African Union Mission in Darfur

UNAMIS . . . . United Nations Advance Mission in the Sudan

UNAMSIL . . . . United Nations Mission in Sierra Leone

UNDP . . . . . . United Nations Development Programme

UNHCR . . . . United Nations Office of the High Commissioner for Refugees

UNIOSIL . . . . United Nations Integrated Office for Sierra Leone

UNJAM . . . . United Nations Joint Assessment Mission

UNMIBH . . . . .United Nations Mission in Bosnia and Herzegovina

UNMIH . . . . United Nations Mission in Haiti

UNMIK . . . . . . United Nations Interim Administration Mission in Kosovo

UNMIL . . . . United Nations Mission in Liberia

UNMIS . . . . United Nations Mission in Sudan

UNMISET . . . . United Nations Mission of Support in East Timor

UNMIT . . . . . . United Nations Mission in Timor-Leste

UNOCI . . . . United Nations Operation in Côte d'Ivoire

UNOL . . . . United Nations Peace-Building Support Office in Liberia

UNOMIL . United Nations Observer Mission in Liberia

UNOMSIL . . . . .United Nations Observers Mission in Sierra Leone

UNOTIL . . . . United Nations Office in Timor-Leste

UNPROFOR . . . . .United Nations Protection Force

UNSMIH . . . . United Nations Support Mission in Haiti

UNTAET . . . . United Nations Transitional Administration in East Timor

UNTMIH . . . . .United Nations Transition Mission in Haiti

USIP . . . . United States Institute of Peace

Part I

Introduction

Chapter 1

Conception and Structure

Introduction

Civilian police were first deployed by the United Nations (UN) in July 1960 (more than 50 years ago). Following a lull of approximately two decades, the number of civilian police in peacekeeping operations increased from 1,677 officers in 1994 to more than 10,000 officers in 2009 (United Nations, 2010p). The role of civilian police has continued to broaden from one of monitoring general elections and providing training and basic security to one of patrolling and developing the capacity[1] of local police.

Despite the extensive literature that has examined the role of the military in peacekeeping and intervention operations, little available literature or information investigates the role and the work of the civilian police or the methods that they use to assist in the reformation of local police.

The inclusion of civilian police in peacekeeping missions is an accepted practice by both academia and practitioners. However, the role of civilian police in peacekeeping missions is not sufficiently understood by policy makers and decision makers.

The purpose of this book is to understand the role that civilian police play in the postconflict context, espe-

cially with regard to reforming indigenous police. This book will examine 23 UN and European Union (EU) peacekeeping missions that took place between 1999 and 2007. The aim of the research is to develop responsive operational tools and policies that will support the effective use of deployed civilian police in their delivery of service and in their development of the capacity of indigenous police. It is also intended that this study will assist in improving peacebuilding outcomes by increasing postconflict security, stability, and development.

Is There a Need to Understand the Civilian Police Role in Peacekeeping Missions?

The deployment of international civilian police to a postconflict zone is a fundamental part of peacekeeping and is vital to commencing the reconstruction of a society. Police play a central role in establishing a sense of security and stability in the lives of people living in postconflict nations. According to Schmidl (1998, p. 3), "[p]olice play a crucial role in securing the transfer from war to peace, enabling the people to return to their 'normal' lives." However, according to Wiatrowski and Pino (2008), when police are deployed into a postconflict situation, they must ensure that their role is consistent with democratic policing and democratic development. Those authors claimed

---

1   Capacity development is the process or method by which "individuals, organizations, institutions, and societies develop (individually and collectively) to perform functions, solve problems, and set and achieve objectives" (United Nations Development Programme, 1997, p. 5). See also pages 20–23.

Table 1.1. Different Types and Forms of Peacekeeping Operations

	Fetherston (1994) and Jett (1999)		Bellamy, Williams, and Griffin (2009)
1.	Nascent Period	1946–56	Traditional peacekeeping
2.	Assertive Period	1956–67	Managing transition
3.	Dormant Period	1967–73	
4.	Resurgent Period	1973–78	
5.	Maintenance Period	1978–81	Wider peacekeeping
6.	Expansion Period	1988–93	Peace enforcement
7.	Contraction Period	1993–99	Peace support
8.	Modern Period	1999–present	Sustainable capacity development

Source: Author.

in an earlier book (Pino and Wiatrowski, 2006) that without democratic forms of security, police can often be repressive.

Despite the increasing level of complexity of missions and the good intentions of the people deployed and involved in the planning and implementation, the success of past peacekeeping operations has been mixed. This inconsistency may be attributed to several factors. Linden, Last, and Murphy (2007) claim that the same types of problems have plagued virtually all peacekeeping missions since the 1980s. Linden and colleagues also claim that some of the major causes of such problems are governance and operational issues, mandate problems, and resource limitations. This situation is exacerbated by the diversity of each mission's mandate, task, and context. As a result, it is difficult to apply the lessons learned in one mission to another (Jett, 1999).

It can be argued that the history of modern peacekeeping cannot be divided into chronological periods because the types of operations are not mutually exclusive (Bellamy, Williams, and Griffin, 2009). However, there is a clear evolution of peacekeeping missions and involvement of civilian police. According to Fetherston (1994) and Jett (1999), seven different eras shape the evolving form of peacekeeping operations. Table 1.1 compares Fetherston's and Jett's chronologically based evolution of peacekeeping with that of Bellamy et al.; the latter presented five types of operations that are based on the mandate and the achievement of each mission. However, Bellamy et al.'s five types of operations are identified by

their desired outcomes rather than by the methods that the mission used to achieve them.

Since the observations of Fetherston, of Jett, and of Bellamy et al., peacekeeping has further evolved. The new type and form, known as the modern period and the sustainable capacity development, have been included in table 1.1.

The most marked progression in mission type and form is between traditional peacekeeping and managing transition. The managing transition form of peacekeeping mission is qualitatively and quantitatively distinct from traditional peacekeeping because of its multifaceted nature (Bellamy et al., 2009) and because the action of the transition is the primary purpose of the mission.

The more modern peacekeeping missions have become broader in scope and longer in duration (Brzoska, 2006) and, as a result, more complex. The broadening scope of peacekeeping missions encompasses laying the groundwork for sustainable social, economic, and political development and the establishment of security frameworks (Brzoska, 2006).

The increased level of complexity of peacekeeping missions has changed the role that civilian police play from one of mentoring the postconflict nation's police to one of developing institutional police capacity, supporting reform, and restructuring and rebuilding local police (Hills, 2009; Murtaugh, 2010). According to Hills (2009, p. 79), "[E]leven of the twelve missions authorized since 1999 refer to monitoring, reforming, and rebuilding local police."

The major governance problem experienced in peacekeeping missions is the use of Western democratic policing models, ideologies, and technologies by international policing deployments. When they use Western democratic policing models, members of the international police usually fail to take into account the local context and culture. Using Western forms of policing raises a number of theoretical and practical questions about imposing such models on postconflict nations. The imposition of Western models also raises questions about (a) the changing role of the nation-state (Garland, 1996), (b) the governance of intervention or reform policing, and (c) the growing use of the police as modes and models of social and state governance (Bayley and Shearing, 2001).

Police reform is acknowledged as a crucial element when establishing a sense of security and when developing a postconflict nation. Although the principles and practices of capacity development can be applied in most development assistance programs, there are some additional challenges to developing or rebuilding police capacity in weak, postconflict, and failed countries. In such situations, rapid capacity development is critical, but this combination is also where the environment is least conducive to success or to the evaluation of technical assistance programs.

Determining how police change during reform programs can provide substantiation and perspective to policy deliberations when identifying, constructing, implementing, and maintaining forms of policing. This support, in turn, contributes to a nation's intended objectives (Bayley, 1995, 2006). Examining how police change during postconflict national stabilization provides a better understanding of state and political development and of the relationship between reform and police institutions. However, in the past, police missions have been vague in describing their tasks, goals, and objectives. This lack of clarity has led to divergent interpretations of mandates, instances of mission creep, and an absence of performance measurement frameworks.

The UN and the EU have struggled to develop useful indicators for measuring the progress toward achieving a mission's short- and long-term goals and objectives, both in reforming local police and in establishing a public sense of security. Regular progress assessments and evaluations are critical for improving the activities of deployed police and for guiding strategic planning and mission direction. Regular assessments also provide the lessons to be learned for future missions.

The lack of mission-specific goals and objectives has been further exacerbated by the fact that efforts to measure the success of the UN's long-term police reform programs have traditionally been ad hoc and inconsistent (Smith, Holt, and Durch, 2007). Report writers' lack of knowledge of police performance measurement compounds this issue. Despite the establishment of the UN Peacekeeping Best Practices Unit, it is unclear to what degree the UN has been able to develop performance measures and to incorporate the lessons learned from previous missions into current missions.

Although the importance of police reform has been widely accepted by researchers and planners of peacekeeping missions in recent years, very little attention has been given to the process for achieving reform or for measuring its implementation. The methods that two different groups of authors advocate for measuring the success or failure of peacekeeping missions are presented in table 1.2. Unfortunately, both sets of performance measures are strategic, vague, and subjective, and although the sets may provide insight at an academic level, they do not provide a framework for a comprehensive evaluation of the implementation of a complex program of indigenous police reform.

As Bayley (2006) notes, most writing about peacekeeping ceases at the beginning of the third stage by Oakley, Dziedzic, and Goldberg (1998), which is when a reasonably secure environment has been created for the international community. Literature relating to police reconstruction and reform in postconflict environments does not make any recommendations about how to build reliable rule-of-law security institutions so that the local population is protected. Nor are recommendations made about how the reforms can be implemented. Furthermore, the literature does not state whether the reforms achieve the objectives of the local government and police.

Beyond measurement, the construction of definitions is the second area of police reform that requires further understanding and research. A number of missions use statements that may be understood at a political level, but generally the statements are wide ranging and do not comprise any technical frameworks that would assist practitioners. For example, the United Nations Mission in Bosnia and Herzegovina (UNMIBH) tasked the police component of the mission to assist with downsizing

Table 1.2. Suggested Methods for Measuring Peacekeeping Mission Success

Oakley, Dziedzic, and Goldberg (1998)	Ratner (1995)
a. Military suppression of organized conflict b. Establishment of an interim civilian police force by the intervening countries to enforce law, prevent crime, and maintain order c. Creation of a local civilian police institution that is both competent and humane	a. Comparison with the mission's mandate b. Comparison with the results of other peacekeeping operations c. Impact on the states concerned d. Impact on the United Nations or implementing organization

Source: Author.

the local police force and to reorganize the force by using "internationally recognised standards of law enforcement" (Durch, 2006, p. 72).

The critical question in the postconflict environment concerns the establishment and the implementation of practical service delivery frameworks that will set up locally effective security and stability. The implementation of such frameworks "will increase the efficacy and effectiveness of specific interventions and initiatives that contribute to sustainable reform and capacity building" (Griffiths, Dandurand, and Chin, 2005, p. 7). Past experience in assisting postconflict nations has demonstrated the benefits of deploying civilian police in association with a coordinated and coherent justice and penal reform program (Organisation for Economic Co-operation and Development, 2007). The police play a linking role in this approach and, as such, provide a means of developing sectorwide strategies. The contribution of civilian police is significant in providing stability and allows a dysfunctional political environment to change by moving the devastated country away from a military regime toward a civilian or democratic political system (McFarlane and Maley, 2001).

With the exception of military researchers, many researchers fail to examine the operational lessons that may be learned from democratic police reform. This failure is part of a larger intellectual analysis gap. Research and debate are required regarding the developmental aspects of security institutions in postconflict environments (Bayley, 1985, 2006; Call, 1999; Wulf, 2000). Although the UN has published volumes of material and given that many analysts around the world have examined at length the causes of military peacekeeping failure

and the inadequate performance of operations, those analysts have not examined in any detail the civilian police component of such missions. Furthermore, an analysis on the strategic planning process of the civilian policing component of the missions has not been undertaken. Nor have researchers undertaken a gap analysis that examines (a) the objectives of the police component of the missions, (b) what was achieved, (c) the policing models that were used, (d) the achievements of the missions as a whole, or (e) the forms of capacity development and technical assistance that were used.

The Theory of Measuring Capacity Development

Capacity development is the process or method by which "individuals, organizations, institutions and societies develop abilities (individually and collectively) to perform functions, solve problems, and set and achieve objectives" (United Nations Development Programme, 1997, p. 5). What differentiates capacity development in an international intervention postconflict situation is that it is planned, instigated, and sustained by providing resources from outside the postconflict nation.

Capacity development, though not unique to aid programs, is the foundation of the majority of current international development assistance and intervention programs following intranational conflict. Such intervention programs are based primarily on achieving a level of transformation and improvement of the local state agencies, departments, and ministries. However, organizations are made up of a mixture of people and systems,

Table 1.3. Capacity Development Principles

	Principle
1.	From the start, plan to leave.
2.	Be flexible and analyze risk.
3.	Remember that capacity development takes time.
4.	Do not overestimate what can be achieved.
5.	Manage expectations.
6.	Take ownership and provide leadership.
7.	Use holistic approaches that are based on sound analysis.
8.	Build on what currently exists.
9.	Take the cultural environment into account.

Source: Adapted from AusAID (2004).

and a capacity development project should comprise intervention strategies on several different levels.

The development community has used a variety of definitions to define capacity development, most of which have been based on the principles and objectives of the mission or the reason for capacity development. Current definitions of sustainable capacity development usually comprise nine major principles, which are presented in table 1.3, and make up the following three components:

1. It is a dynamic, continuous learning process.
2. It emphasizes efficacy through effective use and empowerment of individuals, resources, and organizations.
3. It requires that systematic and relationship-building approaches be considered in formulating strategies and program development (adapted from United Nations Development Programme, 1997; Canadian International Development Agency, 2000).

Those foundation components identify that capacity development is not likely to be linear and should be based on the values held by the postconflict nation. For example, the approach taken by the Regional Assistance Mission to Solomon Islands (RAMSI) included the majority of these components from the beginning of the intervention program. The mission relied principally on the following AusAID (2004) definition of sustainable capacity development:

The process of developing competencies and capabilities in individuals, groups, organizations, sectors, or countries which will lead to sustained and self-generating performance improvement.

This definition acknowledges that there are two levels of capacity development, each of which compose multiple entry points. Any capacity development assistance provided should ensure (a) that it leads to sustainable improvement of the performance of the postconflict nation or organization and (b) that the program enables the nation or the organization to improve itself when the support ceases.

The implementation of capacity development principles underlines the importance of a comprehensive systems approach that will be supported by building long-term cultural and strategic partnerships. Any capacity development program that alludes to a quick fix or to the search for short-term results should include the effective coordination and coherence of structural, organizational, and technological transformation frameworks (Griffiths et al., 2005). As a result of the complexity of capacity development, most programs are multifaceted and incorporate a number of different approaches. Those approaches may include technical assistance, on-the-job training, train-the-trainers, formal short courses, and study tours (AusAID, 2004). They should also be seen as an indigenous process of change and evolution (Morgan, 1998).

Several broader contextual and specific local variables need to be considered when designing and developing capacity development programs. Those variables should center on the capability of the postconflict nation's political and physical infrastructure and on the commitment of the leaders or the nation's elite to reform. If the nation's leadership is not motivated to fully participate or if the country and its institutions are unable to absorb the capacity development effectively, then any "benefits introduced by the programme will not survive the withdrawal of [that] aid" (AusAID, 2004, p. 4). However, the extent to which those issues apply will depend on the level of social disruption that has occurred or is occurring (AusAID, 2004).

The approach taken by planners to assist with the capacity development in a postconflict nation is key to whether the efforts will be successful (AusAID, 2004). The design of any implementation approach of capacity development programs should allow sustainable improvements to be achieved and should take into account the constraints of underlying weak governance. This perspective will increase the ability of the people of the postconflict nation to improve and will allow their organizations to absorb assistance productively.

Furthermore, the measurement of capacity development is an internal validity process that provides retrospective information about a specific program or intervention. Capacity development programs are indisputably difficult to measure. However, it is easier to measure external rather than internal transformative changes, and there is a tendency for evaluations to focus on such perceptions rather than examine internal performance measures. Developing appropriate performance management frameworks, indicators, and measures of achievement in the development program is essential because it influences the implementation of specific projects within the actual program.

According to Eck (2006), there are two objectives in evaluating intervention programs. The first is to produce the maximum amount of information with the least amount of uncertainty about the efficacy of the intervention program. The second is to provide guidance about what should be achieved subsequently. This objective is important because capacity development planners and implementers need such information to determine whether the program should be continued, repeated, or modified in some way (Eck, 2006).

The difficulty in implementing and evaluating most capacity development programs is that there is usually no underlying method for measuring improvement in the receiving individual, organization, or government. Nor is it easy to measure whether any improvement is sustainable. Those gaps mean that most capacity development program evaluations are not comprehensive strategic assessments. Instead, such assessments look for an improvement in "an aspect of organizational performance judged to be important to the ability of the organization to fulfil its mission" (Wing, 2004, p. 155).

The success of a capacity development program should be measured by using the program's original goals, objectives, and planned achievements. Poorly designed performance indicators can challenge the process of capacity development implementation because such measures can reduce local ownership, can encourage incorrect behavior, and can waste resources. Measures to evaluate the capacity-building intervention program should be designed to include identifying where changes are required, the nature of the changes, and how to best effect those changes with the available resources and within any other constraints. Identifying such performance measures is a complex task and will require a systematic approach to the reform of an organization or an individual.

The process of identifying program performance measurement starts (a) with the receiving organization's priorities and objectives and (b) by examining what has occurred in that organization that has indicated a need to change individual or group performance (Harris, 2005). The process then moves on to identify what has caused the gap between the desired performance and the actual performance; then it designs a capacity-building project to close the gap.

In the case of police reform, a measurable systematic approach could include the following six steps, adapted from Harris (2005):

- Establish capacity-building priorities.
- Analyze police tasks, and identify performance standards.
- Identify current gaps in police performance.
- Create capacity-building program specifications.

Table 1.4. The Five Stages of the Project

Stage		Description
1.	Primary literature search and review	Document review and construction of database
2.	Primary Internet search and review	Document findings
3.	Secondary literature and Internet search and review	Completion of phase 1 research questions and documentation
4.	Analysis of primary and secondary literature and Internet searches and reviews	Completion of phase 2 research questions and documentation
5.	Development of conceptual frameworks	Completion of research goals

Source: Author.

- Select capacity-building program design and delivery systems.
- Design an evaluation and monitoring plan.

Such a comprehensive, systematic approach should include a continuous assessment loop that links the receiving organization's objectives to the performance gap identification process. Using this procedure will establish a program of specific measurable projects that will enable a final evaluation of the capacity-building program to be undertaken. Whether or not the original goals and objectives of the program have been achieved can then be assessed.

However, the major issue when measuring an individual or organizational capacity development program is that it is not uncommon to find that the project has multiple goals and objectives. This comprehensive inventory of goals and objectives may encompass the goals and objectives of the capacity development provider and those of the capacity development receiver. The objectives of the provider and receiver may not be aligned. A lack of alignment in the development program complicates the project performance evaluation and raises the question of whose goals are being measured.

Evaluation of the Civilian Police Role in Peacekeeping Missions

This book is based on an extensive literature search and review of specific UN and EU official documents and covers the five stages summarized in table 1.4.

The first stage of the research provided the basis for developing a 39-question template that is used in part III, chapter 17, to analyze what the civilian police role was in postconflict capacity development, what methods and service delivery models were used, and how the programs were evaluated. The primary literature review completed during this stage also enabled the identification of many practical and political problems experienced during previous peacekeeping missions.

The practical and political problems from previous peacekeeping missions are presented in table 1.5 and are listed under five major peacekeeping topics that have been identified from the literature: Police Mission Planning, The Mission, Local Police Capacity, Policing Approach, and Program Evaluation. Included under each of the topics are the topic's respective Mission Component problems and the issue that caused the Component Problem.

The primary literature search and review also enabled the development of a series of research questions, which were grouped into two logical and analytical phases as presented in table 1.6. The questions contained in phase 1 compose the first step in reviewing the role of the civilian police component in the 23 case study missions. The information obtained in phase 1 is subsequently used to form the basis for developing new frameworks in phase 2. The frameworks are used to examine:

- The appropriate role(s) for civilian police in intervention or postconflict missions
- The appropriate policing service delivery and the reform or capacity development model(s) for civilian

Table 1.5. Practical and Political Problems in Previous Peacekeeping Missions

Police Mission Planning	
Mission Component	**Component Problem**
Premission planning	• Failure to match ends (desired outcomes) with means (inputs)
Personnel	• Inconsistent quality and skills
Mission mandate	• Unrealistic • Vague
The Mission	
Deployment[a]	• Not timely • Completed in stages
Security[a]	• Failure to establish a sense of security
Local Police Capacity	
Training	• Inadequate planning, management, and support • Lack of qualified staff members
Mentoring and monitoring	• Poor training standards • Western curriculum
Policing Approach	
Reform program plan	• Nonexistent • Inappropriate doctrines • No performance measures or evaluation process
All-of-government	• Failure to include comprehensive approach
Policing approach	• Use of Western models
Modernization plan	• Nonexistent • No strategic vision
Program Evaluation	
Program assessment	• Half-hearted attempt • No best practice process
Program evaluation	• Not undertaken

Sources: Bayley (2006); Bayley and Perito (2010); Durch (1993, 2006); Greener (2009); Hills (2009); Jakobsen (2006).

Note: a. From author.

police to use in intervention and postconflict environments

• A performance management methodology for civilian police postconflict missions

The applied goal of this research was to use this evidence and the resulting analysis to devise responsive operational tools and policies that will support the effective use of deployed civilian police in their delivery of service and their provision of capacity development assistance. This research will result in better peacebuilding outcomes

by increasing the security, stability, and development of the postconflict nation.

This project comprised reviewing and analyzing the mandates, deployment processes, strategic performance, and achievements of 15 UN and 8 EU peacekeeping missions that either commenced or were completed between 1999 and 2007 and in which the principal task of the civilian police component of the mission was to reform the local police. The list of the missions, each country that the peacekeepers were deployed to, and the date of the deployment are presented in appendix A.

Table 1.6. Project Research Questions

Phase 1
What was the role of police in the mission: security and stabilization or security sector reform (SSR)?
At what stage were police deployed?
What were the strategic goals or objectives of the police mission or deployment? Were they formulated in conjunction with the postconflict nation?
What were the performance measures and evaluation procedures in each intervention?
What policing service delivery model was used?
Did the police undertake capacity development of the local police?
Was there a capacity development plan? What were the goals and objectives?
Was the capacity development program evaluated? What were the capacity development evaluation methods?
What did the police mission achieve? How did the evaluators know that the objectives of the intervention were achieved? How were the results measured?
Phase 2
What are the roles for civilian police in peacekeeping or peacebuilding missions? What are the scope and the parameters?
Can police fill the "security gap"?
Can police be used more effectively in the nation-building or governance-building process postconflict?
Can police reform measures from Western democracies be used in postconflict nations?
Is there an appropriate model of police service delivery in a postconflict environment?
Is there an effective civilian police process for capacity development planning and implementation?
What should an appropriate civilian police program for capacity development include?
What should be included in a civilian police process for strategic planning?

Source: Author.

The 23 peacekeeping missions included in the study represent a rich and disparate sample of cases. Of the missions, 11 took place in Africa, 5 in Europe, 3 in South Asia, 2 in the Caribbean, and 2 in the Middle East. The sample includes many of the best-known and devastating examples of intrastate conflict and perpetrated civilian atrocities. Given the geographical array and operational depth of the 23 case study missions, it should be possible to develop general conclusions about police reform following conflict.

The project was composed of a structured and focused comparison of 23 case studies that enabled a common format for discussion and analysis to take place. This form of case study investigation has been called "controlled comparison" (George, 1979) and was taken because of the small sample size and because it provides a foundation for measuring the change in missions over time. The small sample size of this project does not enable in-depth statistical analysis to be completed. Furthermore, the project is based on the extraction of qualitative information rather than quantitative data.

Druckman and Stern (1997) claim that a case study approach allows the first step to be taken in collecting a qualitative data set with explicit, systematic criteria, which thus enables analytical models to be constructed. The alternative approach of developing an analysis framework from each of the mission mandates was not taken because of the context-specific nature of each of the mission mandates.

The methodical process used in the case study approach ensures that any model developed is robust and should, as Druckman and Stern (1997, p. 160) emphasize, "allow policy makers to evaluate precisely the impact of individual variables on success and, through sensitivity analysis, determine what the impact would be of altering these variables."

Each of the 23 case studies is examined by using the following seven headings:

1. Background to the mission
2. Mandate of the mission
3. Mission deployment environment
4. Actions of the mission (output)
5. Mission implementation (model)
6. Mission achievements (outcomes)
7. Ways the mission was evaluated

The headings used in this research have been designed to provide a framework for eliciting and summarizing the information obtained from the literature search templates, and the summaries consider the inputs, outputs, and the outcomes of each mission. The headings also offer a logical presentation structure and a construct for ensuring that no potentially valuable qualitative data are passed over (Druckman and Stern, 1997).

The project was more about analyzing the differences in the approaches taken over time across the aggregate missions rather than a comparison across the cases. A comparison of the 23 missions would not have provided any information about the improvements or any deterioration in the local police reform programs (Jones, Wilson, Rathmell, and Riley, 2005). This approach was taken because the postconflict countries suffered different forms of unrest and because they were at different stages of reconstruction when the missions began.

Overview of the Book

This book will examine the methods and procedures used by 23 peacekeeping missions, which included the reform of the local police within their mandate over an eight-year period. It is argued that by using a common template approach in analyzing the 23 missions as individual case studies, the role of the civilian police mission component can be investigated and a generic, culturally based police reform model can be developed. The developed or proposed reform model would be adaptable for use in future peacekeeping missions.

The development of the civilian police reform model is premised on several assumptions, which include the following:

- The reform of local police in a postconflict situation is difficult.
- There is no "one size fits all" answer or model.
- Many factors influence the outcome of reform programs, factors that are beyond the control of the advising institution involved.
- Police reform is a long-term commitment.
- Police reform on its own will not create a secure environment.
- Police reform needs to be part of a comprehensive government and political reform program that includes other justice sector agencies, intelligence agencies, and the military.

The goal of this research was to identify a new reform model for civilian police peacekeeping. The model was designed by examining the official documentation of both the UN and the EU that pertained to the 23 missions. In this process, in-depth information was gathered for some missions, but in the case of other missions, information was not found because the official documentation did not provide even the most basic of reporting data. The lack of available information in some documentation is a weakness of this research.

Moreover, accepting that the deficiency of information within the official documents is a weakness of this research also highlights a weakness in the reporting processes of the UN and the EU. When analyzing the 23 missions and when developing a new reform model for civilian police peacekeeping, the author drew not only on official documents and records but also on gathered information from a wide variety of sources, including interviews with peacekeeping practitioners, government officials, and individuals specializing in international police issues. This additional research was necessary because of the gaps in data from the official documentation.

The study comprises three parts. Part I sets the scene for the study by discussing the role of civilian police in peacekeeping missions. Part II presents the 23 case studies. Part III analyzes the information obtained and covers the development of a new reform model for civilian police peacekeeping.

Chapter 2

Police in Peacekeeping

Police Involvement in Peacekeeping Missions

The first deployment of police officers in a United Nations (UN) peacekeeping mission occurred in 1960, when a civilian police contingent was included in the UN forces that were sent to suppress violence in the Congo. In the ensuing 50 or so years, most UN peacekeeping missions have included civilian police officers. As time passed, the role of civilian police in UN peacekeeping missions has changed substantially. In early missions, that role was typically limited to monitoring general elections, training local police, and providing security. In recent years, civilian police activities have included undertaking patrols and developing the capacity of the local police. This broadening of the police peacekeeping role takes the police into unfamiliar areas of state building such as providing assistance to develop sound governance, strengthen democratic institutions, and build government capacity (Linden, Last, and Murphy, 2007).

Changes to peacekeeping missions began in the early 1990s, when the number and complexity of tasks assigned to police grew dramatically. Those changes can be attributed to earlier police involvement in peacekeeping or peacebuilding, which revealed the need for more multifaceted and intrusive police components in mission mandates. The significance of effectively establishing a sense of public security and of developing local police capabilities was increasingly recognized with each subsequent policing mission.

The biggest changes to take place in recent times occurred in 1999 with the deployment of police to two new complex peacekeeping missions with "executive" mandates: the United Nations Mission in Kosovo (UNMIK) and the United Nations Transitional Administration in East Timor (UNTAET). The police not only were directly responsible for public security within mission areas, but also became extensively involved in local governance. As Chesterman (2004) notes, this new direction meant that peacebuilding was starting to resemble statebuilding.

These progressive changes have culminated (a) in every UN mission since 2003, including police aspects that have "transformational" mandates of varying scope, and (b) in a number of later missions that give direct operational assistance to police forces to maintain law and order. This evolution of UN policing in peace missions can be described in terms of three categories of mission types: traditional, transformational, and executive. The three categories are not mutually exclusive, but the composition categories are useful for understanding the different roles performed by civilian police in postconflict situations as well as understanding the evolution of police involvement in peacekeeping missions.

An analysis of the three category mission types was applied to the 23 missions included in this research. The identification of the category of each mission was based on the information contained in the original mandate

Table 2.1. Analysis of the 15 UN Missions from 1999 to 2007

Type of Policing Mission Category	Area of Responsibility	Specific Tasks	Number of UN Deployments
Traditional	Monitoring police or preparing for elections and limited training, or providing guidance and development to local police, or both	Monitoring local police to ensure compliance with peace agreements and human rights Reporting violations of peace agreement Providing limited training, guidance, and development to local police	0
Transformational	Reforming, restructuring, rebuilding, and developing local police Knowing that more missions include capacity development of local police (may include security or law enforcement)	Developing training material Establishing police training academies Vetting prospective police Designing internal processes and checks for police Providing security	MIPONUH, MINUSTAH (Haiti) UNMIBH (BiH) UNOMSIL, UNAMSIL (Sierra Leone) MONUC (DRC) UNMIL (Liberia) UNOCI (Côte d'Ivoire) ONUB (Burundi) UNMIS, UNAMID (Sudan and Darfur)
Executive	Providing primary law enforcement ("Executive Authority") Developing local law enforcement capacity and institutions	Providing law-and-order services Conducting investigations and arresting offenders Managing local police organizational reform and restructure	UNMIK (Kosovo) UNTAET, UNMISET, UNMIT (Timor-Leste)

Source: Adapted from Smith, Holt, and Durch (2007).

and takes into account any subsequent strategic directional change. Table 2.1 presents an analysis of the categories, the areas of responsibility, and the specific tasks of the 15 UN missions that are included in this research. All 8 of the European Union (EU) missions included in this research are identified as transformational.

The UN has undertaken many peacekeeping missions, although peacekeeping per se was not originally envisaged as a function of the UN. The UN Charter "does not explicitly mention the concept [n]or does it contain specific provisions for peacekeeping operations" (Bellamy, Williams, and Griffin, 2009, p. 46). A large number of tra-

ditional peacekeeping missions that were undertaken by the UN between 1948 and 1991 were established without reference to Chapter VII of its Charter[1] (Durch, Holt, Earle, and Shanahan, 2003). Since 1999, all complex operations have been established in whole or in part under Chapter VII (Durch et al., 2003).

---

1   Chapter VII of the UN Charter sets out the UN Security Council's powers to maintain peace. The chapter allows the Council to "determine the existence of any threat to the peace, breach of the peace, or act of aggression" and to take military and nonmilitary action to "restore international peace and security."

The exclusion of peacekeeping from the Charter has had several different but interrelated effects on the development of peacekeeping:

1. Peacekeeping has developed in response to particular crises in an ad hoc fashion.
2. The key concepts of traditional peacekeeping—consent, impartiality, and minimum use of force—were developed through practice. As a result, their meaning is contested and often interpreted differently in contemporaneous missions (Bellamy et al., 2009).
3. Member states have reinterpreted the Charter's provisions to suit the situation over time (Bellamy et al., 2009).
4. The structure of the UN Department of Peacekeeping Operations has evolved to meet the fundamental changes in missions.
5. The Peacekeeping Best Practices Unit was established in 2001 by merging the Lessons Learned and the Policy Planning Units.

The development in the role of peacekeeping can also be seen in the change of form and in the detail of the mission's mandate. Early mission mandates were principally military focused, and civilian police were minor actors. When civilian policing was included in early UN missions, the Support, Monitoring, Advising, Reporting, and Training (SMART) concept was used in the mandate implementation process.

In comparison, civilian police in EU-authorized peacekeeping operations have always undertaken a significant role. The inclusion of civilian policing in UN missions was seen as a vital component and signified a conceptual change in a mission's strategic structure as compared to the historic situation in which "civilian police issues were typically more of an afterthought" (Greener, 2009, p. 2).

The role of civilian police changed fundamentally when police were granted executive authority during UNMIK and UNTAET in the late 1990s. This step was significant because civilian police within a mission became responsible for local law enforcement. However, since 1999, civilian police executive authority has become the standard in most UN missions.

The role of civilian police peacekeeping missions changed again in 2003 when they increased in com-

plexity. The reason for the increased complexity was the inclusion of rebuilding the capacity of local criminal justice sectors as part of mission mandates (Smith et al., 2007).

According to Holm and Eide (2000, p. 3), the new generation of "peace operations [is] more about managing change than about returning to some status quo." Such operations are no longer only about military intervention and the establishment of public security, but are also about political engineering and state building (Durch, 2006), which can include police reform.

The reform of indigenous police has been included in the state-building component of missions since the mid-1990s. However, there is little empirical understanding of what the appropriate application (Druckman and Stern, 1997) of police reform is, what it should include, and how it should be undertaken. There is also little understanding about what a mission can accomplish or how to assess whether a mission has achieved its goals (Druckman and Stern, 1997).

The Changing Police Role in Peacekeeping

In the traditional or first generation (Broer and Emery, 2002) peacekeeping missions, UN civilian police personnel were restricted to the provision of SMART tasks with the role centering primarily on relationships with the local police and population. Following the confusion in the 1990s and as intrastate conflicts became more complex, the value of including civilian police as a fundamental component of peacekeeping missions began to be recognized (Greener, 2009) and was increasingly seen as an essential component in the reconstruction of post-conflict nations.

As the peacekeeping environment changed, the role of the police also changed. The role of civilian police in modern peacekeeping missions evolved from one of providing public security and confidence building—although those remain primary goals—to one of providing an environment that enables the community to commence rebuilding. The manner in which international civilian police provide assistance to local police has also evolved "from being a technical issue to an ideologically specific set of objectives and activities: namely, police reform" (Hills, 2009, p. 74) that was based on their experience in peacekeeping operations during the late 1980s and early 1990s.

It was during this period that civilian police outgrew the SMART concept and that peacekeeping operations revealed the need for more multifaceted police components within mission mandates (Smith et al., 2007). In many situations, civilian police were already pushing the boundaries of the SMART concept and were blurring the distinctions between monitoring and performing law enforcement. Those are the reasons that executive policing emerged in 1999 (Dwan, 2002).

The SMART concept had been applied during the 1990s without significant rethinking (Dwan, 2002) in diverse peace missions in Africa, Asia, Europe, and Latin America. Although SMART still formed the core tasks for civilian police, the role of the civilian police was expanded in the three UN transitional missions of UNMIBH, UNMIK, and UNTAET to include the seven critical roles as noted by McFarlane and Maley (2001) and Bellamy et al. (2009):

1. Establish a stable and secure environment.
2. Dismantle the former structures of oppression and violent conflict.
3. Build and maintain an effective apparatus of law enforcement and criminal investigation.
4. Select and train new members of an indigenous police force.
5. Investigate and prosecute alleged human rights abuses.
6. Assist the courts in reestablishing a criminal justice system.
7. Build confidence through community involvement.

All those actions taken by civilian police culminated in creating a secure environment and providing a foundation for the public to resume normalcy. It is this view that places the reform of the local police following conflict as a part of the security sector reform (SSR) approach to stabilization.

A subtle change in police involvement in modern peacekeeping has occurred, principally in the form of deployment since UNMIK and UNTAET. Although civilian police, who undertake general policing duties, still form a significant number of the police deployed on a mission, they are rapidly being overtaken by formed police units (FPUs). FPUs are defined as "cohesive mobile police units" (Bruno, 2007). Those units are civilian police in most instances, but units of a semimilitary origin have often been deployed as contained, self-reliant companies, and they are capable of filling the security gap within deployments (Bruno, 2007; Department of Peacekeeping Operations, 2010). However, there is dissent about whether FPUs portray a democratic image and whether they are able to undertake community-policing duties (Pino and Wiatrowski, 2006).

Although the role of police within peacekeeping missions appears to be maturing, there is very little understanding of what policing entails, what the role of police should be, or what influence police have in postconflict nations. Most available literature concentrates on the military role in peacekeeping and postconflict situations, while little literature is available on the role of police and policing in postconflict nations.

According to Greener (2009, p. 112), the military prevalence in peacekeeping has arisen simply because peacekeeping missions have historically been military missions and "emphasis has tended to rest with planning the military part of peace missions, [and] not enough thought [has been] given to what will happen after the immediate security pause." Whatever civilian police peacekeeping literature is available focuses on the use of Western policing models, while indigenous forms of policing are totally ignored (Hills, 2009).

The failure to understand the role of the police in postconflict situations cannot be remedied by examining existing definitions of peacekeeping operations. As Jett (1999) notes, the majority of published definitions are broad and could be applied to any conflict. Nor do the definitions identify what is to be accomplished. However, in 1992, the then-UN Secretary-General Boutros Boutros-Ghali attempted to standardize the strategic framework of peacekeeping missions by describing four different types of peace-associated operations: preventive diplomacy, peacemaking, peacekeeping, and peacebuilding (Durch et al., 2003; Jett, 1999).

Lewis (1994) later extended this framework to include five distinct types of operations: peacemaking, peacekeeping, peace enforcement, peacebuilding, and protective engagement. However, since the distinct peacekeeping operations framework that was identified by both Boutros-Ghali (in the Brahimi Report) and Lewis, the boundaries between the different operations and their distinctions have become increasingly blurred.

Mission mandates do not provide a definition of peacekeeping and provide little or no substantive guidance (Rauch, 2002) to civilian police about how they should carry out their duties. Mandates have become more comprehensive and specific and are rarely limited to one activity. The Brahimi Report called for a "doctrinal shift" in the role of civilian police within peacekeeping operations (Greener, 2009). The shift changed the role of civilian police from passive observer to supporter of human rights and the rule of law through the restriction and reformation of local police institutions.

A peacekeeping mission may fail because of a lack of understanding of the role of civilian police and of a common definition of peacekeeping operations. At the least, the absence of a definition and the lack of understanding will complicate the strategic direction of the mission and will confuse the allocation of tasks to different mission components. Furthermore, this situation can lead to mission creep and to the redefinition and expansion of the civilian police role.

The expanding role of police in peacekeeping operations, together with the increased number and expense of peacekeeping missions, has created a situation in which the performance of the police and their contribution to missions need to be evaluated. There is no accepted definition of mission success nor is there any agreement on how to measure a mission's performance. Any evaluation of a peacekeeping mission should include the achievements of the international police in relation to their mandated objectives and their success in reforming the indigenous police.

The main problem with evaluating peacekeeping missions is that "different actors and constituencies have different objectives and criteria for evaluating success" (Druckman and Stern, 1997, p. 160). A set of performance criteria that have not been researched should be used with caution. One of the most comprehensive definitions of success has been developed by Bratt (1996), who lists four distinct criteria for measuring success: completion of the mandate, facilitation of conflict resolution, containment of the conflict, and limitation of casualties.

Attempting to measure the performance of civilian police within a peacekeeping mission is problematic in that peacekeeping missions appear to be on a continuum. The continuum begins when the fighting stops and continues until the postconflict nation holds democratic elections. However, transitional aspects of the policing role in peacekeeping are qualitatively distinct from the traditional role of police law enforcement, and those aspects take place at different stages of the stabilization program.

Police Reform in Postconflict Nations

Despite the increase in interventions in international conflict and in postconflict states, Botes and Mitchell (1995) claim that the success of such missions has been both minimal and disappointing. Little evidence shows that police reform and capacity development efforts have resulted in sustainable outcomes (Griffiths, Dandurand, and Chin, 2005). The obstacles to achieving order and stability during a nation's rebuilding process are extensive and are more political and social than justice related. This lack of success is principally the result of the difficulty in implementing effective reforms and because institutions take time to develop to a level at which there is confidence in their delivery of service. Furthermore, there is little substantiation on whether the implementation of capacity or service improvement programs of police reform have shown any measureable improvement in the performance of indigenous police.

One of the first state service sectors to be reformed in a postconflict nation is security or criminal justice, namely police. The reform of police in postconflict nations is often seen as an essential component of national consolidation and as a means to prevent future conflict. Police reform is necessary to establish public confidence and to create a sense of security so that the rebuilding of the state can commence. The reformation of the police is an important "point of entry" (Griffiths et al., 2005) for reform in the security and criminal justice sector and is also a prerequisite for establishing a transparent and accountable law enforcement sector. Police capacity development differs from more conventional aid or state development programs. Police reform is more complex than conventional programs, perhaps because of the likelihood that police may have been involved in or were one of the causes of the conflict.

Police reform is important in a postconflict society. If reform is not undertaken, the police could become a liability and an obstacle to rebuilding civil society efforts and to democratic governance. Furthermore, "police activity can have a profound influence on the vitality of the processes that are essential to democratic political life" (Bayley, 2006, p. 18). Strengthening the rule of law and reducing crime "are multi-faceted endeavours that go well beyond the capabilities of police forces to influence" (Call, 2003, p. 4). Police are only one agency within the criminal justice sector, and improving the performance of the police will require establishing relationships and enhancing the capabilities of other state institutions.

International police reform or capacity development in postconflict nations usually evolves from peacekeeping operations (as in the Democratic Republic of Congo and Timor-Leste) or as part of a broader nationbuilding or statebuilding program, which may include "agency-specific and sector-wide institutional strengthening activities that [have been] collectively designed to strengthen the state" (McLeod, 2009, p. 149) as in Iraq and Afghanistan. Police reform programs are externally applied initiatives that range from projects of restoring failed or dysfunctional local policing institutions (Sierra Leone, Timor-Leste) to less comprehensive programs that target the development of specific skills, such as criminal investigations and training (EUPOL COPPS) (McLeod, 2009).

Although policy and academic communities have sought to define police reform, little theory has been developed with respect to reforming the roles of police and their functions in postconflict nations and even less on how to implement any proposed reform program (Call, 2003; Pino and Wiatrowski, 2006). The majority of literature that examines police capacity development discusses the issue in general terms and is characterized by universal perceptions about best practice and lessons learned rather than being based on accepted theory and processes.

As Bayley (1995, 2006) discussed, there is much debate, enterprise, difficulty, and uncertainty about how to reform and democratize police in countries that have experienced transitions from authoritarian, totalitarian, and oppressive forms of governance to democracy. The lack of a shared definition and understanding means that plan-

ners, policy makers, and practitioners have no explicit knowledge on how to reform police agencies or how to measure the success of the reform programs that have been implemented. Because of this lack of knowledge, police reforms in postconflict nations are based on foreign policing models and experiences that do not usually take into account the local culture and context. This problem is exacerbated by the number of national police officers who are deployed to postconflict nations to assist with the reform of the police and who inevitably replicate their own understanding and use of Western policing models.

The evaluation of specific police reform programs requires differentiation between a number of alternative perspectives, including human rights, military, law enforcement, economic, and democratization (Call, 2003). The two main goals of police reform in postconflict nations are effectiveness and accountability of the local police forces (Call, 2003). Another major goal is capacity development, but it is only one aspect of postconflict police reform. An intervention program requires a thoroughly systematic approach to the capacity-building initiative to ensure that a desired and sustainable individual and organizational change takes place. The capacity-building program should provide a framework to assist in the reform of the police to enhance their accountability and transparency. This framework will enable the local police to achieve their goals efficiently and effectively. Such an approach extends beyond providing technical assistance directly to the police and must be firmly connected to the whole framework process for government reform.

The problem of measuring police performance in a postconflict situation is inherently difficult because of poor quality data and insufficient resources. Those deficiencies render impossible most statistical techniques for evaluating organizational performance (Bajraktari, Boutellis, Gunja, Harris, Kapsis, Kaye, and Rhee, 2006). Frameworks should be designed to deliver effective reform and development programs that will assist the police in increasing the efficacy and effectiveness of specific program interventions and initiatives that contribute to sustainable capacity development (Wing, 2004).

Given the uncertainties in designing, implementing, and measuring police reform and capacity development programs in a postconflict situation, it would be erroneous to recommend only one evaluation framework or model. The transformational period during the police reform postconflict provides a unique opportunity for researchers to examine what the role of police officers is, how the agency changes within such situations, and how police transform during democratic consolidation. This study will allow the theory to be expanded.

This project will attempt to fill the vacuum that currently exists in relation to the role of civilian police deployed on assistance missions, and it will build on the body of knowledge about reforming and democratizing police in postconflict countries or countries that are in transition from authoritarian governance. The link between the reforms and the service delivery of the police will also be examined as a practical model that will assist in defining ways to rebuild fractured police agencies postconflict and in highlighting how police services should be delivered in those nations.

Policing and Security Sector Reform

SSR is a concept that was developed in Europe in the 1990s and is used to reform or rebuild a state's security sector. SSR can also be viewed as a branch of human or personal security, which is the reason civilian police reform has been included within its parameters. However, viewing postconflict police reforms within the context of SSR portrays "the difficulties and opportunities for reforms in a different light rather than [what a] focus on the police alone provides" (Marenin, 2005, p. 17). SSR identifies civilian police as a component of the wider security sector and considers police reform as a process rather than an outcome.

Whether indigenous police reform and development should be included in an SSR program is questionable. Civilian police reform has been viewed from two perspectives: whether civilian police are part of the security sector or part of the justice sector. Whatever perspective is taken can influence the strategic dimension and approach of the proposed reform program. The SSR perspective is a more bureaucratic or institutional approach, while the justice sector perspective is more community focused.

The constructs of SSR mean that it cannot become the catalyst for democratic change, but it can affect the processes that are adopted postconflict to reform the local police. The reform of the indigenous police will be included in the wider reform of the local security sector. This inclusion means that the role of international civilian police will expand to reflect the broader notion of security, and the role of the local police will also expand.

Including police within the scope of SSR means that policing is viewed at the "high end" and that it is accepted that policing is more about law enforcement than about providing services or maintaining public order. Although policing is part of the governance of security (Marenin, 2005), it is more about the promotion of the community and of democratic values. The debate about whether police or policing is part of SSR will not be determined by further explanation of SSR, because it requires a more in-depth understanding of police, police reforms, and the processes that the police use in both a Western nation and a postconflict nation context.

There is no universal understanding of the purpose of the police as an institution, and as a result, "[a]mbitious claims are regularly made on behalf of police reform" (Hills, 2009, p. 64). Because of this misunderstanding about the role of police and policing, the current reform processes and models of local police in postconflict nations are in confusion. Policy makers and practitioners have misconceptions about what is required postconflict to develop and implement sustainable police reforms in local police.

Part II contains case studies that place an emphasis on the process of evaluating civilian police involvement in 23 peacekeeping missions in fragile, transitional, or postconflict situations. It is hoped that the process will be one step closer to establishing a methodology for understanding police reform in postconflict nations.

Part II

Mission Case Studies

Chapter 3

Overview of Case Studies

Introducing the Case Studies

The majority of the peacekeeping missions included in the case study analysis are of a multidimensional structure. In that context, this form of peacekeeping mission usually includes a number of goals to deal with the different effects of civil or intrastate war, such as human security and humanitarian requirements. The situation has created larger, more expensive, and more complex peacekeeping missions. As well as enforcing the keeping of the peace, such missions are often tasked with assisting with the development of the local political environment.

Evolving multifaceted peacekeeping missions create an environment where many different issues could contribute to the failure of the mission at or during any of its three phases: predeployment, deployment, and postdeployment.

According to Jett (1999), a peacekeeping mission can have three possible outcomes: outright failure, indefinite extension, and declaration of success. Given the wide range of conditions and challenges that confront police in postconflict environments and the wide range of tasks that they are mandated to complete, there is no standard definition of success (Jett, 1999). Diehl (1993) and Druckman and Stern (1997) claim that one method of defining success is the fulfillment of the mission's mandate. Mandates are usually vague and are not itemized lists of what needs to be done. How does one determine when a mission's mandate is fulfilled? What are the performance measures? In comparison to what? Diehl acknowledges that a better

indicator of success is whether the mission prevented any further hostilities and succeeded at conflict resolution. Such indicators are vague, and a peacekeeping mission alone cannot achieve the prevention of further hostilities.

Apart from identifying the criteria for evaluating the success of a mission, one must overcome at least two hurdles in forming a basis to identify the actual level of success. The first hurdle is obtaining reliable data. In most postconflict nations, such information is simply not available. The second hurdle is, as in all policing, finding causal relationships.

To overcome the first hurdle, this research used a number of useful qualitative and quantitative proxy measures, which were created from information contained within official United Nations and European Union documents. The approach resolved the problem of developing lists of criteria. The problem with creating such lists is that potentially rich qualitative information may be passed over (Druckman and Stern, 1997). With regard to the second hurdle, there is little evidence of causal links between the mission's mandate, the deployment environment, the actions of the mission (output), and the mission implementation (model). Research attempts to identify the links by examining 39 areas of specific analysis are discussed in part III, chapter 17.

The 23 missions are presented alphabetically in part II by the country of origin. As explained earlier in chapter 1, to help readers better analyze each individual mission and compare the missions, this research presents each mission by using the following seven-heading framework:

1. Background to the mission
2. Mandate of the mission
3. Mission deployment environment
4. Actions of the mission (output)
5. Mission implementation (model)
6. Mission achievements (outcomes)
7. Ways the mission was evaluated

Exploring the Analysis of the Case Study Missions

The examination of the 23 mission case studies identifies a number of similarities between and across the missions from 1999 to 2007. The similarities include the following:

- Many postconflict countries had more than one failed peace agreement before the mission was deployed.
- Except for the European Union Police Advisory Team in the Former Yugoslav Republic of Macedonia, all of the missions' mandates were extended.

- All missions included some form of training.
- Governing bodies, often comprising local officials, were established to oversee the reform program.
- Local government or police displayed passive resistance in implementing reforms.

The brief analysis of the case studies highlights that—although there are a number of similarities in mission approaches and their mandates—there is significant variation in the ability of the international community to design and implement effective reform programs. As will be discussed in part II, this mission variation is compounded by the significant variation in the indigenous police's ability to absorb training and to reform.

What does the analysis of each of the case studies suggest about overall efforts to reconstruct or reform the local police? In particular, which countries experienced an improvement in the performance of the local police following the reconstruction efforts? By analyzing the case studies in more depth, we attempt to answer those questions in part III, chapter 17.

Chapter 4

Afghanistan

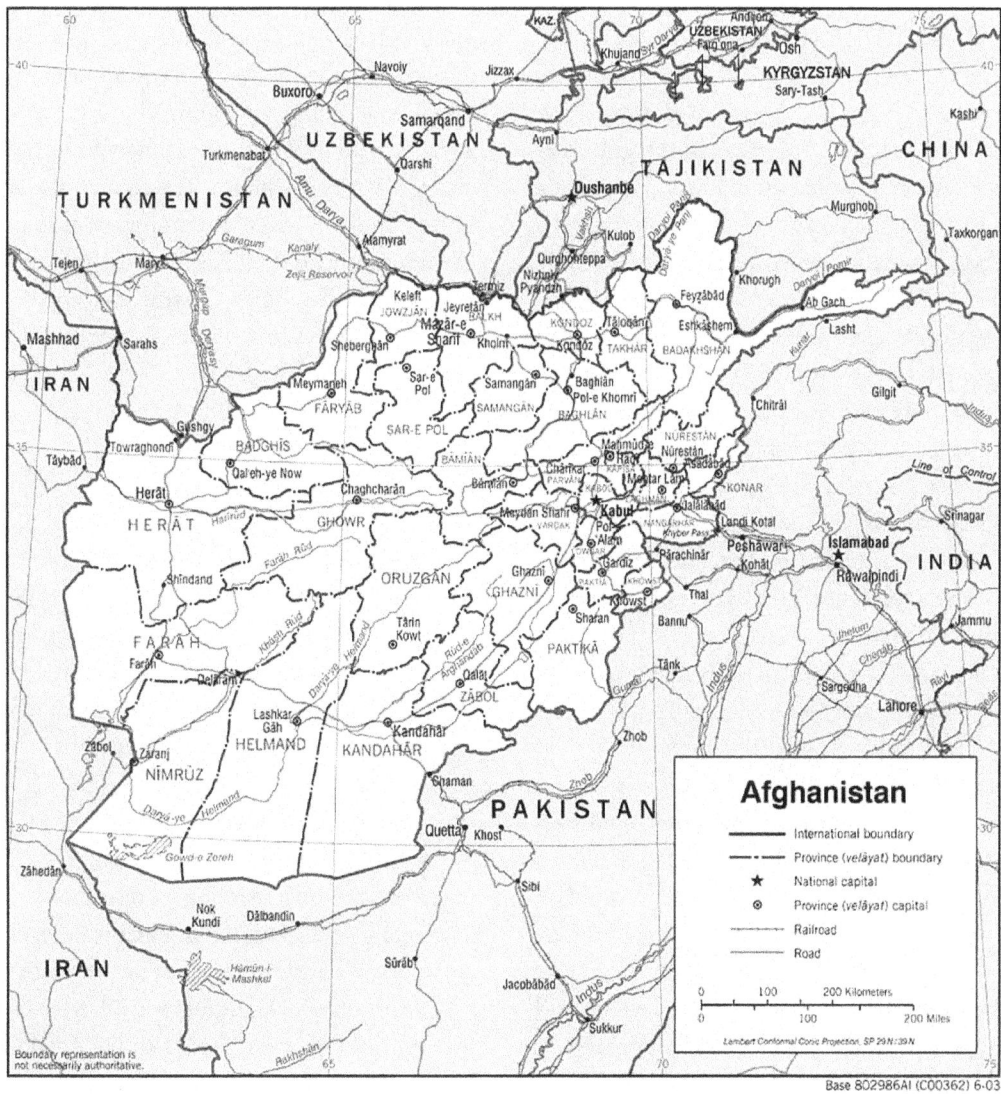

Map 4.1. Afghanistan
Source: Courtesy of the University of Texas Libraries, The University of Texas at Austin.

Case Study: European Union Police Mission in Afghanistan

Background to the Mission

The reconstruction of Afghanistan's police began in February 2002 with a conference held in Germany to discuss international support for the Afghan police. A comprehensive plan to create a national Afghan police force was presented to another conference, which was held one month later in Berlin (Jones, Wilson, Rathmell, and Riley, 2005).

On October 13, 2006, the Joint European Union Assessment Mission to Afghanistan presented a report to the Council of the European Union's Political and Security Committee, which detailed an analysis of the state of the rule of law in Afghanistan. The report contained a number of recommendations that would strengthen the European Union's (EU's) strategic contribution to the law enforcement sector in Afghanistan, and it recommended that consideration be given to the EU's "contributing support to the police sector through a police mission." To explore further the feasibility of such a mission, the report recommended that a fact-finding mission be sent to Afghanistan (Council of the European Union, 2007b).

The fact-finding mission visited Afghanistan between November 27 and December 14, 2006. From this mission, the council "approved the crisis management concept (CMC) for an EU police mission to Afghanistan in the field of policing that would have linkages to the wider rule of law. It was agreed that the mission would provide added value" (Council of the European Union, 2007b). The council noted that the mission would be a long-term commitment that would provide assistance in reforming the Afghan police force. The reform would be based on local ownership and respect for human rights, and it would operate within the framework of the rule of law. The mission would build on international efforts and would follow a comprehensive and strategic approach. In adopting this program of reform, the mission would "address issues of police reform at central, regional, and provincial levels" (Council of the European Union, 2007b).

On April 23, 2007, the council approved the concept of operations for a European Union Police Mission to Afghan-

istan (EUPOL Afghanistan), which would cover the entire country (Council of the European Union, 2007e) and would include primarily police reform programs with links to the wider rule of law (Council of the European Union, 2007b). The council noted that the proposed mission would build on the efforts of the German Police Project Office and would be set in the wider context of the "international community's effort to support the Government of Afghanistan in taking responsibility for strengthening the rule of law, and in particular, in improving its civil police and law enforcement capacity" (Council of the European Union, 2007e).

The council identified that the minimum time frame of EUPOL Afghanistan would be three years and that the mission would require close coordination with other international actors, including the international security assistance force (ISAF), which would be involved in providing security assistance. The council also noted that because the deployment environment was unpredictable, the mission would take a flexible approach. As a result of this unpredictability, the size and scope of the mission would be subject to six monthly reviews (Council of the European Union, 2007b).

Mandate of the Mission

On May 30, 2007, the Council of the European Union passed Council Joint Action 2007/369/CFSP, which established, for an initial period of three years, EUPOL Afghanistan. The joint action noted that the mission would include an initial planning phase, which would begin on May 30, 2007, and an operational phase, which would commence no later than June 15, 2007 (Council of the European Union, 2007b).

The council tasked the initial planning phase team with preparing and documenting an operational plan and with developing the technical instruments necessary for the deployment of EUPOL Afghanistan. The team was to undertake a comprehensive risk assessment, which was to identify the security risks associated with the mission. The assessment was to be designed to take into account any changes in the mission's operational environment and would include a security plan (Council of the European Union, 2007b).

The EUPOL Afghanistan mission statement specified that the objectives of the mission were to contribute significantly to the establishment—under Afghan ownership—of sustainable and effective civilian policing arrangements. The mission was to be nonexecutive in form and was to be completed by monitoring, mentoring, advising, and training. The mission would also undertake "appropriate interaction with the wider criminal justice system, in keeping with the policy advice and institution building work of the community, member states, and other international actors" and was to "support the reform process towards a trusted and efficient police service"(Council of the European Union, 2007b). This approach would be in accordance with international standards of the rule of law and respect for human rights (Council of the European Union, 2007b).

As the Council of the European Union (2007b) describes, the objectives of the mission statement established an operational-level framework through which the EUPOL Afghanistan was to accomplish the following:

- Develop strategic initiatives, while placing an emphasis on work toward a joint overall strategy of the international community in police reform.
- Support the government of Afghanistan in coherently implementing its strategy.
- Improve cohesion and coordination among international actors.
- Support links between the police and the wider rule of law.

The mission was tasked to "work closely with Afghan police officers, assisting them to make practical arrangements for security and law enforcement in their areas of responsibility" and to achieve tangible benefits for Afghan communities (Council of the European Union, 2007b). The structure of the mission included the deployment of staff members to the central, regional, and provincial offices. Technical arrangements, resources, and accommodations were sought in conjunction with the ISAF and provincial reconstruction teams (PRTs) (Council of the European Union, 2007b).

The joint action also specified that the mission was to be reviewed every six months in order to adjust its size and scope, if necessary, and that the mission was to be reviewed "no later than three months before its expiry in order to determine whether the Mission should be continued" (Council of the European Union, 2007b).

Mission Deployment Environment

The EU Council Secretariat sent two exploratory missions to Afghanistan. The first was in July 2006, and the second was in September 2006. The exploratory missions composed a Joint Council–Commission European Assessment Mission (JEUAM), which assessed the situation of the Afghanistan police forces and judiciary.

The EU member states had deployed approximately 27,000 soldiers to Afghanistan within the framework of ISAF. The council noted that the solutions in Afghanistan would be political, not military, and, to this end, would continue "to focus its activities largely on governance and the rule of law" (Council of the European Union, 2009b).

Actions of the Mission (Output)

The mission placed an emphasis on enhancing the coordination between EUPOL Afghanistan and the member states bilateral program (Council of the European Union, 2009c). EUPOL Afghanistan initially concentrated on raising the level of security in Kabul by improving the standard of local policing (Common Security and Defence Policy European Union, 2010). Improvement of the standard was to be achieved by implementing specific training, especially in criminal investigation.

EUPOL Afghanistan trained more than 1,000 Kabul police officers in crime scene investigation and developed a training curriculum for civilian police and the anticrime police. The mission also established an Anti-Corruption Prosecutor's Office (ACPO), in which specialist prosecutors developed cases against a number of high-profile public officials suspected of corruption. To support the ACPO, the mission trained more than 300 Ministry of Interior inspectors in basic anticorruption investigation techniques (Common Security and Defence Policy European Union, 2010).

Mission Implementation (Model)

The initial EUPOL Afghanistan consisted of 160 police officers, who were deployed to Kabul; five regional police commands; and a number of PRTs (Council of the

European Union, 2007e). However, the number of mission personnel doubled progressively from December 2008 to approximately 400 staff members to allow the mission, on the basis of a renewed mandate, to reinforce its activities in support of the Afghan national police (Common Security and Defence Policy European Union, 2010).

The mission relied extensively on the creation of partnerships, especially with the international community, to enhance Afghan ownership of reforms. In conjunction with the International Police Co-ordination Board (IPCB), the mission consolidated its strategic priorities along these six objectives: intelligence-led policing; police chain of command, control, and communication; criminal investigation; anticorruption; police–prosecutor links; and human rights and gender mainstreaming within the Afghan police force (Council of the European Union, 2007a). Implementation of those objectives ensured the continuing progress of the mission at the strategic, operational, and tactical levels (Council of the European Union, 2009d).

Mission Achievements (Outcomes)

Although progress has been made in some areas of police reform, reconstruction efforts have not minimized security threats to the country. Jones et al. (2005) note that two of the reasons for the continuing security threat are that the police-to-population ratio is low and that the reconstruction of the justice sector has taken place only in the capital region. The other reasons noted by Greener (2009) include conflicting approaches to reform by donor countries, lack of reform efforts directed at the judicial sector, and ethical and professional issues within the Afghanistan Nation Police (ANP).

The mission provided the environment for the reform of the local police, which would ensure that the police were progressing toward respecting human rights and delivering their services within the framework of the rule of law. The mission was pivotal in the provision of support to the Afghan justice sector by (a) strengthening the criminal investigation system, (b) establishing intelligence-led policing, (c) implementing an anticorruption strategy, and (d) improving the role of police in securing Kabul and Herat. This model of security policing was also to be introduced in other key cities, such as Kandahar and Mazar-e-Sharif (Common Security and Defence Policy European Union, 2010).

EUPOL Afghanistan is influential in developing relationships with the wider rule of law sector and in conducting several "train-the-trainers" training programs throughout Afghanistan. The mission also provided criminal investigation services and delivered training on the handling of a crime scene to Afghan Police Investigators (Common Security and Defence Policy European Union, 2010).

Ways the Mission Was Evaluated

The Council of the European Union noted during its External Relations Council Meeting in 2008 that although the EUPOL Afghanistan had experienced a number of achievements, challenges still remained. The challenges that remained were mainly in the "areas of development and governance, and the underlying factors, notably corruption and a lack of security—with narcotics being linked to both—continue to undermine the functioning of the Government of Afghanistan" (Council of the European Union, 2008a).

The EU approach to those challenges was to double the original number of experts working in the mission with the view that this approach would provide an important additional capacity to assist with key police reform issues (Council of the European Union, 2008a). However, the mission emphasized that reforming a police force at a strategic and operational level required long-term planning and communication between stakeholders, with all parties participating in a phased implementation (European Mission in Afghanistan, 2008). As a result of these requirements, and "due to the challenging operational environment, thorough preparation, timely planning, prior full operational capability and continued contribution of high-calibre staff are essential" (Council of the European Union, 2008a).

Conclusion

The mission was established after six years of war, which was the result of a U.S.-led invasion following the 9/11 terrorists' attacks in New York City and Washington, DC. The initial invasion to dispose of the Taliban rulers was successful but gradually lost momentum and became a hostile situation involving local mercenaries and insurgents.

The major issue facing the mission is the history of Afghanistan and the profound effect the disposing of the Taliban has had on the ANP. This problem is compounded by a weak central government and by the country's dependence on foreign assistance and intervention to provide stability.

The mission faced a number of challenges. The first major challenge was the poor state of the ANP and the extent of organizational corruption. The second major problem was the discrepancy between the civilian model of police reform advocated by the mission and the more militarized approach, supported by the United States, in which the police complement the role of the army.

The focus of the mission was at a very high level, principally concentrating on strategic policing reform. Although the mission has made progress toward achieving some aspects of its mandate, the issue will be whether those achievements are sustainable.

The mission is ongoing and was extended on May 18, 2010, for a further three years until May 31, 2013.

Chapter 5

Bosnia and Herzegovina

Map 5.1. Bosnia and Herzegovina

Source: Courtesy of the University of Texas Libraries, The University of Texas at Austin.

Case Study: United Nations Mission in Bosnia and Herzegovina

Background to the Mission

The breakup of Yugoslavia and the end of the Cold War were the major factors leading to the war in Bosnia and Herzegovina. There is some debate as to whether the war in 1992–95 was interstate or intrastate. The war was extremely violent and principally targeted civilians. More than 200,000 people were estimated to have been killed and more than 1.2 million people displaced (United Nations, 2010d). The conflict was also very complex as it involved a number of different actors who frequently changed their objectives and their allegiances, leaving a legacy of hatred and widespread fear of retribution.

Fighting ceased on October 11, 1995, and war was brought to a formal end after the General Framework Agreement for Peace in Bosnia and Herzegovina (GFAP) was signed in Paris on December 14, 1995. This agreement was made up of 11 annexes and covered a broad range of issues including the establishment of an international police task force (IPTF). Following the signing of the GFAP, peace negotiations were held in Dayton, Ohio, and were made final on December 21, 1995 (United Nations, 2010d). Those accords later became known as the Dayton Agreement.

The United Nations Protection Force (UNPROFOR) was deployed from October 11 to December 20, 1995, to monitor the cease-fire agreement. A United Nations (UN) police reconnaissance mission, which was made up of the current and two previous UN police force commissioners and a member of the UN Department of Peacekeeping Operations, traveled to Bosnia and Herzegovina to plan for the proposed civilian police deployment (United Nations, 2010d).

On December 15, 1995, the North Atlantic Treaty Organization (NATO), on the basis of the UN Security Council Resolution 1031 (United Nations, 1995a), was given the mandate to implement the military aspects of GFAP and to endorse the establishment of the multinational implementation force (IFOR) for about 12 months. IFOR was the largest military mission un-dertaken by the Western Nations Alliance and replaced UNPROFOR on December 20, 1995, as Operation Joint Endeavour (NATO, 2010a). IFOR was itself replaced by the multinational stabilization force (SFOR) in December 1996.

Mandate of the Mission

The UN Security Council adopted two resolutions that established the United Nations Mission in Bosnia and Herzegovina (UNMIBH), initially for one year. The first, Resolution 1031 (United Nations, 1995a) was passed December 13, 1995, and the second, Resolution 1035 (United Nations, 1995b) was passed December 21, 1995.

This mission comprised two principal components: the IPTF and the UN civilian office (United Nations, 2010a), which exercised a wide range of functions that related to law enforcement and police reform (United Nations, 1995b). The mission was nonexecutive and was to have an authorized strength of 1,721 unarmed civilian police officers and 5 military liaison officers. The mission was to have a nationwide presence. It was to establish regional headquarters in Banja Luka, Bihać, Doboj, Mostar, Sarajevo, and Tuzla and a district headquarters in Brčko (United Nations, 2010a).

UNMIBH's mandate was fairly generic and related to the welfare of refugees, humanitarian relief, demining, human rights, elections and rehabilitation of infrastructure, and economic reconstruction. The mission was to contribute to establishing the rule of law in Bosnia and Herzegovina by helping reform and restructure the local police. This goal was to be achieved by assessing how the existing judicial system functioned and by monitoring and auditing the performance of the police and other agencies that were involved in the maintenance of law and order (United Nations, 2010a).

As suggested by the United Nations (1995a), the IPTF's tasks, in accordance with the GFAP, were more specific and included the following:

- Monitor, observe, and inspect law enforcement activities and facilities, including associated judicial organizations, structures, and proceedings.
- Advise law enforcement personnel and forces.

- Train law enforcement personnel.
- Facilitate law enforcement activities.
- Assess threats to public order and advise on the capability of law enforcement agencies to deal with such threats.
- Advise government authorities about the organization of effective civilian law enforcement agencies.
- Assist by accompanying law enforcement personnel as they carry out their responsibilities.
- Consider requests for assistance from local law enforcement agencies, with priority given to agencies that need to ensure free and fair elections and that need to protect international personnel present because of the elections.

Over time, as the mission evolved and the country became more stable, the UN Security Council added a number of specific tasks and responsibilities to the original mandate of UNMIBH. Those tasks included the following:

- Undertake investigations of allegations of human rights abuses by police (United Nations, 1996e).
- Increase the mission by 186 civilian police who would specifically assist with the monitoring, restructuring, and retraining of the police in the Brčko area (United Nations, 1997e).
- Increase the mission by 120 civilian police that would increase the mission's capability in investigating human rights, monitoring local police, strengthening police training, restructuring police administration, and developing guidelines for democratic principles (United Nations, 1997f).
- Create specialized training units to (a) address key public security issues such as refugee returns; organized crime, drugs, corruption, and terrorism; and public security crisis management (including crowd control); (b) detect financial crime and smuggling; and (c) assist in a program of judicial and legal reforms, including assessing and monitoring the court system, developing and training legal professionals, and restructuring institutions in the judicial system (United Nations, 1997i).
- Increase the mission by 30 civilian police personnel to carry out new intensive programs for the local

police in a number of specialized fields (United Nations, 1998k).
- Assist in a program to monitor and assess the court system as part of an overall program of legal reform (United Nations, 1998n).

Mission Deployment Environment

When the war ended, three issues of concern for the mission were created. The first area of concern was the number of demobilized soldiers who would become unemployed and might turn to crime or seek revenge for lost family members and property. The second area of concern was the large number of highly powered weapons that would be available at the end of the hostilities because of the demobilization of the military.

The third issue pertained to the Bosnia and Herzegovina police. As a result of the war, the number of police officers in the country was more than 44,000, which was three times the prewar strength. Of that number, more than 32,000 were deployed in the Federation of Bosnia and Herzegovina (the Federation) and 12,000 in the Republika Srpska–controlled area (United Nations, 1995a).

The Bosnia and Herzegovina police force was not suited to undertake civilian law enforcement duties because it was politically dominated and had a history of corruption. The police force consisted of a single ethnicity and was organized along paramilitary lines in three parallel structures (United Nations, 1995a). This negative security situation was reinforced by members of the police harassing and intimidating citizens not of their own ethnicity and by the establishment of checkpoints that restricted travel between communities. As a result, the police failed to provide the population with any sense of security.

Actions of the Mission (Output)

Within the highly volatile setting of Bosnia and Herzegovina, the UNMIBH's main objective was to provide civilians with a sense of security by creating a stable environment. Stability was to be achieved through the presence and the joint patrolling of local police with IPTF officers and by changing the primary focus of the local police from the security of the state to the security of the individual (United Nations, 2010a).

The IPTF was charged with monitoring all of the activities of the Federation Police Force and the Republika Srpska Police. The IPTF was to introduce the principles of democratic policing to these police forces by leading by example (United Nations, 1996c). Initially, the IPTF's major responsibility was to help plan the reduction of, the restructuring of, and the training of local police. The composition of the police force needed to be changed from the overrepresented ethnic groups and war-period numbers to the maximum numbers set by the restructuring agreements with the Federation and the Republika Srpska. This process was to be achieved by the IPTF in cooperation with the Federation within a timeline that was agreed to on April 26, 1996. It provided the guidance to reduce the number of uniformed officers from more than 20,000 to a maximum of 11,500. During this period, the Republika Srpska's government agreed to (a) the IPTF statement of internationally accepted principles for policing in a democratic state, (b) the related operational standards of policing, and (c) a new code of conduct for police officers. However, the government did not agree to downsize its own police force (United Nations, 1996b). Not until 1998 did the Republika Srpska agree to restructure and downsize the police (United Nations, 2010a).

As the immediate postconflict crisis began to diminish, the IPTF started to address the broader issues of the mandate, which would lay the foundations for future police reform in both entities. The IPTF began a comprehensive training, restructuring, and vetting program for selection and recruitment, and it introduced community policing into a number of areas. The IPTF also introduced a program into schools that was designed to educate students at all levels in their civic duties and the principles of democratic policing (United Nations, 1996c).

This approach was supported by placing IPTF advisers in the cantonal and entity interior ministries, public security centers, and police stations, which enabled closer monitoring of the activities of local bureaucrats. IPTF advisers were deployed to 5 regional police headquarters, 17 central police districts, and 109 police stations. This arrangement permitted monitoring, observing, and inspecting law enforcement activities and facilities and

resulted in a ratio of 1 IPTF officer to 30 local police officers (United Nations, 2010a). The deployment of IPTF advisers within the cantonal and entity interior ministries also allowed for progress in integrating the Federation's Ministry of Interior into the new police structure, and in establishing the Federation Police Academy in Sarajevo. This change created the environment to complete the negotiations and to reach an agreement on the installation of a fully unified Federation police organization on June 6, 1997 (United Nations, 1997a).

The IPTF was extensively involved in recruiting, selecting, training, and deploying police cadets from underrepresented ethnic and gender groups, as well as in encouraging the return and the transfer of experienced officers. The task force provided basic training, transitional training, and advanced training courses for command and senior officers of the Federation and the Republika Srpska. After the UN Security Council Resolution 1144 (United Nations, 1997i), the IPTF also provided specific specialized training in organized crime, drugs and crowd control, and major incident management (United Nations, 2010a).

The IPTF provided operational and tactical advice to local police, which included advice on investigating special cases and improving the day-to-day lives of residents. For example, the IPTF advised the local police on how to establish road checkpoints that would ease civilian movement. It also acted as liaison between the population and the police forces of the Federation and the Republika Srpska (United Nations, 1997a).

To ensure that the IPTF approach created a multiethnic, professional, and effective police force, the role of the task force expanded from restructuring and reforming the ministries of interior and the police forces of the two entities to providing advice on establishing and training the court police and the State Border Service (SBS). However, the IPTF accepted the reform program more slowly than had been initially anticipated. This delay was mainly caused by political disputes between the entities and disagreements about, for example, the type and design of police identification cards that would be issued to the restructured Federation police force (United Nations, 1996c).

By late 1999, the security environment had stabilized, and displaced persons were able to return to their prewar homes. At this time, the IPTF realized that establishing sustainable police reform and restructuring the police forces could not be completed by using two approaches of recruit training and co-location within the ministries of interior and police stations (United Nations, 2010a). As a result, the IPTF developed a conceptual model that incorporated a baseline of tangible measurements to reform and restructure the police forces.

The conceptual model formed the future direction of the mission and was the basis of a comprehensive and measurable two-year implementation plan, which constituted detailed goals, projects, benchmarks, and timelines. The plan would become the primary reference document for the activities undertaken by the mission and would address specific strategic capacity development areas and levels. Those areas and levels were identified as (a) the individual police officer level, (b) the law enforcement institutional level, and (c) the police and the public relationship level (United Nations, 2010a). The plan was also organized into six core programs (see table 5.3 on page 39) and identified the mission's three goals. The United Nations (2010a) identified the goals in the six core programs as the following:

- Certification of individual officers
- Accreditation of police administrations
- Establishment of self-sustaining mechanisms for state- and regional-level interpolice force cooperation

To increase the acceptance of the implementation plan by each of the entities and to minimize political interference, the IPTF advised establishing independent police commissioners at the cantonal level and directors of police at the entity level. This structure allowed for independent police commissioners to be appointed in all 10 Federation cantons and for one director of police in each of the Republika Srpska and the Federation (United Nations, 2010a).

Mission Implementation (Model)

The approach taken by the IPTF in implementing its mandate comprised two time-based phases. The first phase was implemented during the period of 1996–99. The second phase, begun in 2000 following the introduction of the conceptual model and the implementation plan, was completed when the mission withdrew on December 31, 2002.

Table 5.1. UNMIBH Civilian Police Staff Numbers, March 1995 to May 2002

Year	Month	Total Civilian Police Officers
1995	March	45
	November	366
1996	February	392
	March	828
	April	1,302
	June	1,562
1997	June	1,812
	September	2,015
	December	2,004
1998	March	2,011
	May	2,011
	September	1,980
1999	June	1,919
	September	1,691
	December	1,795
2000	May	1,602
2001	May	1,798
	November	1,673
2002	May	1,586

Source: Author drawing from United Nations documents.

First Phase: 1996–99

Primarily, the first phase constituted establishing the mission, getting staff on the ground, and concentrating on the immediate issues so that a secure environment could be created for the civilian population. The mission reached its UN Security Council–authorized strength of 1,721 police officers in late 1996 and, as presented in table 5.1, remained above or close to that number throughout the mission. However, the skill sets of IPTF officers needed to change as the mission matured. Patrol officers were required in the early stages of the mission, but in the later stages of the mission, officers were required who possessed training, management, and mentoring skills.

As a result of the need to establish the mission in the first phase, the IPTF focused its delivery strategies on joint patrolling, training, and co-location. The task force carried out its activities by using two main components: operations and development. The operational component primarily covered monitoring the local police to ensure civilian freedom of movement, adherence to professional police procedures, and respect for human rights. The developmental component covered assisting the local authorities in restructuring their police forces. This restructuring was achieved by downsizing and by vetting and screening officers for criminal records and previous human rights abuses of local residents. Upon certification by the IPTF, officers were tested, trained, and approved for service in the new police organization (United Nations, 1997b).

Co-location of IPTF officers with local police senior managers in their place of work was identified as an effective means of influencing local police reform (United Nations, 1998e). The strategy included establishing 800 positions across the Federation and the Republika Srpska ministries of interior and local police forces. By establishing those positions, IPTF officers could seek clarification of local police practices, identify deficiencies in their skills, and observe the competency of individuals and the organization.

This comprehensive capacity development framework was supported, in conjunction with SFOR, by an assertive weapons inspection program in local police stations. The weapons inspection program ensured that the local police maintained only the equipment that they needed to fulfill their duties. The standard applied across the Federation and the Republika Srpska police forces was one long-barreled rifle for every 10 officers and one side arm for each officer (United Nations, 1997d).

UNMIBH was also responsible for investigating a large number of allegations of human rights violations that had been committed by local police officers. It appeared that the majority of those violations were usually a product of nationalist political agendas that had corrupted the local police forces at all levels. To minimize those types of violations in the future, UNMIBH identified that police forces in both entities would require greater transparency and public accountability (United Nations, 1999g).

The training initially provided to existing or serving local police officers by the IPTF was designed to increase the ability of the local police forces to operate according to internationally accepted policing standards. This training, initially delivered by IPTF officers, but later by trained local police officers, consisted of certified local police officers attending (a) a two-day information course, (b) a three-week transition course, and (c) a one-week human dignity course. At the same time, task force officers introduced (a) a field officer training course (in cooperation with the International Criminal Investigative Training Assistance Program), (b) a six-month recruit training course, and (c) a supervisor training course (United Nations, 1997b).

In the case of the Republika Srpska, coordinating the training and the transition of suitable serving officers from the special police to the new civilian police was aided by forming a working group of officials from the IPTF, the SFOR, and the ministry of the interior (United Nations, 1997d).

The second strategic area of training in which the IPTF provided assistance was the rehabilitation and the development of professional police academies and the establishment of a six-month police recruit training curriculum in the Federation and Republika Srpska (United Nations, 1997d). The new curriculum implemented a modern professional approach to recruit training compared to the "secondary school style program" that was in place (United Nations, 1998b).

To address the country's security concerns, the IPTF also established the following three specialized police training units, according to the United Nations (1998b):

- Critical Incident Management Unit for training and advice in the field of public security crisis management, crowd control, and disaster preparedness and response
- Organized Crime Unit for training and advice about organized crime, corruption of public officials, smuggling, and financial crime
- Drug Control Unit for training and advice on narcotic prevention, local and international interdiction, and street-level enforcement

Six specialists in each of the training units were to develop, deliver, and manage the training program; to prepare training materials; and to provide technical training advice to the governments of the Federation and Republika Srpska (United Nations, 1998b).

The Federation's first phase of police restructuring was near completion in March 1998 with 8 of the 10 cantons fully inaugurated by reducing staff members and by training and certifying officers (United Nations, 1998b). At this stage, UNMIBH and IPTF began to review the direction and the achievements of the mission to assess the quality of the police component. This systematic assessment evaluated the extent to which joint police forces were succeeding at breaking down ethnically based, parallel command structures and establishing standards of democratic policing (United Nations, 1998h).

Two components were used in the systematic assessment. The first component was undertaken by the newly created police assessment teams (PATs), formerly called contract assurance teams (CATs). The PATs completed an in-depth reference guide on the status of police reform in both entities. The guide provided a benchmark from which the strategies for the second phase of the mission and the police reform could be developed (United Nations, 1998h).

The second component was an audit of the ministry of the interior and police forces by a special response team of the UNMIBH Human Rights Office, termed Operation Transparency. The audit was in response to the findings of an investigative support team of the Human Rights Office. The special response team focused on the inadequate performance of the cantonal ministry organization and the failure of the ministry to integrate and unify its organizational structures, which were operating in parallel in Croat-dominated institutions (United Nations, 1999d).

The reviews, as suggested by the United Nations (1999g), concluded the following:

- In the Federation, the achievement of professional policing would require a shift from parallel policing in which Bosniac and Bosnian Croat police work in separate structures to unified policing in which they are effectively integrated into a multiethnic force.
- In the Republika Srpska, greater ethnic representation, decentralization, transparency, and accountability that was essential for a successful integration was still required.

From the review, UNMIBH made local police reform the principal long-term task of the IPTF (United Nations, 1998e). In addition to undertaking this concentrated role, the IPTF was to continue to monitor the local police's operations.

Any misconduct by the local police in the delivery of their general operational duties would provide information about the type of additional training that would still be required. This approach meant that monitoring would become the basis for police reform and that the results from the monitoring would feed directly into future reform efforts. The proposed monitoring framework would provide a means by which the IPTF would be able to measure its performance in increasing the capacity development of the local police. With the mission shifting its focus toward training and advising in the field and, in particular, selecting monitors who would work permanently alongside local chiefs of police or inside the ministries of interior, officers with sound professional skills and a confident grasp of democratic policing principles would be required (United Nations, 1998e).

Second Phase: 2000–02

The second phase of the police reform was based on the findings of a review completed by the IPTF in 1998 and on the development of a conceptual model and an implementation plan. This second phase consisted of a philosophical shift from the operational and developmental approaches to one of monitoring the performance and the recording of the newly inaugurated police services to ensure that the new services complied with agreed standards. The monitoring was to ensure that minority representation was increased and that the capacity for self-sufficiency was improving. The IPTF noted that the implementation of the second phase would require intensive support, especially in providing advice and in delivering training as well as in constant monitoring of the implementation in every municipality (United Nations, 1998b).

The conceptual model that formed the foundation of the future direction of the UNMIBH and the IPTF mission is presented in table 5.2. The strategic direction of the mission was made up of two parts: the first pertained to the individual officer and the second to the police organization. Each of the parts contained areas that were identified as contributing to the competence or the integrity of the individual or the organization. The model also

Table 5.2. UNMIBH Police Reform and Restructure Matrix

	Individual	Organization
Competence	• Basic competence and human rights training • Public order training • New crime challenges training	• Adequate resources • Effective management and human resource systems • Interpolice force cooperation
Integrity	• Law enforcement personnel registry • In-depth checks (housing status, criminal records, academic credentials, wartime conduct)	• Multiethnic and gender • Depoliticization—police commissioner and director of police project • Transparency and public accountability
Endpoints	**Certification of personnel**	**Accreditation of institutions**

Source: Adapted from United Nations (2002a).

identified an endpoint benchmark that needed to be obtained to ensure that the individual and the organization met the international standard of professionalism.

To achieve the mission's three goals, the implementation plan was organized into six core IPTF programs, which enabled evaluation and measurement to take place. Table 5.3 presents the six core programs with their benchmark measures, the required actions taken by the IPTF from 2000 to achieve the benchmarks, and the IPTF performance measurements.

To enable the UNMIBH and the IPTF to monitor the progress of the local police toward achieving the benchmarks of the conceptual model and implementation plan, the mission extended the co-location strategy to include the police force's legal, finance, and budget departments. According to the United Nations (2001e), the following two evaluation mechanisms were introduced in February 2001:

- Performance reports, which recorded minor acts of inadequate performance that could be remedied through training or other supportive measures
- Noncompliance reports, which recorded serious lapses of duty or violations of the law and obliged police officials to initiate internal disciplinary measures and to place the officer concerned under intensive IPTF scrutiny

At the same time, UNMIBH and IPTF introduced a professional and accountability disciplinary code and a number of specialized training courses for management. Those courses covered handling hazardous materials,

counterterrorism, and riot control. The practical curriculum for joint training in riot control was developed in consultation with the SFOR (United Nations, 2001i).

The deployment of minority ethnic police officers was a major issue for UNMIBH and IPTF when implementing the reform strategies in both of the entities. To increase ethnic representation and to address the gender balance in both of the Federation and Republika Srpska police forces, the mission implemented four programs in conjunction with the implementation plan. The United Nations (2002k) described the following programs:

- Voluntary redeployment for minority law enforcement personnel
- Selection of minority cadets for the two police academies
- Refresher training program for returning former police officers
- Recruitment campaigns to encourage female enrollment at the academies

The mission also provided a housing assistance as a further incentive to encourage the return of minority officers (United Nations, 2002k).

In December 2001, the UNMIBH began a comprehensive analysis of systems to restructure all of the key areas of law enforcement administrations. The review involved (a) development of a manual of law enforcement standards and procedures, (b) local self-assessment of compliance with those standards and procedures, (c) onsite assessment by IPTF, (d) establishment of local police change

Table 5.3. Six Core Programs of the Implementation Plan

Core Program	Number	Benchmark	Required IPTF Action	IPTF Performance Measure
Police Reform	1.1	Individual police officers meet international standards of professionalism and integrity.	Check the following: Wartime background Professional performance Legality of housing Educational credentials Completion of training Citizenship Criminal records	(a) Registration of serving police officers (b) Initial screening before awarding provisional authorization (c) Final in-depth check leading to full certification
	1.2	Program raises skills of local police officers.	Develop and deliver training courses and a mentoring program to a recognized international standard.	Satisfactory completion of mandated training
Police Restructuring	2.1	Program develops a sustainable police force.	Ensure that local police have the following: Adequate resources Efficient organizational structure Insulation from political interference Appropriate ethnic and gender representation	(a) Voluntary redeployment for minority law enforcement personnel (b) Selection of minority cadets for the two police academies (c) Refresher training program for returning former police officers (d) Recruitment campaigns to encourage female enrollment at the academies
Police and Criminal Justice System	3.1	Police forces are a partner in the justice sector.	Foster relations between justice sector agencies. Monitor court cases. Train local police.	(a) Maintenance of support and advisory function (b) Provision of liaison (c) Advice about legal procedures
Institution and Interpolice Force Cooperation	4.1	Program achieves the ability to combat national, regional, and transnational crime.	Establish a state border service (SBS). Establish intelligence capability. Establish physical security capability.	(a) Establishment of SBS (b) Implementation of intelligence framework (c) Establishment of State Investigation and Protection Agency (SIPA) (d) Implementation of special trafficking operations program (STOP)
Public Awareness	5.1	Program is established to create trust and confidence in local police.	Arrange the following: Community open days School visits Police demonstrations Website	Implementation and maintenance of all actions
Participation in United Nations Peacekeeping	6.1	Local police officers are able to be deployed on United Nations missions.	Ensure that local police have appropriate skills to be considered for United Nations deployments.	United Nations' acceptance for local police to be deployed on missions

Source: Author (from various United Nations documents).

management teams in each law enforcement agency, and (e) implementation of both short- and long-term recommendations by the change management teams (United Nations, 2002f). A package of reforms and recommendations was developed in cooperation with local authorities (United Nations, 2010a). Upon completion of the analysis, the framework ensured that the local police administrations had assumed the increased responsibility for future police restructuring.

Mission Achievements (Outcome)

At the time that the UN Security Council authorized the UNMIBH, the mission to Bosnia and Herzegovina was the most extensive police reform and restructuring program undertaken by the United Nations to date (United Nations, 2010a). The mission achieved its mandate and reached the performance measures that were set in consultation with local authorities in the conceptual model and the implementation plan. The mission provided the stability and the foundation for sustainable capacity development of the police forces. This approach ensured the smooth transition during the hand-over of long-term monitoring to the EU.

The UNMIBH demonstrated its ability to undertake and implement a complex mandate in accordance with a strategic plan that included completion timetables and realistic and finite performance measurements. The IPTF was able to quickly establish a high level of security that allowed Bosnia and Herzegovina to develop and establish mechanisms and institutions to fully participate in the regional and international fight against organized crime and terrorism (United Nations, 2010a). The mission implemented a comprehensive training framework to ensure that all police officers from the Federation and Republika Srpska had completed the human dignity course and the transitional training by the end of 1999 (United Nations, 1999g).

The high level of public security provided by the mission and the mission's approach to reforming and restructuring the police laid the foundation for the Bosnia and Herzegovina postwar recovery and development. The sense of stability provided the environment for the return of more than 250,000 refugees to their prewar homes (United Nations, 2010a).

Organized and transnational crime was reduced by the establishment of an SBS, which saw a dramatic decrease in the flow of illegal migrants, a deterrence in narcotics and human trafficking, and a reduction in smuggling (United Nations, 2010a).

An innovative implementation plan for the mandate was fundamental to the mission's operational and strategic achievements. The mission's approach was to develop and to reassess its reform and restructuring progress. The implementation plan was adopted by the UN and was emulated in other UN peacekeeping missions and in the office of the high representative (United Nations, 2010a).

Ways the Mission Was Evaluated

Some of the major problems encountered in the mission were whether the police personnel offered by member states were available and professionally suitable (United Nations, 1996b). In the first three months of the mission, more than 80 monitors were repatriated because they could not meet the minimum language qualifications or pass the driving test. In some cases, the majority of a contingent failed one or more of the tests (United Nations, 1996a).

The IPTF had very limited resources following its transfer from the UNPROFOR. The IPTF had only 150 police monitors because of the delay in deploying more monitors. The difficulties encountered in the mission's initial stages were especially acute. A large number of officers were urgently required because of tense conditions in the Sarajevo suburbs (United Nations, 1996a). Those conditions included violent clashes between Serbs and Croatians.

One of the major obstacles faced by the mission in a number of the Federation cantons was not the reform of the police forces per se. It was the lack of political will in issues pertaining to uniform insignias and minority representation. The failure to resolve such issues caused extensive delays in the inauguration of restructured police forces and extended the timeframes of the mission. To address the operational difficulties that arose because of the inauguration of the cantons, the IPTF formed CATs. Those CATs assessed each cantonal police force's level of compliance with the standards set by the Bonn-Petersberg Agreement of April 25, 1996, and carried out an extensive evaluation of the role and operations of the mission. The

CAT review, according to the United Nations (1998e), focused on the following seven agreement standards:

1. Ethnic composition of the cantonal police services
2. Degree of cooperation between and among police officers of different ethnic groups
3. Quality of that cooperation
4. Operation of the cantonal police chains of command and the free flow of information between commanders of different ethnic groups
5. Degree to which the orders emanating from the chain of command are obeyed by officers of the different ethnic groups
6. Freedom of movement within the canton
7. Quality and thoroughness of investigations carried out by the cantonal criminal police sections

The evaluation highlighted the need for greater coordination and sharing of information between the IPTF and local police forces. In light of the reassessment, the IPTF shifted the emphasis from police monitoring to police development as the principal long-term goal of the mission. Clearer performance goals were set to measure progress on this and other IPTF objectives (United Nations, 1998e). The findings were supported by the results of the CAT assessments, which were used to do the following (United Nations, 1998e):

- Identify and address reform and restructuring problems that had arisen.
- Evaluate the level at which the cantonal police services were operating.
- Introduce changes to oblige police throughout the Federation to adhere to democratic standards of policing.

The mission undertook a further comprehensive audit of six police stations in the city of Mostar in September and October 1999. The audit revealed deficiencies in fulfilling the ethnicity requirements of police structures. At the same time, an inspection in the majority Bosnian Croat areas of Bosnia and Herzegovina confirmed the existence of (a) parallel budgets and parallel personnel systems, (b) undeclared police personnel, (c) separate crime databases, and (d) shortcomings in the chain of command that con-

stituted major impediments to professional and democratic policing. To develop and implement change in the local police, the mission designed "an enhanced and potentially more effective strategic approach." This approach specifically built on existing reform strategies by targeting the areas of risk and targeting resources. It consisted of a full co-location of IPTF with key local police managers, extensive use of audits, and vigorous implementation of noncompliance and decertification policies (United Nations, 1999l).

Conclusion

After the earlier UN mission in Haiti from September 1993 to June 1996, UNMIBH was the most expansive transformational operation the UN had ever undertaken (Smith, Holt, and Durch, 2007). The IPTF task was primarily one of monitoring, but the mandate was subsequently expanded to include the reform of the local police.

The mission was successful in completing a number of key aspects of its mandate, including (a) reducing the size of the local police from 45,000 to 16,000 officers, (b) increasing the ethnic composition of the local police, and (c) restoring freedom of movement by introducing a common vehicle license plate. The mission also helped establish the state border police and introduced international policing standards to the police academies.

UNMIBH was terminated on December 31, 2002, following the completion of its mandate (United Nations, 2010a) and following the July 12, 2002, passing of UN Security Council Resolution 1423 (United Nations, 2002n). The mission was replaced by the European Union Police Mission (EUPM) on January 1, 2003.

Case Study: European Union Police Mission to Bosnia and Herzegovina

Background to the Mission

During the meeting of the General Affairs Section of the Council of the European Union on January 28, 2002, the council announced it had given approval to deploy a "follow-on" European Union Police Mission (EUPM) to the United Nations International Police Task Force (IPTF) in Bosnia and Herzegovina (European Union, 2002), which would begin January 1, 2003. The mission would be a seamless transition from the IPTF, and the deployment would comprise more than 400 experienced officers (Solana, 2002a). The EUPM would ensure the continuing professional development of the police forces in Bosnia and Herzegovina for three years (Peace Implementation Council, 2002).

The seamless transition from the United Nations Mission in Bosnia and Herzegovina (UNMIBH) to the EUPM was achieved by the EUPM's retaining 119 IPTF police advisers and adopting the same priorities that had guided the work of the preceding mission (Merlingen and Ostrauskaite, 2006).

The EUPM's aim would involve a broad effort to strengthen and address the area of rule of law in Bosnia and Herzegovina (Solana, 2002a) and would include police activities that would "be mutually supportive and reinforcing" (European Union, 2002). The approach would "be comprehensive and would include both the EUPM and European Union's training and institution building programme"(European Union, 2002). This police reform framework would contribute to the overall implementation of peace in Bosnia and Herzegovina and would ensure that Bosnia and Herzegovina was able to fulfill the remaining 10 points "of indispensable reforms" required by the European Union Road Map as noted by Solana (2002a).

The EUPM was based on the understanding that the IPTF had made strides in assisting police reform in Bosnia and Herzegovina and in the postwar context in which members of the IPTF were deployed. The mission's primary task was to restructure the existing police services; examine individual police officers; and help recruit, select, and train police forces that would contribute positively to the peace implementation in Bosnia and Herzegovina (Solana, 2002b). The European Union (EU) noted that a framework for democratic policing existed (Solana, 2003). In regard to those activities, the IPTF had performed with distinction. However, the EU was aware that it also had a responsibility to assist with the reform of police in Bosnia and Herzegovina, and that the mission should not duplicate the IPTF's efforts as the

Bosnia and Herzegovina police forces were at a different stage than they were in 1995 (Solana, 2002b).

The EU noted that it was time for the Bosnia and Herzegovina authorities to fully assume their law enforcement responsibilities. To assist the Bosnia and Herzegovina police with this task, the EU, in conjunction with the UNMIBH, IPTF, and Organisation for Security and Co-operation in Europe (OSCE), identified the main priority of the EUPM. Priority was given to assist the Bosnia and Herzegovina police to establish sustainable police arrangements under Bosnia and Herzegovina ownership aligned with the best European and international practice. It was the EUPM's task to monitor, mentor, advise, and assist in this process.

The overarching strategy of the EUPM called for all of the initiatives and programs to be founded on the principle of human rights. All professional European police services saw this principle as being a fundamental benchmark and considered that any reformed police organization must reflect the standards in its own structure and practice. To ensure that this approach was implemented during the mission, the mission field reports were to include reporting on human rights (Solana, 2002b).

The mission did not have executive authority to investigate allegations of human rights abuse. To allow the mission to examine the investigation of such cases that had been conducted by the Bosnia and Herzegovina police, the EUPM established a system of benchmarking. Benchmarks and targets were set in consultation with the Bosnia and Herzegovina police and were designed to provide a basis for the review and monitoring of police violence against Croatian refugees and the recruitment of police, promotions, and discipline (Solana, 2002b).

Mandate of the Mission

On March 11, 2002, the Council of the European Union passed Joint Action 2002/210/CFSP, which established the EUPM in Bosnia and Herzegovina for an initial period of two years. It was based on the council's February 18, 2002, announcement that the EU was ready to ensure that they would be able to deploy the EUPM to replace the IPTF in Bosnia and Herzegovina by January 1, 2003. The EU also announced that it aimed to take a broad approach in its activities to address "the whole range of Rule of Law aspects, including institution building programmes and police activities which should be mutually supportive and reinforcing" (Council of the European Union, 2002).

The mission was based on the general objectives of Annex 11 of the Dayton Agreement. That agreement was designed to establish sustainable policing arrangements under Bosnia and Herzegovina ownership in accordance with best European and international practice and thereby raise the current standards of the Bosnia and Herzegovina police. The council envisaged that the EUPM would not hold executive powers or deploy an armed component. Instead, the EUPM would be entrusted with the necessary authority to monitor, mentor, and inspect the indigenous police, and it should achieve its goals by the end of 2005 (Council of the European Union, 2002).

To ensure that there was a seamless transition from the IPTF to the proposed EUPM, the council authorized a planning team to be established to develop the mission from April 1 to December 31, 2002. The council also proposed that the EUPM's headquarters would be in Sarajevo and that an initial 24 monitoring units would be co-located within the "[p]olice structures at [the] medium-high level, including within entities, Public Security Centres, cantons, [the] State Intelligence Protection Agency, [the] State Border Services and within the Brčko district" (Council of the European Union, 2002).

The EUPM mission statement detailed the objectives of the mission. According to the Council of the European Union (2002), the EUPM was to do the following:

- Preserve, through continuity with the achievements of the IPTF mission, the existing levels of institutional and personal proficiency.
- Enhance, through monitoring, mentoring, and inspecting, the police managerial and operational capacities through specific focus of delegation of power and quality-oriented management principles, as well as improving the operational planning capacity that is based on analysis.
- Strengthen professionalism at the strategic and senior officer level within the ministry of interior through advisory and inspection functions.
- Monitor the exercise of appropriate political control over the police.

The Council of the European Union (2002) describes the objectives of the mission statement that established the operational-level framework by which the EUPM was to ensure that members of the Bosnia and Herzegovina police force would do the following:

- Act in a professional manner and in accordance with relevant legislation and regulations.
- Be free of national government political interference and be led by apolitical, qualified, and accountable personnel.
- Possess the integrity, knowledge, and means to perform their duties in a transparent and objective manner.
- Adopt a professional culture at ministries and at the senior police officer level that would be based on a fair, transparent, and accountable system of internal management, including the exercise of internal controls and disciplinary procedures of the highest standard.
- Ensure that management practices are carried out through fair and impartial personnel policies for recruitment, training, specialization, promotion, and discipline.
- Be based on a transparent structure that considers the multiple ethnic composition of the society and that deals satisfactorily with gender-related issues.
- Manage personnel and resources effectively within an affordable and appropriate institutional framework.
- Standardize data recording and analysis systems to facilitate information sharing for operational planning and investigations with a view to promoting a crime statistics system for all of Bosnia and Herzegovina.
- Develop police cooperation among all Bosnia and Herzegovina police forces, including at interentity and intercanton levels (for example, building structures for coordination, exchange of information, and confidence building).
- Undertake criminal investigations of major corruption cases regardless of political implications and the person involved.
- Be capable of investigating and countering the full range of criminal activities, including organized crime and terrorism with a state-level capability for forming an effective part of the administration of justice, cooperating closely with the prosecution, and operating within a reformed criminal justice system.

- Develop—in close cooperation with the stabilization force (SFOR)—specialized information sharing in support of the state-level capability and other appropriate authorities.
- Possess capacity to respond to public disorder in accordance with modern police standards and without political or ethnic bias.
- Constructively cooperate with police services of neighboring states and EU members.

To achieve the objectives set, the EUPM recommended to member states that only qualified personnel be deployed to the mission and that such personnel would be sent to the mission for a minimum of one year. Furthermore, the EUPM should also do the following, as suggested in the Council of the European Union (2002):

1. Co-locate the international police alongside commanders at the various entities, public security centers (PSCs), cantons, Brčko district, state investigation and protection agency (SIPA), and state border service (SBS) at medium and senior levels of the Bosnia and Herzegovina police.
2. Remove noncompliant officers from office through a recommendation by the EU police commissioner to the high representative.
3. Coordinate with the office of the high representative to further overall objectives in the rule of law of the international community, as well as with other organizations within the international community.
4. Act as a liaison with SFOR on public security issues including the assurance of SFOR support in extremis.

The Council Joint Action 210 Mandate was extended for another two years from January 1, 2006, by the Council Joint Action 824 (Council of the European Union, 2005e). The mission has since been extended every two years when the previous year's mandate expires.

Each renewal of the mandate has consisted of a carry-over of objectives and tasks. However, the renewal in 2007 included an article that established a six-month review. This review process was to be carried out with criteria specified in the concept of operations and the op-

erational plan and was to take into account developments in police reform and "enable adjustments to be made to the EUPM's activities, as necessary"(Council of the European Union, 2007d).

Mission Deployment Environment

The environment in Bosnia and Herzegovina was regarded as being reasonably secure, but it was capable of erupting into violence. Since the conclusion of the war in 1995, a number of violent civilian riots have resulted in extensive damage and injured peacekeepers.

Although the UNMIBH had been successful in achieving some aspects of their mandate and that the IPTF had made strides in assisting police reform in Bosnia and Herzegovina (Solana, 2002b), it was accepted that the local police could not be counted on to enforce the law. The local police were identified as corrupt and inconsistent with the application of the law, especially to organized criminal activity and ethnic violence.

The EUPM was the first mission undertaken by the EU within the framework of the European Security and Defence Policy (ESDP) and was to carry on the reform of the Federation and Republika Srpska police forces that had been started by the UNMIBH. A number of programs were not fully implemented by the UNMIBH because they had been subverted by political obstruction or by intentional police action.

Actions of the Mission (Output)

The EUPM made considerable advances in developing a sustainable police arrangement under the Bosnia and Herzegovina government. This improvement was achieved by local ownership of the police reform process, which was realized by establishing the Directorate for Police Co-ordination at the state level and the following three boards at the provincial level, according to the European Union (2010b):

1. Project Implementation Board
2. Senior Management Board
3. Police Restructuring Commission

The four strategic priorities of the mission, as identified by the United Nations (2005a), were the following:

1. Undertake institution and capacity building at the management level.
2. Combat organized crime and corruption.
3. Develop financial viability and sustainability.
4. Promote police independence and accountability.

In partnership with local police, other international stakeholders, and bilateral donors, the mission developed and implemented seven core programs. The programs addressed the key areas of expertise and the methods required to raise the level of policing in Bosnia and Herzegovina to meet the best of European standards including being free from inappropriate political interference (United Nations, 2005a). To paraphrase, four of the seven core programs were identified as follows:

1. Institution and capacity building
2. The fight against organized crime and corruption
3. Financial viability and sustainability of the local police
4. Development of police independence and accountability

Three organizations were developed and established by the mission: the Ministry of Security (MoS), the SIPA, and the SBS. The MoS was fully staffed and the divisions of the organization that covered all areas of responsibility were operational by mid-2005. A new series of laws was also adopted, thus creating and regulating a new Immigration Service. Moreover, a further law, which governed the working of the SBS, was introduced (United Nations, 2005a).

The SIPA has been transformed into an operational police agency that has enhanced executive powers that enable it to fight organized crime and corruption (European Union, 2010a). The majority of heads of departments have been appointed, and a total of 279 police officers were recruited for the SIPA. Legal and guidance framework by which the SIPA operates was established, along with a headquarters and two regional offices. By late 2004, the criminal investigation department had begun to conduct investigations (United Nations, 2005a).

All aspects of police education were brought together under a separate program in May 2004, and an agreement was reached about the creation of a standardized, countrywide training system. The first level of training was delivered to new recruits in the lower ranks, and a project was launched to fully complement the curriculum of all three training schools in Bosnia and Herzegovina (United Nations, 2005a).

A nationwide police intelligence system was designed and introduced so that officers could submit information. Intelligence meetings were held regularly in all areas, and there was an effective flow of intelligence between the public security centers and the state-level agencies (United Nations, 2005a).

To achieve a sustainable and financially viable local police, the mission implemented a program to develop the capacity of administrators in planning budgets for organizational units, managing resources, rationalizing the use of police equipment, controlling inventories and payrolls, and implementing general budgets (United Nations, 2005a). Staff members of the Federation and Republika Srpska ministries of the interior were trained to establish and monitor budgets at a local level and, in particular, to match operational planning to the budget process (United Nations, 2005a).

Mission Implementation (Model)

The EUPM comprised 862 personnel, of whom 472 were seconded police officers, 61 were international civilians, and 329 were national staff members from Bosnia and Herzegovina. All but one of the 25 EU member states participated in the mission (United Nations, 2005a).

To assist in implementing the mission mandate, the EUPM developed "an innovative police reform model" (Merlingen and Ostrauskaite, 2006). The model required comprehensive local participation. The mission established a structure that provided a relationship between local police practitioners with the newly created police steering board (PSB) and the working groups responsible for specific mission programs and projects.

The development of a strategic implementation plan (SIP) coordinated the efforts of the EUPM and the PSB. The SIP codified the criteria for achieving the benchmarks "that were operationally useful as systemic instruments of countrywide police reforms" (Merlingen and Ostrauskaite, 2006, p. 63). Furthermore, the aim of the EUPM interventions was to achieve the four strategic objectives that were stated earlier. Those four strategic objectives were developed into seven program implementation plans (PIPs), which were subsequently used to form the basis for the framework to monitor and mentor the SIPA.

Mission Achievements (Outcome)

The EUPM made considerable achievements in developing sustainable policing arrangements in Bosnia and Herzegovina, including the following (United Nations, 2005a):

- Transformation of the SIPA into an operational police agency with enhanced executive powers to fight organized crime and corruption
- Solid development of other state-level institutions, in particular the MoS and the SBS

Ways the Mission Was Evaluated

The mission made measurable progress in strengthening the state-level law enforcement agencies of Bosnia and Herzegovina. The mission achieved a sustainable level of delivering local police services, and it successfully encouraged local ownership of the reform process. As the mission entered the final stages of its mandate, it was well placed in partnership with the local authorities "to complete its prime directive and to leave in place sustainable

and effective policing arrangements in Bosnia and Herzegovina that are in line with the best European practices." The professionalization of the Bosnia and Herzegovina police forces will take several years to complete. With the mandate of EUPM ending on December 31, 2005, consideration should be given as to how best support the further development of the local police of Bosnia and Herzegovina (United Nations, 2005a).

Conclusion

There has been a series of EUPM missions since January 1, 2003. The first EUPM, referred to as EUPM I, was authorized for an initial period of three years and was the first mission launched under the European Security and Defence Policy. Following an invitation by the Bosnia and Herzegovina authorities on the expiry of EUPM's mandate in December 2005, the EU decided to continue the mission with a modified mandate and with a reduced number of police officers. The latest EUPM mandate was extended until December 31, 2011.

The EUPM was a higher-level mission than that undertaken by the UNMIBH. The EUPM focused primarily on medium-term capacity-building projects. As noted by J. J. D. (Paddy) Ashdown, the former high representative of Bosnia and Herzegovina (2003), the EUPM peacebuilding activities were possibly more shaped by the prospect of Bosnia's integration into the EU (and the North Atlanta Treaty Organization) than by the risk of descent back into civil war.

Chapter 6

Republic of Burundi

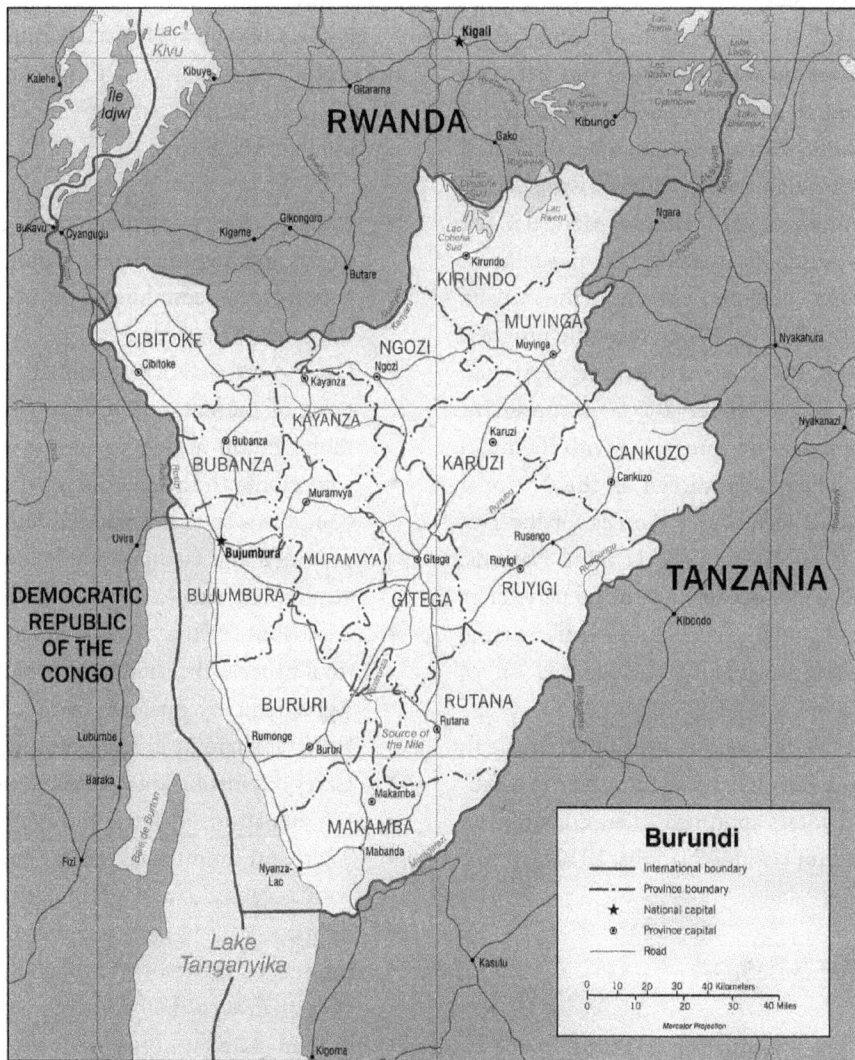

Map 6.1. Burundi

Source: Courtesy of the University of Texas Libraries, The University of Texas at Austin.

Case Study: United Nations Operation in Burundi

Background to the Mission

The Burundi Civil War, an armed conflict that lasted for 13 years (between 1993 and 2005), was based on long-standing ethnic divisions between the Hutu and Tutsi tribes. The conflict began October 21, 1993, when members of the Tutsi tribe assassinated the first democratically elected president since independence was gained from Belgium in 1962 (United Nations, 2004ac). As a result of the assassination, violence broke out between the two tribes, leading to an estimated 300,000 fatalities in Burundi and to the 1994 mass murder of an estimated 800,000 people in the neighboring nation of Rwanda.

The conflict continued until Nelson Mandela, the president of South Africa, facilitated cease-fire talks in Tanzania in 2000. That meeting, known as the Arusha talks, closed on November 30, 2000, with little progress made (United Nations, 2004ab). At a summit of African leaders in Tanzania in November 2003, the president of Burundi signed a cease-fire agreement with the main Hutu rebel group, which was known as the National Council for Defense of Democracy–Forces for the Defense of Democracy (CNDD–FDD) (United Nations, 2004o). The CNDD–FDD became a political party after signing the agreement, and the rebel Hutu militia became integrated into the predominantly Tutsi armed forces (United Nations, 2004ac).

By early 2005, many developments had been made in the peace process. The Burundi president agreed to establish a new army, and voters approved a new constitution in a national referendum (United Nations, 2010k).

Mandate of the Mission

After determining that the situation in Burundi continued to constitute a threat to international peace and security in the region, the United Nations (UN) Security Council adopted Resolution 1545, which established the United Nations Operation in Burundi (ONUB) for an initial period of six months (United Nations, 2004ac).

The mission was established to "support and help to implement the efforts undertaken by Burundians to restore lasting peace and bring about national reconciliation, as provided under the Arusha Agreement" (United Nations, 2010k).

The UN Security Council authorized the mission "to use all necessary means to ensure respect for cease-fire agreements through monitoring their implementation and investigating their violations" (United Nations, 2004ac; 2010n). The mission's authorized strength was 5,560 military personnel and 120 civilian police personnel (United Nations, 2004e; 2004ac; 2010n).

As described by the United Nations (2004ac; 2010n), the ONUB was mandated to provide advice and assistance and to contribute to the efforts of the transitional government as follows:

- Monitor the implementation of cease-fire agreements and investigate any violations.
- Promote the reestablishment of confidence between the Burundian forces.
- Carry out the disarmament and demobilization portions of the national program of disarmament, demobilization, and reintegration of combatants.
- Contribute to the creation of the necessary security conditions so that humanitarian assistance could be provided and facilitate the voluntary return of refugees and internally displaced persons.
- Contribute to the successful completion of the electoral process that had been stipulated in the Arusha Agreement by ensuring a secure environment for free, transparent, and peaceful elections to take place.
- Carry out institutional reforms, including the integration of national defense and internal security forces.
- Train and monitor the police to ensure compliance with accepted standards of democracy and human rights.
- Implement the reform of the judiciary and correction system, in accordance with the Arusha Agreement.
- Extend state authority and utilities throughout the territory, including police and judicial institutions.

The main task of the ONUB civilian police was to provide support to the transitional government so it could prepare a comprehensive plan to integrate and to develop the Burundi National Police (BNP). By developing curriculum, vetting candidates, and instructing trainers, the ONUB civilian police would also help plan and implement a training program for the police (United Nations, 2004d).

The mission's mandate was subsequently extended in six monthly increments until December 31, 2006 (United Nations, 2006g; 2010n).

Mission Deployment Environment

The Arusha Agreement created the framework for establishing the new Burundi National Defense and Security Forces, a national police of Burundi, and a General Intelligence Service. Approximately 7,189 persons in Burundi delivered the main policing functions that were spread across four different institutions: "the gendarmerie under the Ministry of Defence, the prosecutorial Judicial Police under the Ministry of Justice; and the Public Service Police and the Police of the Air, Borders, and Foreigners under two different sections of the Ministry of Public Security" (United Nations, 2004d).

The Arusha Agreement determined that all four police institutions would be restructured under the Ministry of Public Security, and an integrated police chief of staff would be appointed to head the approximately 20,000-officer national police force. The new police chief of staff was to prepare a strategy to form the new national police force. The transitional government agreed to the new national police force, which would make up 65 percent of the force for the transitional government and 35 percent for the CNDD–FDD (United Nations, 2004d).

Actions of the Mission (Output)

In August 2004, the ONUB police component assessed the organizational structure and the training capability of the BNP (United Nations, 2004o). The assessment formed the basis of the strategy to develop a comprehensive security plan for the national elections and to form a strategic plan that would enhance how the local police function (United Nations, 2004o).

To enable the monitoring and training of the new BNP, the ONUB created a security sector reform cell. It provided advice to the government about planning and implementing the integration and reform of the defense and security forces (United Nations, 2004o).

The transfer of former combatants to the BNP was assisted by the ONUB. As part of the transfer, the ONUB provided basic police training in the integration and reconciliation of 6,896 former combatants in 20 police training centers around the country. When the training was completed, the new police officers joined the 8,300 former members of the gendarmerie and the 1,400 former internal security police at 143 police posts throughout the country (United Nations, 2005u).

To improve the BNP training advisory capacity, the ONUB civilian police instructed 160 police trainers in operations and security (United Nations, 2005u). When the trainers completed their instruction, they were deployed to the police training centers (United Nations, 2005b). The ONUB civilian police also instructed approximately 500 BNP officers and 194 trainers in election security and other procedures and, jointly with the BNP, developed a number of new training modules (United Nations, 2005x).

The ONUB civilian police assisted the BNP in designing and implementing the electoral security plans. To ensure that coordination was achieved among the ONUB civilian police, the BNP, and the government during the elections, the ONUB and the BNP established a joint operations center (United Nations, 2005x).

In September 2005, the ONUB implemented a framework to ensure that coherency existed among the various international partners who provided support for the national police. The framework would manage donor funds that paid for the construction of six new police training centers, the establishment of a rehabilitation program for the provincial police commissariats, and the training of 20,000 police personnel (United Nations, 2005x).

By November 2005, the ONUB civilian police had integrated approximately 20,000 officers into the national police, implemented the new BNP organizational and rank structure, and finalized appointments of BNP executives (United Nations, 2005x). The ONUB had also delivered training in human rights (United Nations, 2006g), criminal investigation, and forensics to 183 officers. Moreover, the ONUB delivered a three-month training program to 2,300 officers (United Nations, 2005u).

In March 2006, the ONUB civilian police trained BNP senior officers and corporals in management and leadership. They also delivered specialized training courses in traffic management and investigations, airport security, and prison management to operational personnel (United Nations, 2006n).

In December 2006, the ONUB civilian police assisted the BNP in establishing a special unit to investigate cases of sexual and gender-based violence. The ONUB designed and developed specialized training modules in sexual and gender-based violence and standard operations procedures for the investigative unit (United Nations, 2006n).

Mission Implementation (Model)

The ONUB civilian police component was projected to have an authorized strength of 120 officers (United Nations, 2006g). However, the mission never attained that strength and by May 2005 had only reached 107 police advisers (United Nations, 2005p).

The major responsibility of the ONUB civilian police was to assist and provide advice to l'État-Major Général Intégré de la Police Nationale. Thus, l'État-Major Général Intégré was a national coordinating committee that comprised the police institutions and the signatories to the Arusha Agreement. The Burundi government established the committee on March 23, 2004, to develop a timetable, internal rules, and procedures for creating a national police service (United Nations, 2004o).

On July 6, 2004, l'État-Major Général Intégré finalized a plan that would form, train, and equip an interim police force to lead the country into the elections (United Nations, 2004o). The plan included a proposed structure and training of the BNP (United Nations, 2005u). To provide security for the elections, the BNP was to consist of 14,400 police officers who had completed a two-month training course in public order and who would form 20 tactical police units (United Nations, 2004o).

The August 2004 plan by l'État-Major Général Intégré formed the basis of the assessment undertaken by members of that group and by the ONUB civilian police (United Nations, 2004o). The assessment and the promulgation of a number of laws by the Burundi government on December 31, 2004, outlined "the creation, organization, composition, and functioning of the new National Defence Force and the new National Police service" (United Nations, 2005h) and formed the framework of the ONUB civilian police approach to the reform of the BNP.

The ONUB civilian police approach to the reform of the BNP was further supported by the Ministry of Public Security paper titled "Concept for the Integration of the Burundi National Police," which was released on January 19, 2005. The paper established the process and the "responsibilities of the different actors in the integration and transformation of the National Police" and detailed the two-phase approach to reform and integration as follows (United Nations, 2005h):

- Phase I—to develop the BNP capacity to ensure security during the national elections
- Phase II—to complete consolidation activities and long-term reform and capacity development initiatives

As part of Phase I, the ONUB civilian police assisted the BNP to select, vet, and screen potential candidates for the national police. The ONUB developed a 10-day training course to develop the BNP trainers who would deliver basic police training to identified candidates (United Nations, 2005h).

In early 2005, the ONUB civilian police developed a security sector reform strategy that outlined steps for the integration of the police force, "including timelines, the size of each force, and actions required of both the government and the international partners" (United Nations, 2005p).

During the mission, the ONUB civilian police and the BNP developed more than 40 police training manuals on a range of policing topics, including areas of specialization. The development of the manuals was aimed at building the capacity of the BNP, especially in the areas of investigating human rights and sexual and gender-based offenses (United Nations, 2005x).

In late 2005, the ONUB civilian police began a plan to draw down the mission and to withdraw personnel. During that period, the ONUB provided mentoring and advice to the BNP "on operational police matters, including investigations, patrols, report writing, and supervision" and provided "support to the Burundi National Police in logistics planning, human resources, training, and the development of legal frameworks" (United Nations, 2006g).

From March 2006, the remaining 15 ONUB police advisers assisted the BNP in developing core policing skills that included leadership training, specialized training, and reconciliation training. The development program delivered courses and seminars in criminal investigation, public order policing, patrol procedures, human rights, sexual exploitation and gender-based violence, community policing, traffic management, border control, jail procedures, rapid reaction, communications, and airport security (United Nations, 2006g).

In late 2006, the ONUB civilian police assisted the Ministry of Interior and Public Security to develop and establish operation centers that linked the various police components to provide swift and effective responses to security situations. The centers were to manage the police operational intervention on the ground (United Nations, 2006x).

Mission Achievements (Outcome)

The mission had made progress in stabilizing the security situation although the situation remained tenuous. The incidence of crime, including murder, theft, and rape, remained high. Many of the crimes committed were attributed to both police and military elements, thus compounding the effect of human rights violations.

The police component of the mission assisted the Ministry of Interior and Public Security to establish a more transparent human resource management system for the BNP. That component also planned the resources and the capacities required by the BNP (United Nations, 2006z). The police component assisted the BNP in establishing a special unit to deal with cases of sexual and gender-based violence.

Ways the Mission Was Evaluated

In late 2006, the UN secretary-general noted that although the ONUB had made progress in the Burundi security sector reform, this reform was limited by the BNP's operational experience, the large number of new personnel, and the limited delivery of training (United Nations, 2006x; 2006z). The secretary-general also identified that the BNP professionalization was impeded by its limited logistic framework, its low professional standards, and a culture of use of excessive force and corruption (United Nations, 2006g).

Conclusion

The ONUB civilian police successfully completed its mandate on December 31, 2006. The mission was succeeded by the United Nations Integrated Office in Burundi, which was established by UN Security Council Resolution 1719 (United Nations, 2006af) on October 25, 2006. The new mission, known as BINUB (Bureau Intégré des Nations Unies au Burundi), began on January 1, 2007, for an initial period of 12 months (United Nations, 2010k).

The mandate of BINUB extended the programs of the ONUB and included support to the government in the following six areas (United Nations, 2010k):

1. Strengthen the capacity of national institutions to address the root causes of conflict.
2. Develop a comprehensive plan for security sector reform (involving the BNP and the national army and combating the proliferation of small and light weapons).
3. Complete the program for the demobilization and reintegration of former combatants.
4. Facilitate the reintegration of returnees and internally displaced persons into their communities.
5. Establish a national human rights commission, and establish transitional justice mechanisms.
6. Promote freedom of the press.

Chapter 7

Republic of Côte d'Ivoire

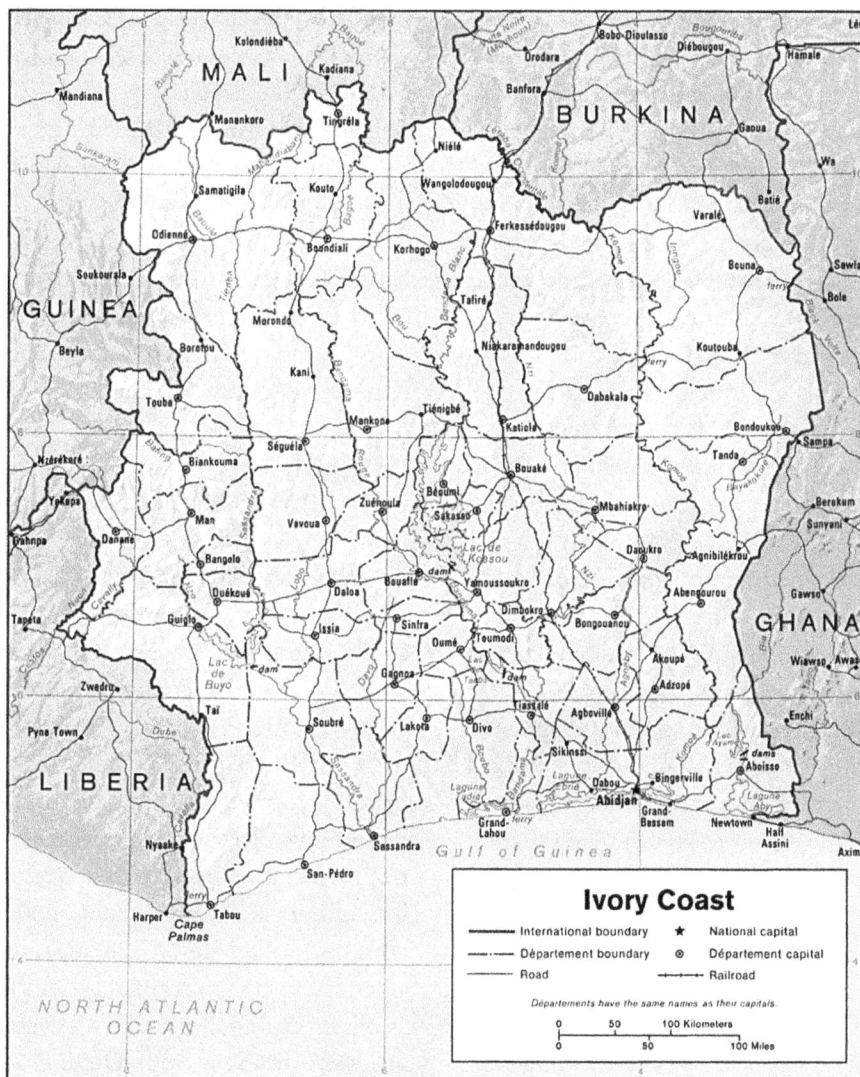

Map 7.1. Côte d'Ivoire
Source: Courtesy of the University of Texas Libraries, The University of Texas at Austin.

Case Study: United Nations Operation in Côte d'Ivoire

Background to the Mission

Following the gaining of independence in 1960, Côte d'Ivoire experienced political stability and relative socio-economic prosperity under its founding leader, President Félix Houphouët-Boigny. After the president's death on December 7, 1993, Côte d'Ivoire descended into a military and political power struggle causing intense political instability that resulted in a military coup d'état in December 1999 (United Nations, 2010b).

Despite a second unsuccessful coup attempt in January 2001, national elections took place in March of the same year. Following the election, the newly elected president "pursued a policy of national reconciliation and sought to decentralize State authority by organizing provincial elections" (United Nations, 2010b).

The president also sought to reform and to decrease the size of the army. This action led to attacks by approximately 800 soldiers on military installations in Abidjan and on two large provincial cities to protest against the soldiers' planned demobilization in 2003. Although loyalist security forces regained control of Abidjan, the rebels increased their control over the northern and western regions of the country, "as other disgruntled soldiers and civilians swelled their ranks" (United Nations, 2010b).

By the end of 2002, the rebel forces had strengthened their hold on the northern area and had transformed themselves into a political movement titled the Patriotic Movement of Côte d'Ivoire (MPCI). The situation became more complex with the emergence of two new armed groups: the Ivorian Popular Movement of the Great West (MPIGO) and the Movement for Justice and Peace (MJP), which, in November 2002, seized control of two western region towns (United Nations, 2010b).

Peace intervention talks between Côte d'Ivoire conflict groups were coordinated by the Economic Community of West African States (ECOWAS) and took place on September 30, 2002. Those peace efforts led to a ceasefire agreement on October 17, 2002, between the government and the MPCI, and they enabled negotiations to begin about governing the country. However, both parties to the agreement were slow to implement a number of its requirements, which caused ECOWAS to deploy a peacekeeping force on December 31, 2002 (United Nations, 2010b).

A number of meetings took place in late 2002 and early 2003, which culminated in the signing of the Linas-Marcoussis Agreement on January 23, 2003 (United Nations, 2010b). However, all parties raised concerns over different aspects of the agreement, which led to friction and a number of aspects not being implemented. The friction led the UN Security Council to adopt Resolution 1479 (United Nations, 2003s) on June 23, 2003, which authorized the establishment of the United Nations Mission in Côte d'Ivoire (MINUCI) (United Nations, 2010b).

The MINUCI's mandate was to facilitate the implementation of the Linas-Marcoussis Agreement by the Ivorian parties and to monitor the security situation. In late 2003, parties to the agreement could not agree on the structure of governance, which resulted in sporadic violence erupting between the parties and among the civilian population (United Nations, 2010b).

Mandate of the Mission

The unstable environment led to the UN Security Council's adopting Resolution 1528 (United Nations, 2004y) on February 27, 2004, which approved the United Nations Operation in Côte d'Ivoire (UNOCI) (United Nations, 2010b). The mission was established on April 4, 2004, for an initial period of 12 months. UNOCI comprised personnel from the MINUCI and the ECOWAS peacekeeping forces and had an authorized strength of 6,440 military personnel and 350 police officers (United Nations, 2004y). However, the authorized strength of the mission was revised and amended on a number of occasions because of the situation in the country and the needs of the mission (United Nations, 2010b). On June 24, 2005, the authorized strength of the civilian police component was increased to 725 officers, which included three formed police units (FPUs) (United Nations, 2005ad).

The UN Security Council, as part of Resolution 1528 (United Nations, 2004y) also authorized the deployment of a small civilian police planning team to Abidjan. The planning team was to provide support for the government and for the deployment of the UNOCI (United Nations, 2004a).

The objective of the UNOCI mandate was primarily to assist the government of Côte d'Ivoire—in conjunction with ECOWAS—to restore a civilian policing presence throughout Côte d'Ivoire. The mission was to advise the Côte d'Ivoire government about reestablishing the authority of the judiciary and the rule of law throughout the country and about restructuring the internal security services (United Nations, 2004z; 2010e). The UNOCI police advisers provided "a key role in instilling confidence in the population so as to facilitate the restoration of a police presence and to strengthen the judiciary in northern Côte d'Ivoire" (United Nations, 2004a). The UNOCI police were to "advise the Government on restructuring the [Côte d'Ivoire] Gendarmerie and the National Police [FANCI, or Forces Armées Nationales de Côte d'Ivoire]" (United Nations, 2004a).

In the southern part of the country, the UNOCI police advisers were to focus on advising and observing the operations of law enforcement authorities. This approach was adopted to ensure that police abuse was reported and to strengthen the professionalism in FANCI and the gendarmerie (United Nations, 2004a).

In March 2005, the mandate of the UNOCI was extended for 12 months until April 4, 2006, (United Nations, 2005k) and was extended again for 12-month periods when the mandate expired. As of June 2010, the mission was ongoing.

On November 1, 2006, the UN Security Council adopted Resolution 1721 (United Nations, 2006ag), which amended the UNOCI mandate to include the design and development of a plan to restructure the Côte d'Ivoire Defense and Security Forces (United Nations, 2010b).

Mission Deployment Environment

The implementation of the Linas-Marcoussis Agreement encountered a number of serious obstacles, which included massive and violent demonstrations in Abidjan and in other towns. Protesters demonstrated against the allocation of the Ministries of Defense and Interior to the rebel movements. During those demonstrations, French interests and installations in Abidjan were targeted and deliberately attacked (United Nations, 2010b).

Following a speech from the president, the street demonstrations in Abidjan ceased. The president's speech and the acceptance of the rebel leaders into a new government had a calming effect on the volatile security situation.

The Côte d'Ivoire FANCI and the gendarmerie had the responsibility for the country's internal security. Those two law enforcement agencies were administered by two different ministries. The FANCI was made up of approximately 12,000 officers and was administered by the Ministry of Internal Security. The gendarmerie, which was made up of approximately 8,522 officers, was administered by the Ministry of Defense (United Nations, 2004a).

Actions of the Mission (Output)

The UNOCI police advisers initially focused on providing technical assistance for the reform and restructuring and on the training of the Ivorian police and gendarmerie. By March 2005, the UNOCI developed training modules for courses about maintaining public law and order, protecting human rights, policing the community, and investigating crimes (United Nations, 2005k). However, because of the prevailing political stalemate, the UNOCI was not able to complete some of the core elements in its mandate (United Nations, 2005a). The UNOCI could not restore a civilian police presence throughout the country, and neither was it able to provide advice about restructuring the internal security services (United Nations, 2005k).

The main reason the UNOCI had not been able to provide advice about restructuring the internal security services was the violent demonstrations in Abidjan in November 2004. Following those demonstrations, the UNOCI changed its assistance from developing capacity in the internal security services to advising about the police response to the security situation and to "improving public confidence in the Ivorian law enforcement institutions through community policing activities" in key Abidjan neighborhoods (United Nations, 2005k).

In December 2004, the UNOCI assisted the FANCI in establishing the Common Security Co-ordination Centre.

The center consisted of senior representatives from the Ivorian internal security agencies and the UNOCI, and it coordinated the increasing police presence in Abidjan through the implementation of joint patrols in Bouaké, Daloa, Yamoussoukro, and Bondoukou (United Nations, 2005k).

The UNOCI police component also supported the disarmament, demobilization, and re-integration (DDR) program by securing the disarmament and cantonment sites, escorting and transporting former combatants, "responding to any violent disturbances in and around the [DDR] camps, ... providing weapons control and destruction facilities, and ensuring a secure environment" (United Nations, 2006a). The police advisers also implemented an action plan to end the use of and recruitment of child soldiers in the militias. They developed and delivered a number of different training courses. In fact, advisers trained 600 Ivorian security auxiliaries in basic security functions and 630 FANCI and gendarmerie officers in child protection procedures (United Nations, 2006h; 2006o).

Mission Implementation (Model)

In May 2004, the initial deployment of the civilian police component of the mission consisted of 49 officers whose task it was to develop a national training program for the FANCI and the gendarmerie and to provide advice in relation to their reform and restructure (United Nations, 2004p). Although the UN Security Council agreed to the mission in February 2004, and given that the authorized civilian strength had increased from 350 to 725, the mission did not reach its authorized strength until mid-2006. The major reason that the mission did not meet its authorized strength was it could not recruit French-speaking civilian police officers, who were needed to undertake duties in training, ethics, criminal investigations, and border patrol (United Nations, 2006a).

The mission's authorized strength was increased substantially. In November 2004, in response to the security crisis, its composition changed to include an FPU component. The increase in personnel was to provide security and protection for the UN force and to increase the operational reserve of UNOCI (United Nations, 2005r). Table 7.1 presents the composition of the UNOCI police component from May 2004 to December 2009.

The mission's civilian police were deployed to Abidjan, San-Pédro, Yamoussoukro, and Man, as well as to sector headquarters in Daloa and Bouaké (United Nations, 2004d). Police advisers assisted the FANCI and gendarmeries in training and mentoring and in facilitating cooperation between the two sides. The training modules developed by the UNOCI included maintaining public law and order, policing the community, and investigating major crimes. In September 2004, the UNOCI delivered a train-the-trainers course about close protection to 10 FANCI officers and 10 gendarmerie officers. Those training programs were tied to the progress in the DDR initiative, "with a view to establishing adequate security conditions for the protection of civilians during the disarmament of the armed elements of the Forces [N]ouvelles [the rebel forces]" (United Nations, 2004p).

By December 2004, UNOCI police advisers were deployed to "the National Police School, the Operation Centre of the Prefecture of Police, the Judicial Police, the Traffic Unit, and the international airport in Abidjan." Procedures were initiated to eliminate illegal police checkpoints and to implement community policing in sensitive Abidjan neighborhoods (United Nations, 2004v).

By January 2006, the UNOCI had provided basic training to 533 security auxiliaries, and it had trained 240 gendarmerie officers in community policing, human rights, forensics, and traffic accident management. The security auxiliary officers were "deployed to 54 locations in the northern part of the country, which [had] been left without any law enforcement presence following the displacement of [approximately] 4,000 police and gendarmes by the conflict" (United Nations, 2006a).

UNOCI police advisers, by mid-2006, were deployed throughout the country to all 18 sites that included 9 locations in areas controlled by the Forces Nouvelles, 2 sites in the zone of confidence, and 7 locations in the government-controlled areas (United Nations, 2006o; 2006w). Those officers provided advice and mentored the FANCI by participating in joint patrols, and they provided refresher courses and specialized police training (United Nations, 2006o).

In early 2007, the UNOCI assisted "in training and building the capacity of the police in the north and with [the] integration [of FANCI] into the national police." They also assisted the government with implementing

Table 7.1. Composition of Total Number of UNOCI Civilian Police Officers, May 2004 to December 2009

Year	Month	Civilian Police Officers	Formed Police Units	Total Civilian Police Officers
2004	May	49	N/K	49
	November	212	N/K	212
2005	June	218	N/K	218
	December	697	N/K	697
2006	March	321	375	696
	July	353	375	728
	October	324	625	949
2007	February	400	750	1,150
	May	400	750	1,150
	September	348	750	1,098
2008	July	402	750	1,152
	October	388	748	1,136
	December	387	750	1,137
2009	March	362	750	1,112
	July	433	750	1,183
	September	432	748	1,180
	December	394	744	1,138

Source: Author (from various United Nations documents dated 2004 to 2009).

Note: N/K = not known.

the Ouagadougou Agreement, which sought to resolve the crisis in Côte d'Ivoire by the following, as described by United Nations (2007g):

- Merge the Forces Nouvelles and the national defense and security forces by establishing an integrated command center.
- Replace the zone of confidence with a green line marked by UNOCI observation points that would be dismantled gradually.
- Deploy mixed Forces Nouvelles and national police units to maintain law and order in the area formerly covered by the zone of confidence.
- Reestablish state administration throughout the country.
- Dismantle the militias.

- Disarm combatants and enroll them in a civic service program.
- Organize a free, fair, open, and transparent presidential election in accordance with the Linas-Marcoussis and Pretoria agreements.

To measure the progress of achievement of the Ouagadougou Agreement, the UNOCI developed the following benchmarks and indicators as described by the United Nations (2009e):

- Profiling and cantonment of 5,000 Forces Nouvelles elements at four sites in the north
- Deployment of 3,400 Forces Nouvelles police and gendarmerie elements under supervision of the integrated command center

- Storage of weapons by the integrated command center under the supervision of the impartial forces
- Profiling and dismantling of militia groups
- Reinsertion of demobilized combatants and militias
- Effective and complete redeployment of the corps préfectoral (local authorities)
- Transfer of authority from zone commanders to the corps préfectoral
- Deployment of mixed police and gendarmerie units in the north
- Deployment of magistrates and court clerks supported by the judicial police expected to play a role in adjudicating electoral disputes
- Deployment of correction officers and prison directors

Mission Achievements (Outcomes)

Security was stabilized by the mission, but in mid-2010, there was an upsurge in armed robberies and other criminal activities, particularly in the west of the country. The mission also had assisted in the demobilization of more than 16,000 Forces Nouvelles members (United Nations, 2009e).

More than 526 microprojects were implemented that offered reinsertion assistance to former combatants, militias, youths, and women affected by the conflict. Those programs provided opportunities for 3,483 beneficiaries and contributed to creating a generally stable environment (United Nations, 2009e).

The UNOCI contributed to the development and implementation of capacity-building projects about areas such as forensics and crowd control. The mission also delivered crowd-control training to the Ivorian gendarmerie and police units. This training was to equip the officers with the skills that were required to conduct law enforcement duties in line with international human rights standards (United Nations, 2009e).

Ways the Mission Was Evaluated

By mid-2006, the north of the country remained insecure (United Nations, 2006h), principally because of the "continued absence of the national law enforcement agencies and a functioning justice system" (United Nations, 2006g). This situation remained even though the UNOCI police component had delivered basic police training to "600 police personnel operating in the north" (United Nations, 2006h).

The major challenge facing the FANCI was the limited capacity of the key national institutions that were to implement the tasks in the Ouagadougou Agreement and the constraints on the capacity of the integrated command center and the mixed police units (United Nations, 2007g).

Conclusion

The history of Côte d'Ivoire and the political interference of its neighboring states were two major issues that the mission faced. Weak and corrupt governments compounded the situation.

Although the mission has been reasonably successful in assisting ECOWAS in restoring a civilian police presence, an overall improvement in the security situation would not be completed quickly. Recruiting and training new officers could not be completed within a short time frame.

The mission was ongoing as of June 2010.

Chapter 8

Democratic Republic of the Congo

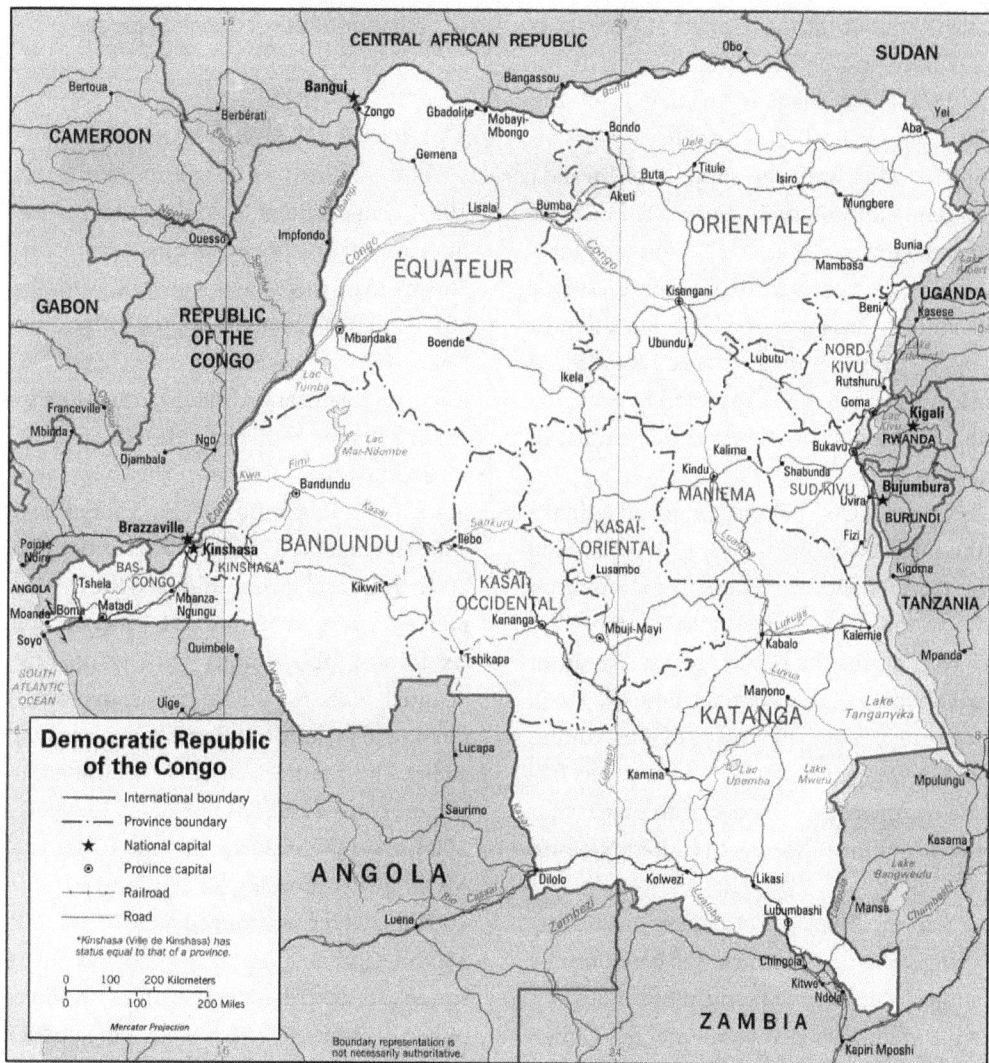

Map 8.1. Democratic Republic of the Congo
Source: Courtesy of the University of Texas Libraries, The University of Texas at Austin.

Case Study: United Nations Mission in the Democratic Republic of the Congo (Mission de l'Organisation des Nations Unies en République démocratique du Congo)

Background to the Mission

The Democratic Republic of the Congo (DRC), formerly Zaire, has been in political turmoil since its independence in 1960 from Belgium. In May 1997, the Alliance of the Democratic Forces for the Liberation of Congo–Zaire (AFDL), with the support of Rwanda and Uganda, marched into Kinshasa and ousted dictator Mobutu Sese Seko. However, within 12 months of forcing Seko's resignation, tensions arose between President Laurent Kabila and his Rwandan and Ugandan allies. In August 1998, open conflict erupted between Kabila and the Congolese forces, which were supported by Rwanda. Angola, Namibia, and Zimbabwe entered the conflict in support of Kabila.

The United Nations (UN) initially deployed military personnel to the DRC on September 3, 1999, following the approval by the UN Security Council of Resolution 1258 (United Nations, 1999r) on August 6, 1999. The resolution was to monitor the peace process agreed to by the Lusaka Ceasefire Agreement on July 17, 1999. The resolution authorized a deployment of a maximum of 90 officers who were to liaise with all warring factions, to provide technical assistance, and to prepare for the deployment of military observers (United Nations, 2000k).

The United Nations Mission in the Democratic Republic of the Congo, the title of which was based on the French translation of Mission de l'Organisation des Nations Unies en République démocratique du Congo (MONUC), was established by the UN Security Council Resolutions 1279 (United Nations, 1999q) and 1291 (United Nations, 2000k).

Resolution 1291 was passed on February 24, 2000, and authorized the deployment of a maximum of 5,537 military personnel to the mission (United Nations,

2000k). The initial mandate of MONUC, as described by the United Nations (2000k), was to do the following:

- Monitor the implementation of the cease-fire agreement and the redeployment of belligerent forces.
- Develop an action plan for the overall implementation of the cease-fire agreement.
- Work with the parties to obtain the release of all prisoners of war and military captives, as well as the return of all remains.
- Facilitate humanitarian assistance, and assist the facilitator of the national dialogue.

Mandate of the Mission

The first mandate of MONUC adopted by the UN Security Council in 1999 was for an initial term of six months. The mandate was renewed every six months until May 28, 2010, when the council adopted Resolution 1925 (United Nations, 2010q), which renamed MONUC as the United Nations Organization Stabilization Mission in the Democratic Republic of Congo (MONUSCO).

The first MONUC mandate to include a police component was Resolution 1355 (United Nations, 2001m), which was adopted by the UN Security Council on June 15, 2001. This resolution authorized the deployment of 1,034 police officers, including 391 general duties officers and six formed police units (FPUs) of 125 officers each (United Nations, 2008q). The mandate extended the mission to include training in human rights, humanitarian affairs, child protection, and medical and administrative affairs (United Nations, 2003q). However, on October 1, 2004, the UN Security Council revised the mandate of MONUC by adopting Resolution 1565 (United Nations, 2004af), which authorized an increase in the strength of MONUC by 5,900 personnel, including 341 police personnel. As described by the United Nations (2010e), the police component of MONUC, in cooperation with the Congolese authorities, the UN country team, and the donors were tasked to do the following:

- Provide advice to strengthen democratic institutions and processes at the national, provincial, regional, and local levels.

- Promote national reconciliation and internal political dialogue—including the provision of good offices (noncorrupt services)—by supporting the strengthening of civil society and multiparty democracy and by giving support to those processes in Goma and Nairobi.
- Assist in promoting and protecting human rights, with particular attention to women, children, and vulnerable persons; investigate human rights violations and publish its findings, thereby putting an end to impunity; assist in developing and implementing a transitional justice strategy; and cooperate in national and international efforts so that the perpetrators of grave violations of human rights and international humanitarian law are brought to justice.
- Coordinate with international partners and the UN country team to provide assistance to the Congolese authorities—including the National Independent Electoral Commission—in organizing, preparing, and undertaking local elections.
- Contribute to the promotion of good governance and respect for the principle of accountability.
- Coordinate with international partners to advise the government of the DRC as to how to strengthen the capacity of the judicial and correctional systems, including the military justice system.

The police component of MONUC was to contribute to the efforts of the international community and to the Congolese government in initially planning the security sector reform. The mission was "to build credible, cohesive, and disciplined Congolese armed forces and to develop the capacities of the Congolese national police and related law enforcement agencies" (United Nations, 2010e).

The mandate was amended in 2004 to include providing support and guidance to the transitional government and authorities in security sector reform, which included providing training and monitoring local police. The mission was to ensure that the local police displayed democratic principles and fully respected human rights and fundamental freedoms (United Nations, 2004af).

The strategic initiatives of the security sector and local police reform, as described by the United Nations

(2007u), were extended by the 2007 mandate to include the following:

- Ensure the security and freedom of movement of UN and associated personnel.
- Carry out joint patrols with the riot control units of the national police to improve security in the event of a civil disturbance.
- Provide basic training in the area of human rights, international humanitarian law, child protection, and prevention of gender-based violence to various members and units of the integrated brigades of the Forces Armées de la République Démocratique du Congo (FARDC), who were deployed in the eastern part of the DRC.
- Continue to develop the capacities of the Congolese national police and related law enforcement agencies in accordance with internationally recognized standards and norms relating to human rights, proportionate use of force, and criminal justice, including the prevention, investigation, and prosecution of cases of gender-based violence. Improve those capacities by providing technical assistance, training, and mentoring support.
- Advise the government about strengthening the capacity of the judicial and correctional systems, including the military justice system.
- Contribute to the efforts of the international community to assist the government in initially planning the reform of the security sector.

To support the implementation of the 2007 mandate in regard to security sector reform, the UN Security Council requested that the DRC government develop a national security strategy. The government of the DRC was to "establish professional security organizations in the areas of defence, police, and the administration of justice" that were well managed, that were capable of protecting civilians, and that acted "in accordance with the Constitution and with respect for the rule of law, human rights, and international humanitarian law" (United Nations, 2007u).

The police reform strategy in the updated mandate is described by the United Nations (2007u) as developing the capacity of the national police and related law enforcement agencies "in accordance with internationally recognized human rights and criminal justice norms and standards" in the following ways:

- At the command and field levels,
  a. Provide policy advice, technical assistance, and training.
  b. Supply mentoring and on-the-job training by co-location of MONUC police advisers.
- At the national provincial levels,
  a. Provide on-the-job training in operational and resource planning.
  b. Create coordination mechanisms.
  c. Establish professional standards and disciplinary units.

Mission Deployment Environment

The need to establish a civilian police component in MONUC was first identified in the secretary-general's eighth report to the UN Security Council on June 8, 2001 (United Nations, 2001n).

The secretary-general proposed that civilian police should be deployed within MONUC to assist members of the local police to enhance their capacity to maintain law and order. The MONUC civilian police would be deployed to areas from which foreign military forces could withdraw. That withdrawal would allow the disarmament, demobilization, repatriation, resettlement, and reintegration process to take place (United Nations, 2001n).

The UN Security Council approved the establishment of a civilian police component in MONUC on June 15, 2001, with the adoption of Resolution 1355 (United Nations, 2001m). The initial civilian police component of the mission conducted an in-depth assessment of policing institutions, needs, and capabilities. Ultimately, it prepared recommendations for an expanded MONUC civilian police component. The UN Security Council envisioned that the MONUC police would "advise and assist the local authorities in the discharge of their responsibilities to ensure the security of the local population, particularly in regard to the internal security situation following the withdrawal of the foreign forces" (United Nations, 2002i).

The secretary-general presented an organizational plan and focus for the proposed police component of MONUC in his second special report to the UN Security Council on May 27, 2003. As described by the United Nations (2003g), the police component would focus on doing the following:

- Assist in the security arrangements in Kinshasa.
- Contribute to the training of an integrated police unit.
- Continue the assessment and planning of its future role in key strategic geographical areas.
- Continue the assessment and planning of its future role in key strategic areas, such as Ituri and some locations in the Kivus.

The report envisioned an organizational structure that would serve as a headquarters that included a training and a planning police staff. The deployment of MONUC would allow for a multilayer mission security system (United Nations, 2003g). The report also proposed the following:

- The existing Congolese police structure (national police, including rapid intervention police, traffic police, and territorial police units) would continue to carry out normal law and order functions in Kinshasa.
- The close protection corps, made up of personal bodyguards, would be reinforced by a newly formed integrated police unit.
- The mission would also contain a military contingent consisting of approximately 740 personnel.

Actions of the Mission (Output)

The security environment within the DRC was extremely volatile, with numerous outbreaks of violence occurring in Kinshasa. Therefore, the initial deployment of MONUC police in 2002 provided technical advice and liaison with Congolese counterparts about the security zone at the Ndjili airport and the en route security between the airport and the Gombe district, between the airport and the city center, and in the Gombe district itself. As a result of the security assessment, MONUC police advised, monitored, and reported on the conduct of the various Congolese entities that were responsible for providing security (United Nations, 2003g).

In Kinshasa, MONUC police provided advice about administration, planning, strategic management, and coordination. Those officers also served as "liaison officers 24 hours a day, 7 days a week to the Joint Security Operations Centre, Congolese police elements, and close protection arrangements." They served as "security technical advisers to various Congolese police and security entities," as well as to the "MONUC military contingent charged with security tasks in Kinshasa" (United Nations, 2003g).

MONUC trained and equipped Kinshasa's 1,200-officer integrated police unit. MONUC also completely refurbished the training facility and established a communications system that would allow the unit to function within Kinshasa security mechanisms (United Nations, 2003g).

The mission staff members designed and implemented, in consultation with the Congolese authorities, a number of benchmarks that were to be achieved (United Nations, 2003g). During this transitional phase, the overarching objective of the mission was to reform the security sector and to restructure the Congolese National Police (CNP) (United Nations, 2004n). Benchmarks were designed to include aspects of these objectives and to provide a sense of trust in the new local police service. The benchmarks identified by the United Nations (2003g) covered the following:

- Regular payment of adequate salaries
- Transparency in recruitment, promotion, and discipline
- Deployment of personnel based on the type of training received
- Development and implementation of internal accountability mechanisms
- Program for building maintenance

To provide a framework to implement the mission benchmarks, MONUC helped prepare and develop a national security plan for the national elections. MONUC advised, trained, and mentored the CNP and specialist units such as the integrated police unit in Kinshasa. The mission also increased its geographical spread across the country to 12 less populated areas (United Nations, 2004n). This approach allowed MONUC to concentrate on the capacity building of local police, "particularly in areas of potential ci-

Table 8.1. MONUC Civilian Police Staff Numbers, February 2002 to October 2007

Year	Month	Total Civilian Police Officers
2002	February	15
	June	14
	October	52
2003	January	49
	October	99
2004	February	115
	August	143
2005	September	368
2006	August	1,019
2007	February	1,024
	October	1,013

Source: Author (from various United Nations documents dated 2002 to 2007).

vilian unrest, where the main effort was focused on political dialogue and problem solving" (United Nations, 2005o).

Mission Implementation (Model)

The mission began on November 30, 1999, but did not include a civilian police component until February 2002. The size of the civilian police contingent within MONUC remained very small until the mission was reconfigured in late 2005 to include FPUs. Table 8.1 outlines the number of MONUC civilian police officers deployed between February 2002 and October 2007.

To facilitate the reform and restructuring of the CNP, MONUC created partnerships with the transitional government and established three joint commissions, which were to formulate a five-year plan that would comprehensively revise the internal security sector. As described in the UN Security Council Resolution 682 (United Nations, 2004o), the plan would also provide a mechanism of interaction in the following:

- Introducing legislation
- Reforming the security sector and police

According to the United Nations (2004n), the partnerships created an environment that would advance the strategy of the "critical path of the transition" in the following ways:

- Improve security in Kinshasa for the transitional institutions and processes.
- Establish a joint police reform planning mechanism.
- Rehabilitate police training centers.
- Begin training new police officers.
- Restructure the CNP.

MONUC implemented the UN Security Council resolution in three phases. The first, the preelection phase, lasted for approximately eight months. The primary goals of this phase were (a) to prepare and to begin implementing a five-year national police reform plan and (b) to establish a coordination framework to train and deploy 6,000 police officers in conjunction with the Ministry of Interior. The deployment would include 3,000 rapid intervention police officers who would provide security services during the transition and election phase in 2004–05 (United Nations, 2004n).

During the four-month electoral or second phase, the MONUC police provided additional on-the-ground training, as well as on-the-job monitoring and mentoring of the CNP. In the third, postelectoral phase of six months, MONUC continued "to support local police crowd-management units [and] train additional police reserve units and units of police d'intervention rapide." At the conclusion of this phase, MONUC focused on border control and provided the necessary support for full implementation of the five-year police reform program (United Nations, 2004n).

To support this structured approach, MONUC staff members were co-located, and seminars, workshops, and train-the-trainers programs were held to increase the senior CNP officers' awareness and knowledge of democratic policing (United Nations, 2004x; 2005i). Such programs were delivered at five locations throughout the DRC and included the training of 250 CNP instructors (United Nations, 2005i).

During 2005, MONUC revised its concept of operations as it developed a new concept that would enhance the role of the CNP in the electoral process and would address the CNP's long-term institutional and capacity develop-

ment. This concept entailed "a two-pronged approach that included the co-location of MONUC senior police officers at general and provincial inspector level." Those officers advised about "operations planning and management, while at the same time building capacity from the bottom up." The revised approach included deploying MONUC police officers to 16 major cities including Bukavu, Bunia, Goma, Kalemie, Kananga, Kindu, Kinshasa, Kisangani, Lubumbashi, Mahagi, Matadi, and Mbandaka, and to nine provinces so that practical advice could be provided to CNP officers (United Nations, 2005i).

The mission, in conjunction with the Ministry of Interior, developed a plan that outlined financial, logistic, and human resources that were necessary for the national police to maintain security during the electoral process. The plan included training 9,000 police officers in public security and crowd control and providing for 18,500 officers in static security duties at the registration and polling centers (United Nations, 2005i).

During 2006, MONUC completed an evaluation of the CNP's operational, technical, and administrative requirements and capabilities and drafted a reform plan for comprehensive institutional capacity development (United Nations, 2006m). As part of the reform plan, MONUC conducted a census of CNP, vetted and certified officers, implemented a salary payment process, and established an effective payment system (United Nations, 2006u).

Following the implementation of the reform plan, MONUC, in conjunction with a technical assessment team from the UN Department of Peacekeeping Operations, developed a new concept of operations for implementing its new mandate, Resolution 1756 (United Nations, 2007u), and it set benchmarks and an indicative timeline for the gradual drawdown of the mission (United Nations, 2007q).

Mission Achievements (Outcome)

The establishment and deployment of MONUC helped bring peace to most of the DRC. As described by the United Nations (2009m), the mission achieved the following from February 1999 to December 2007:

- Overseeing implementation of the Lusaka Ceasefire Agreement (1999)

- Monitoring cease-fires between foreign and Congolese forces
- Brokering local truces
- Disarming and repatriating thousands of foreign armed combatants
- Creating an environment conducive for the national dialogue in Sun City, South Africa, which was the proposed location for the peace conference
- Assisting the transition to democratic rule
- During 2006, facilitating the first democratic elections in 40 years
- Helping the government dismantle remaining armed groups in Ituri and the Kivus
- Supporting regional reconciliation
- Dismantling the Forces for the Democratic Liberation of Rwanda (FDLR)
- Protecting vulnerable communities from rebel violence
- Helping establish state authority and the rule of law

In June 2004, despite the lack of security and the level of violence that was perpetuated in the DRC, progress was made in the reform of the 80,000-member CNP by the appointment of a number of executive and senior officers (United Nations, 2004n). MONUC also developed a train-the-trainers program, through which 446 national police became certified trainers (United Nations, 2005o). A framework was established to train and deploy 9,000 police and rapid intervention officers who were to provide security during the 2004–05 transition and election (United Nations, 2004n).

Despite the achievements of the MONUC, a number of areas within the CNP required development and completion. The CNP lacked equipment, logistics, and training and did not have a personnel management record system (United Nations, 2005o). The difficulties faced by the administrative, logistical, and operational structures of the national police affected the envisaged multiplication of programs such as train-the-trainers. The difficulties also limited the achievements of the mission (United Nations, 2005o).

Ways the Mission Was Evaluated

In 2007, a technical assessment team from the UN reviewed MONUC and surveyed officers of the CNP. The review identified two strategic level benchmarks that measured MONUC's progress toward achieving its mandate: (a) the establishment of an overall stable security environment and (b) the consolidation of the country's democratic institutions. As described by the United Nations (2007q), the assessment team determined that any downsizing plan of the mission and eventual withdrawal should be based on these three key preconditions:

1. That the Congolese and foreign armed groups are disarmed and demobilized or repatriated, and that they no longer pose a threat to peace and stability in the DRC or neighboring countries
2. That FARDC and the CNP have achieved levels of capacity that would enable them to assume responsibility for the country's security, including duties now performed by MONUC
3. That MONUC remain deployed at its current strength at least through the completion of the local elections

Identifying the strategic performance benchmarks of the mission enabled MONUC to develop operational performance measures. The identification also enabled progress in achieving and measuring the principal objectives of the mandate to be made and for a stable security environment to be established (United Nations, 2007q). The operational benchmarks described by the United Nations (2007q) included the following:

- Stabilize sensitive areas.
- Complete disarmament and demobilization of former combatants and disarmament and repatriation of foreign armed groups.
- Extend state authority throughout the territory of the DRC.
- Reform the security sector by developing a unified national police that was entrusted with public security and that was capable of protecting the people and their property while maintaining law and order and respect for human rights.

MONUC observed in 2008 that although the mission had been in the country for nearly 10 years, progress in the reform of the security sector had been modest. Little progress had been made toward achieving the security sector reform benchmarks and establishing a secure environment that could provide a basis for the country to move forward. However, progress on police reform had been more promising (United Nations, 2008e) with a number of projects implemented and many objectives achieved. Those achievements included establishing an internal accountability regime and developing a building maintenance program.

Conclusion

Civilian police were not included in the mission until 18 months after it began. Even then, the police component consisted of only 15 officers. After two years of civilian police deployment, only 115 police officers were on the ground.

The mandated tasks of the civilian police component were very ambitious given the authorized strength, even after the mission was reconfigured in late 2005. However, the mission was successful in bringing peace to most of the country.

As noted earlier, on July 1, 2010, MONUC was renamed the United Nations Organization Stabilization Mission in the Democratic Republic of Congo.

Case Study: European Union Police Mission in Kinshasa

Background to the Mission

Following the establishment and deployment of the police component of MONUC in 2003, the United Nations (UN) police assessment team saw that it needed to train and equip the Kinshasa-based Congolese National Police Integrated Police Unit (CNP IPU) that was based in Kinshasa, Democratic Republic of Congo (DRC). This need was caused by the threat of public disorder and rioting in Kinshasa. Because the demand was immediate and the UN would not be able to identify and deploy an IPU, the UN requested the European Union (EU) undertake the task. After identifying this security need and signing both (a) the agreement about the transition in DRC in

Pretoria, South Africa, on December 17, 2002, and (b) the memorandum about security and the army on June 29, 2003, the EU agreed to establish an IPU that would be deployed to Kinshasa in the DRC (Council of the European Union, 2004b).

To ensure that a police response capability was maintained in Kinshasa until the EU's IPU was deployed, the UN Security Council agreed that the role could be undertaken by MONUC. This interim arrangement was formally recognized on October 1, 2004, with the UN Security Council adoption of Resolution 1565 (United Nations, 2004af). The resolution determined that MONUC would have the mandate to contribute to the security of the institutions and to the protection of Kinshasa transition officials until the IPU was ready to take on this responsibility. The resolution also called for MONUC to help the Congolese authorities maintain order in other strategic areas (Council of the European Union, 2004b).

In April 2005, the EU, in close coordination with the UN, launched a police mission to Kinshasa. That mission would support the CNP IPU within the framework of the European Security and Defence Policy (ESDP) (European Union Council Secretariat, 2005d).

Mandate of the Mission

On December 9, 2004, the Council of the European Union adopted Joint Action 2004/847/CFSP, which established the European Union Police Mission (EUPOL Kinshasa) to help form an IPU in Kinshasa in early January 2005. To prepare for the mission, a EUPOL police planning team was established and remained operational until the start of the mission (Council of the European Union, 2004b).

EUPOL Kinshasa's mission was to monitor, mentor, and advise about the formation and initial operation of an IPU. The mission was also to ensure that the proposed CNP IPU performance was in line with the training received in the academy center and that the performance was in accordance with international best practices in this field. Training was given to CNP IPU supervisors and managers to improve their unit leadership capabilities and to monitor, mentor, and advise operational units as the units executed tasks (Council of the European Union, 2004b).

Initially, the Joint Action 847 (Council of the European Union, 2004b) was to last for 12 months and was to expire on December 31, 2005. The development of the IPU continued to ensure that the unit integrated correctly with the CNP. The mission was extended a number of times by the council, with approval for a final extension until June 2007 (Council of the European Union, 2006a). The mission's mandate was amended during the extension to include providing advice to the CNP about facilitating the security sector reform process in the DRC (Council of the European Union, 2006b).

Mission Deployment Environment

In response to an invitation by the DRC government, the EUPOL Kinshasa was the first civil mission for crisis management established in Africa within the ESDP framework (European Union Council Secretariat, 2005c). The focus of the mission was to consolidate the volatile security situation in Kinshasa.

Tensions were high in Kinshasa because of the presence of several politically based militias in the city center. Except for those who could afford to pay for security, policing was nonexistent. Militias had a free hand, and political factions could easily mobilize the population to launch large demonstrations that could lead to violent riots and civil disorder. This highly volatile situation had the potential to jeopardize elections (Vircoulon, 2009).

Actions of the Mission (Output)

The role of the mission was (a) to provide advice directly to the command element of the CNP IPU and (b) to ensure that the unit undertook its duties in accordance with the best international police practices and human rights doctrine.

The mission's objectives were to improve and facilitate unit communication and management decision making. The objectives also included applying operational directives and supervising maneuvers of the units in charge of maintaining order in the capital (EUPOL Kinshasa, 2006).

To achieve those objectives, the mission's activities, as described by EUPOL Kinshasa (2006), covered these three areas:

- Establish a continuous training program for the CNP IPU.
- Strengthen the operational capacities of the unit officers and the planning and leadership capacities of the headquarters staff managers and of the basic unit commanders through theoretical lessons and practical exercises.
- Train officers on how to protect human rights.

The mission initially comprised 30 EUPOL officers and was temporarily reinforced by the deployment of a "police co-ordination support element" during the electoral process. The increase in authorized officer strength was to ensure that there would be an "enhanced and coordinated response of the CNP crowd control units in Kinshasa in case of disturbances during the electoral period" (Council of the European Union, 2006b).

Mission Implementation (Model)

The mission deployed 30 EUPOL officers as a headquarters element and as police monitors. The headquarters staff had one officer who acted as the head of mission and who provided administration support to the mission (Council of the European Union, 2006a). The police monitors, who were also mentors, advisers, and trainers, were co-located in the CNP IPU operational base. Before the election, the mission established "a dedicated co-ordination element in charge of specific tasks assigned to the mission during this period" (Council of the European Union, 2006b).

EUPOL Kinshasa officers were deployed within the 1,008-officer CNP IPU in different levels of the Congolese police chain of command (EUPOL Kinshasa, 2006). This approach was taken "in order to monitor, mentor, and advise their Congolese counterparts with the aim of ensuring that the CNP IPU met international best practice" (European Union Council Secretariat, 2005c) and to advise the CNP on reform and reorganization.

The mission did not have executive authority, and it primarily provided technical advice about supervising staff members and planning crowd management operations. The active presence of EUPOL officers within the CNP IPU structure boosted morale and increased the level of cohesion within the unit (EUPOL Kinshasa, 2006).

The mission adopted a second strategy to achieve its mandate. The mission would use police officers from other African nations within the mission. The integration of third-country officers underscored a new dimension in EU missions (EUPOL Kinshasa, 2006).

Mission Achievements (Outcomes)

Through mentoring and training members of the CNP IPU, the mission contributed to strengthening the level of stability in Kinshasa. The IPU increased its capability in handling, maintaining, and reestablishing public order in the capital. The mission trained a total of 4,500 CNP officers in IPU tactics and management (EUPOL Kinshasa, 2006).

At a practical level as described by the Council of the European Union (2004b), the mission also contributed to the following:

- Inspection, verification, and management of CNP IPU
- Drafting of relevant rules and regulations for the IPU

Ways the Mission Was Evaluated

The Mixed Reflection Group on the Reform and Reorganization of the Congolese National Police was formed on the initiative of the Congolese Minister of Interior to review the EUPOL mission. The group included members from EUPOL Kinshasa, MONUC, Angola, South Africa, France, and the United Kingdom. A final report was completed and published by the group in June 2006. The report positively supported the EUPOL mission and was adopted by the new Congolese government as the basis for future police reform (Geberwold, 2007).

Conclusion

The mission appears to have been successful in achieving its mandate and building the capacity of the CNP IPU. Se-

curity remained fragile following the national elections in the DRC. To increase the level of security, on July 1, 2007, the European Union Police Mission to the Democratic Republic of the Congo followed the EUPOL Kinshasa mission to help the Congolese authorities with police reform.

Case Study: European Union Police Mission to the Democratic Republic of the Congo

Background to the Mission

On December 9, 2004, the Council of the European Union adopted the Joint Action 2004/847/CFSP on the European Union Police Mission in Kinshasa (EUPOL Kinshasa), the first mission undertaken by the EU in Africa (European Union, 2009a). The objective of the mission was to provide advice to the Congolese National Police Integrated Police Unit (CNP IPU) in Kinshasa about public order and crowd control.

On December 7, 2006, the council adopted Joint Action 2006/913/CFSP, which amended and extended Joint Action 2004/847/CFSP. The new mandate, which ran until June 30, 2007, enlarged the original mandate to include the provision of advice to the CNP that would facilitate the security sector reform progress in the Democratic Republic of the Congo (DRC) (Council of the European Union, 2007c).

To ensure that there was not going to be a break in the continuity of the mission when the EUPOL Kinshasa finished on June 30, 2007, the council, on May 14, 2007, approved a police mission conducted under the European Security and Defence Policy on security sector reform (SSR) and its interface with the DRC's justice system. The new mission would be called EUPOL RD Congo (European Union Police Mission in the Democratic Republic of the Congo) and was to begin on July 1, 2007 (Council of the European Union, 2007c).

Mandate of the Mission

The Council of the European Union adopted Joint Action 2007/405/CFSP on June 12, 2007, which established EUPOL RD Congo. As part of the preparatory mission process, the head of the mission prepared an operational plan that was for the mission and that was to be submitted to the council for approval (Council of the European Union, 2007c).

As described by the council, the mission strategy was to "support SSR in the field of policing and its interface with the justice system" (Council of the European Union, 2009a). This objective was to be achieved by monitoring, mentoring, and providing advice to the CNP with an emphasis on the strategic dimension. Specifically, as described by the Council of the European Union (2007c; 2009a), the mission was to do the following:

- Contribute to the reform and the restructuring of the CNP through support for the establishment of a viable, professional, and multiethnic police force. That force accounted for proximity policing throughout the whole country with the direct involvement of the Congolese authorities in that process.
- Contribute to improving the interaction between the police and the criminal justice system in the broader sense.
- Contribute to ensuring the consistency of all SSR efforts.
- Operate in close interaction with the projects of the commission, and coordinate its action with the other international efforts in the field of reform of the police and the criminal justice system.

The mission was required by the council to design and implement policies that are founded on human rights and international humanitarian law; democratic standards; and principles of good governance, transparency, and respect for the rule of law. The mission would provide advice and support at the governmental level to the Congolese authorities and through the police reform monitoring committee (CSRP) and the joint committee on justice (Council of the European Union, 2007c).

Mission Deployment Environment

In the mid- to late-1990s, following the 1994 genocide in Rwanda, the DRC underwent two successive wars: the first in 1996 and the second in 1998. Those wars nearly engulfed the African continent, killing millions of people and destroying "decades of development" (European Union Police Mission for the DRC, 2006).

There were two earlier missions in the DRC before the cease-fire agreement was signed in Pretoria on December 17, 2002. The first was the United Nations Mission in the Democratic Republic of Congo (MONUC), and the second was EUPOL Kinshasa. During June 2003, the EU deployed a temporary multinational force, known as Operation Artemis, to the DRC. The aim of Operation Artemis was to reinforce MONUC because the security situation in the Ituri region was deteriorating. This operation was launched on June 12 and was completed in three weeks upon the arrival of the United Nations Multinational Emergency Force to Bunia (European Union Police Mission for the DRC, 2006).

Both MONUC and EUPOL Kinshasa were designed to support the stabilization and the transition in the DRC and played an important part in achieving peace in the region (European Union Police Mission for the DRC, 2006).

Actions of the Mission (Output)

The mission was primarily based in Kinshasa, although staff members delivered advice to police in other geographic regions of the DRC (Council of the European Union, 2007c). The mission provided advice and support about the reformation and the restructuring of the police sector through the CSRP. The CSRP was a joint consultative body comprising the ministries that were involved with the police reform, the CNP, and the international partners (European Union Police Mission for the DRC, 2006).

The mission's specific tasks, as described by the Council of the European Union (2008b), included the following:

- Form working parties on police reform.
- Assign staff to the CNP.
- Provide an interface with other justice sector agencies.
- Provide expertise on police SSR.

Mission Implementation (Model)

Included in the mission were 53 international staff members who possessed knowledge in policing, criminal justice, and security sector reform (European Union Police Mission for the DRC, 2006). The mission was to deliver services jointly with the European Union Advisory and Assistance Mission for Security Reform in the DRC (EUSEC RD Congo) in the fields of human rights, children associated with armed forces or armed groups, and gender equality (Council of the European Union, 2009c).

The mission had a permanent presence in eastern DRC and in Bukavu and Goma and was to provide assistance in the stabilization process. A headquarters was established in Kinshasa (Council of the European Union, 2007c; 2008b). As the Council of the European Union (2007c; 2008b) shows, the headquarters comprised the following:

- Police advisers at the operational and strategic level
- Legal advisers at the strategic and operational level
- Administrative support

Mission Achievements (Outcomes)

The mission focused on reforming the CNP and associated aspects of policing, which included the legal framework, police organizational structures, administration, and management.

The mission provided assistance in establishing the border police and the police inspectorate. The mission also created an environment to develop more operational and visible activities, such as establishing a research and intervention police unit in Kinshasa (Vircoulon, 2009).

Ways the Mission Was Evaluated

On November 17, 2009, the council supported the achievements of EUPOL RD Congo and its interaction with the justice sector (Council of the European Union, 2009c). The council noted that the "reform is beginning to achieve some positive results" especially in the "coordination work conducted by the" CSRP (Council of the European Union, 2009c).

Conclusion

The main challenges that the mission faced and that undermined reforms were the lack of ownership of the reform process and the unwillingness of the DRC authorities to complete the reform of the local police. The core of the problem was the lack of coordination and the inability to integrate police reform into the broader nation-building and development program.

The mission had a specific and ambitious mandate for the number of police advisers deployed. Moreover, the mission appeared to be achieving its mandate and was ongoing June 15, 2010.

Chapter 9

Former Yugoslav Republic of Macedonia

Map 9.1. Former Yugoslav Republic of Macedonia
Source: Courtesy of the University of Texas Libraries, The University of Texas at Austin.

Case Study: European Union Police Mission to the Former Yugoslav Republic of Macedonia

Background to the Mission

On September 8, 1991, the Former Yugoslav Republic of Macedonia (FYROM) became independent of Yugoslavia. FYROM remained peaceful following the declaration and during the Yugoslav wars of the early 1990s. However, the stability of the country was seriously threatened by the 1999 Kosovo war, when an estimated 360,000 ethnic Albanian refugees from Kosovo took refuge in FYROM.

Although the refugees departed after the Kosovo war ceased, Albanian radicals on both sides of the border pursued autonomy or independence for the Albanian-populated areas of FYROM and Kosovo. A civil war was fought mostly in the north and west of FYROM between the government and the ethnic Albanian insurgents from March to June 2001. Following an intervention by the North Atlantic Treaty Organization (NATO), a cease-fire was agreed to under the terms of the Ohrid Framework Agreement.

On September 16, 2003, the government of FYROM invited the European Union (EU) to assist with reforming the country's police (Council of the European Union, 2003).

Mandate of the Mission

On September 29, 2003, the Council of the European Union adopted Joint Action 2003/681/CFSP, which established the European Union Police Mission to the Former Yugoslav Republic of Macedonia (EUPOL Proxima) (Council of the European Union, 2003). EUPOL Proxima was the second European Security and Defence Policy (ESDP) police mission, but unlike the European Union Police Mission (EUPM) in Bosnia and Herzegovina that followed the United Nations (UN) international police task force (IPTF), it was the first mission to start from scratch (Grevi, Helly, and Keohane, 2009). The initial mandate approved by the EU expired on December 15, 2004. However, the EU extended the mandate for a further 12 months, until December 14, 2005 (Council of the European Union, 2004a).

The EU also authorized establishing a planning team that was to begin on October 1, 2003, and was to remain in operation until the EUPOL Proxima personnel were deployed on December 15, 2003 (Council of the European Union, 2004a). The planning team was to be a liaison with the Organisation for Security and Co-operation in Europe (OSCE), to complete a risk assessment for the mission, and to develop a concept of operations (Council of the European Union, 2004a).

Furthermore, the mission was to establish a headquarters in Skopje and was to operate under a broader rule of law perspective (Council of the European Union, 2004a). The approach taken by the mission was to monitor, mentor, and provide advice to the country's police, thus enhancing the ability of the local police to cope with organized crime more effectively and to consolidate public confidence in policing (Council of the European Union, 2003).

EUPOL Proxima was to "support the development of an efficient and professional police service and to promote European standards of policing." It was to comprise approximately 200 police officers and civilians (European Union Council Secretariat, 2003). As the Council of the European Mission (2004a) describes, the mission's focus was on the middle and senior management of the local police and was to support the following:

- Practical implementation of the comprehensive reform of the Ministry of Internal Affairs, including the police force
- Operational transition toward and creation of a border police as a part of the wider EU effort to promote integrated border management
- Local police in building confidence within the population
- Enhanced cooperation with neighboring states in the field of policing

The mission's mandate included contributing assistance and providing advice "in partnership with the Ministry of Internal Affairs and other relevant authorities" and undertaking police reforms to comply with the 2001 Ohrid Framework Agreement (European Union Council Secretariat, 2003).

Mission Deployment Environment

Following the cease-fire, there were two interventions in FYROM. The first was the NATO operation, Allied Harmony, which deployed approximately 300 troops to provide security to EU monitors that were overseeing the implementation of the Ohrid Framework Agreement. The second intervention, which followed Allied Harmony, was the EU mission, Concordia. This mission deployed EU troops to watch over the growing civil unrest in FYROM because of the ethnic tensions between the Macedonian majority and the Albanian minority in the east of the country. Despite those two interventions, the political and security situation in late 2002 was stable but was capable of deteriorating, with potentially serious repercussions to international security (Council of the European Union, 2003).

The fragile security situation was exacerbated by the proliferation of private firearms possession, the weak government, and the nonexistence of law enforcement in ethnic Albanian-dominated areas (Grevi, Helly, and Keohane, 2009). The Council of the European Union (2003) noted that the commitment of the EU political effort and its resources could assist in embedding stability in the region.

Actions of the Mission (Output)

The EUPOL Proxima police advisers were co-located and supported the local police in full partnership at the central, regional, and police station level (European Union Police Mission Proxima, 2003). By monitoring, mentoring, and advising the local police, EUPOL Proxima advisers assisted in increasing their "level of proficiency" and supported "the development of an efficient and professional police service" (European Union Police Mission Proxima, 2003).

The mission mandate was renewed in 2004 and changed the focus of the EUPOL Proxima. The mission continued to give particular attention to police senior and middle management but focused mainly on the police reform process and on organized crime, public peace and order, and border police (Grevi, Helly, and Keohane, 2009). During this stage, the mission expanded its geographical coverage while it maintained a presence in the former crisis areas.

Mission Implementation (Model)

The EUPOL Proxima mission comprised approximately 200 uniformed and civilian police personnel. Senior advisers were deployed to the central headquarters of the ministry of internal affairs in Skopje, and police advisers were deployed to regional headquarters (Skopje, Tetovo, Kumanovo, and Gostivar), to subregional headquarters (Debar, Struga, and Kicevo), and to the police station level (European Union Police Mission Proxima, 2003).

The mission developed five programs that included 28 activities from the tasks listed in the mission mandate. The five programs included (a) uniform police, (b) criminal police, (c) department for state security and counterintelligence, (d) internal control, and (e) border police (Grevi, Helly, and Keohane, 2009). The mission also deployed police advisers to border crossings and to the Skopje and Ohrid international airports. Those actions were designed to support and strengthen regional cooperation and to assist with restructuring the border police.

The mission provided assistance to increase the level of cooperation between the agencies in the criminal justice sector and with the establishment of an internal control and professional standards unit in the Ministry of Interior (Grevi, Helly, and Keohane, 2009). In the later stages of the mission, police advisers focused on improving the leadership capability, crime scene management, border policing, and capacity of the department of state security and counterintelligence to plan and manage operations to fight terrorism and organized crime.

To achieve the objectives of the mandate, the mission developed a results-based activity plan that was tied to a monitored weekly time frame. This benchmarking system enabled the mission to tackle very specific projects according to a process endorsed by the Ministry of Interior (Grevi, Helly, and Keohane, 2009).

Mission Achievements (Outcomes)

In line with the objectives of the Ohrid Framework Agreement and the stability and association process (SAP), EUPOL Proxima's objective was to promote the gradual stabilization of the country (Grevi, Helly, and Keohane, 2009).

The mission was successful in (a) implementing a comprehensive reform of the Ministry of Interior, (b) creating a border police, and (c) increasing the level of confidence between the local police and the population. It also enhanced police cooperation with neighboring states (Grevi, Helly, and Keohane, 2009).

Ways the Mission Was Evaluated

There were no formal EU documents relating to how the mission was evaluated. However, Merlingen and Ostrauskaite (2006) note that although the mission had identified five thematic reform priorities, those themes were not initially developed into broad objectives or into detailed project plans. This lack of development culminated in a lack of strategic direction and in an uncoordinated noncoherent reform effort.

By June 2004, the EUPOL Proxima began to reorganize the mission to enhance its effectiveness (Merlingen and Ostrauskaite, 2006). Overall effectiveness was achieved by producing a "programme-driven reform agenda" that centered resources on three clearly defined priorities: enforcing the law, policing the border, and increasing confidence and trust between the police and the public. The three priorities comprised five programs and 28 projects (Merlingen and Ostrauskaite, 2006).

Conclusion

The mission was terminated on December 14, 2005, even though many programs were not completed. The mission was not able to complete its mandate because it lacked a common EU view about policing and because it was hampered by the slow pace in which the FYROM authorities adopted legal changes (Grevi, Helly, and Keohane, 2009).

EUPOL Proxima was a complex mission, and the development of a programmatic approach proved significantly more difficult than the EUPM expected (Merlingen and Ostrauskaite, 2006). The mission failed to create projects that generated added value, and difficulties arose because many of the tasks included in the mission mandate were undertaken by other international donors.

As with EUPM, there was a series of short EUPOL Proxima missions. When each mandate expired, a new mission was established that usually adopted its predecessor's reform agenda but had a revised operation plan. Each new mission also had a leaner deployment strategy and a more focused approach (Merlingen and Ostrauskaite, 2006).

Case Study: European Union Police Advisory Team in the Former Yugoslav Republic of Macedonia

Background to the Mission

In late 2005, the government of the Former Yugoslav Republic of Macedonia (FYROM) indicated to the European Union (EU) that it would approve the deployment of a European Union Police Advisory Team (EUPAT). The team would bridge the gap between the EUPOL Proxima, which was completing its mandate on December 14, 2005, and the start of the planned project of practical technical assistance that would be funded by the EU program titled Community Assistance for Reconstruction, Development, and Stabilisation (CARDS) (Council of the European Union, 2005f).

The government of FYROM was concerned about consolidating the security situation and wanted to ensure that police reform was continued and sustainable.

Mandate of the Mission

On November 24, 2005, the Council of the European Union adopted Joint Action 2005/826/CFSP, which established EUPAT in FYROM for six months from December 15, 2005, to June 14, 2006 (European Union Council Secretariat, 2005b). The mission was to begin after the termination of the European Union Police Mission to the Former Yugoslavia Republic of Macedonia (EUPOL Proxima) on December 14, 2005 (European Union Council Secretariat, 2005b).

The strategic objective of EUPAT was "to further support the development of an efficient and professional police service based on European standards of policing." The EU's assistance to FYROM was based on the Ohrid Framework Agreement and included institution-building programs and police activities that were to be mutually supportive and reinforcing (Council of the European Union, 2005f).

The EUPAT mandate specified that the mission was to operate in partnership with local authorities to support the development of an efficient and professional police service, which would be based on European standards of policing. The EU police advisers were to focus on the middle and senior levels of local police management and were to monitor and to mentor the police "on priority issues in the field of Border Police, Public Peace and Order, and Accountability, and in the fight against corruption and organised crime" (Council of the European Union, 2005f). Specifically, the Council of the European Union (2005f) called for the EU police advisers to assist in the following:

- Implementation of police reform in the field
- Police-judiciary cooperation
- Professional standards and internal control

Mission Deployment Environment

The mission was established because the Council of the European Union thought that a continued EU presence was necessary in FYROM, especially in rural areas and outside Skopje. The council was also concerned about instability arising from the opening of the Kosovo status negotiations (Ioannides, 2009).

As part of EUPAT, the European Commission planned to establish the Local Implementation Component (LIC) Project, which focused on the reform of the local police at the field level and on building the capacity of the Ministry of Interior (Ioannides, 2009).

Actions of the Mission (Output)

The EU deployed approximately 30 police advisers to advise and support the local police in their "development of an efficient and professional police service based on European standards of policing" (Council of the European

Union, 2005f). Advice and support was given by monitoring and mentoring the local police about general policing and about specific law enforcement issues in border policing, accountability, corruption, and organized crime (Council of the European Union, 2005f).

The mission established a small headquarters in the capital Skopje and placed teams in Tetovo, Ohrid, Bitola, and Štip (Merlingen and Ostrauskaite, 2006).

Mission Implementation (Model)

The EUPAT's goals, mission, and organization were similar to that of the EUPOL Proxima. The mission built on the results achieved by EUPOL Proxima and principally monitored, advised, and mentored the police at the local level about border policing, public peace and order, corruption, and organized crime. EUPAT focused on implementing police reforms, encouraging cooperation between the police and the justice sector, raising professional standards, and establishing internal controls (Ioannides, 2009).

Mission Achievements (Outcomes)

The security of the country improved after the end of the civil war in 2001 and stabilized following the EU intervention in 2003. The two EU missions, EUPOL Proxima and EUPAT, created an environment that enabled the "implementation of key Ohrid Framework Agreements" and that enabled the local authorities to address other reform priorities, including those in the field of rule of law (Council of the European Union, 2005f).

Ways the Mission Was Evaluated

No documents were available relating to how the mission was evaluated. However, EUPAT's performance framework included a "consultation mechanism" (Ioannides, 2009), which was an improvement on EUPOL Proxima's "benchmarking system." The new mechanism determined that the mission should report monthly to the FYROM government about progress in reforming the local police.

Conclusion

EUPAT was a short bridging mission between the completion of EUPOL Proxima and a 12-month, 35-person CARDS-funded project. This project was tasked with monitoring and assessing local police and implementing the on-going police reform (Merlingen and Ostrauskaite, 2006).

EUPAT identified that the EU police planners were able to learn from experience and were able to adjust rapidly to changing operational demands (Ioannides, 2009). The mission adopted and improved a number of mechanisms that had been developed by EUPOL Proxima, such as the performance measurement framework and the interagency consultation process.

Chapter 10

Haiti

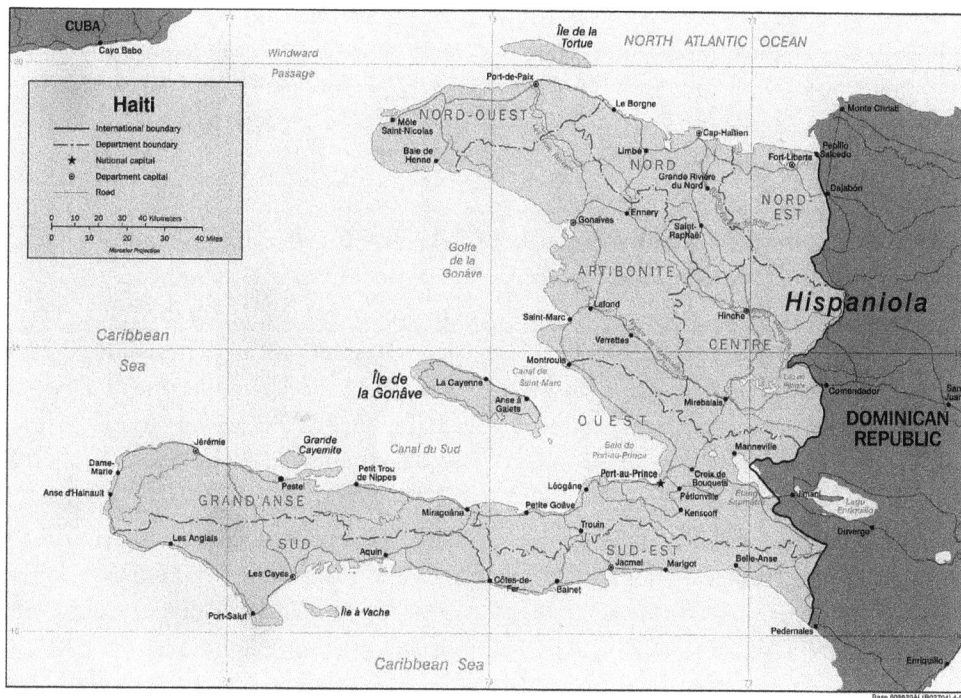

Map 10.1. Haiti

Source: Courtesy of the University of Texas Libraries, The University of Texas at Austin.

Case Study: United Nations Police Missions in Haiti

Background to the Missions

There have been three United Nations (UN) missions to Haiti since 1993:

1. The United Nations Mission in Haiti (UNMIH)—September 1993 to June 1996
2. The United Nations Support Mission in Haiti (UNSMIH)—July 1996 to July 1997
3. The United Nations Transition Mission in Haiti (UNTMIH)—August to November 1997

On September 23, 1993, the UN Security Council adopted Resolution 867 (United Nations, 1993), which established UNMIH (United Nations, 2009l). The mission was to principally support the implementation of the Governor Island Agreement, which was signed by the three Haitian parties involved in the conflict (United Nations, 2009a): Haiti's President Jean Bertrand Aristide, the Haitian Military, and the UN Special Envoy. Its mandate was to assist in modernizing the Haitian military and to establish a new police force (United Nations, 2009l). However, members of the Haitian military were initially uncooperative until the UN Security Council adopted Resolutions 940 (1994) and 975 (1995c) that enabled the mission to assist the Haitian government in professionalizing the military and creating a separate police force (United Nations, 2009l).

The UNMIH achieved its mandate on December 17, 1995, with the successful completion of the presidential elections (United Nations, 2009l). However, the mandate was extended to June 30, 1996, at the request of the president of Haiti.

On June 28, 1996, UNSMIH was established to support the government of Haiti to maintain a secure and stable environment by establishing a multinational force and by assisting the UNMIH (United Nations, 1996d). The mission, as detailed by the United Nations (2009n) was mandated to assist the Haitian authorities in the following:

• Professionalize the Haitian National Police (HNP).

• Maintain a secure and stable environment that is conducive to the success of current efforts to establish and train an effective national police force.

The mission was initially established for six months but was extended further for two six-month periods and was finally completed on July 31, 1997 (United Nations, 2009n).

UNTMIH followed the UNSMIH and was established by the UN Security Council on July 30, 1997, with the adoption of Resolution 1123 (United Nations, 1997g). The mission was established to train special units of the HNP in crowd control, rapid reaction, and presidential palace security for a single four-month period ending on November 30, 1997 (United Nations, 1997g).

Mandate of the Mission

On November 20, 1997, the UN Security Council adopted Resolution 1141 (United Nations, 1997h), which established the United Nations Police Mission in Haiti (MIPONUH). The mission was based on the May 1997 Haitian National Police Development Plan (HNPDP) for 1997–2001 and was to help establish a fully functioning HNP force of adequate size and structure. The HNP was identified in the HNPDP as being an integral element to consolidate democracy and to revitalize Haiti's system of justice (United Nations, 1997h).

The MIPONUH's mandate was to be limited to one year and was to end on November 30, 1998 (United Nations, 1997h). The mission was to comprise 300 armed civilian police officers (United Nations, 1997c) and was to support and contribute to "the professionalisation of the Haitian [N]ational [P]olice in accordance with the arrangements, including mentoring Haitian [N]ational [P]olice field performance" (United Nations, 1997h). The police advisers were not to undertake patrolling activities, but were to assist HNP supervisors and senior management and were to provide training for specialized units (United Nations, 1997c).

The mission was to be deployed in all nine HNP departments including the six commissariats in the Port-au-Prince metropolitan area, HNP headquarters, and several specialized units (United Nations, 1997c).

The UN Security Council agreed when discussing Resolution 1064 (United Nations, 1998j) that the MIPONUH's mandate should be extended for another year until November 30, 1999. The proposed extension was to broaden the mandate to include the provision of training to middle and senior cadres of the HNP. It was also to provide advice about the creation of a "proper command structure and administration" and the concept of community policing (United Nations, 1998j).

The mission's mandate was extended on November 25, 1998, until November 30, 1999, with the adoption of Resolution 1212 (1998o). The extension was to strengthen "the capability of the central directorate of the police force to manage aid provided to it from bilateral and multilateral sources" (United Nations, 1999a).

Mission Deployment Environment

During the 1990s, the UN undertook a number of transformational missions, including those to Haiti and the Balkans. In 1994, the UN Security Council authorized UN police to assist Haiti create a separate police force (United Nations, 1994). The mission, UNMIH, in conjunction with the United States Department of Justice's International Criminal Investigative Training Assistance Program (ICITAP), advised and assisted with recruiting, vetting, and training a new HNP force. The two successive UN missions, UNSMIH and UNTMIH, were to provide technical advice and were to professionalize the HNP by focusing primarily on training and mentoring HNP specialized units and supervisors (Smith, Holt, and Durch, 2007). Those missions concentrated primarily on reforming the HNP and did not include the coordination of the activities undertaken by the courts and the prisons. As a result, the missions did not succeed in fulfilling their mandates.

Haiti had faced political turmoil and civil unrest since President Aristide was overthrown by a military coup d'état in September 1991. The coup placed General Raoul Cedras in power and forced President Aristide into exile. During the period of military rule from 1991 to 1994, an estimated 3,000–5,000 Haitians were killed. Between 1991 and 1992, more than 40,000 refugees were interdicted in the United States.

In mid-September 1994, the United States prepared to enter Haiti by force, but President Cedras stepped down and President Aristide returned to power.

The political situation from the late 1980s until the mid-1990s saw public confidence in the HNP depreciate and saw an increase in rampant crime, popular justice, and mob and gang violence. The HNP was often implicated in this violence and in a number of media-fueled human rights violations.

Because of the political instability and the military involvement in the HNP in the early 1980s, the HNP suffered from mismanagement, from corruption, and from a lack of funding.

Actions of the Mission (Output)

The MIPONUH police component monitored the HNP daily and provided operational technical assistance, in particular to specialist units in relation to crowd control, rapid reaction, presidential palace security, and investigations. Police advisers accompanied HNP officers and provided assistance and ongoing training during their daily duties. The mission also provided assistance to the directorate-general, the inspector-general, and the national police staff at each of the departmental headquarters. This action was to establish a framework to professionalize the force in its operational development as well as in its institutional development (United Nations, 1997c).

In the early phase of the mission, the MIPONUH assisted the HNP to implement a uniform in-service training program for all HNP officers. "The practices of the rapid intervention team [were reviewed] to ensure its adherence to Haitian law and [to] the spirit of civilian policing" (United Nations, 1997c).

In February 1998, the MIPONUH trained 500 HNP recruits and implemented a recruiting and training program that enabled the HNP "to grow from under 5,000 in 1997 to its targeted strength of 6,726" (United Nations, 1998a). This program allowed the MIPONUH to provide in-service training to an average of 400 HNP officers every week (United Nations, 1998j).

Mission Implementation (Model)

The MIPONUH was designed to be a technical assistance program that would provide the HNP with top-

Table 10.1. Composition of Total Number of MIPONUH Civilian Police Officers, October 1997 to February 2000

Date	Special Police Units	Civilian Police Officers	Total Civilian Police
October 1997	N/K	N/K	242
February 1998	139	146	285
May 1998	140	145	285
August 1998	140	144	284
November 1998	140	145	285
February 1999	140	142	282
May 1999	130	147	277
February 2000	110	109	219

Source: Author (from United Nations documents).

Note: N/K = not known.

level law enforcement expertise over the next three years. The mission was based on a number of diagnostic studies that were conducted in July 1996 and in January and July 1997. These studies covered the three areas of justice, police, and prisons. The studies also aimed to track progress in developing and consolidating the HNP and to pinpoint problem areas that then became the focus of concerted attention (United Nations, 1997c).

The adoption of Resolution 1141 (United Nations, 1997h) by the UN Security Council authorized the maximum strength of 300 civilian police officers in the MIPONUH. Despite the early deployment of the mission's civilian police component and the adoption of the resolution, the mission never reached its authorized strength. Table 10.1 illustrates that civilian police numbers reached a maximum of 285 officers and remained around that number until the mission was completed in March 2000.

The MIPONUH assisted the HNP in designing and implementing a command center at the HNP headquarters and in redeploying HNP officers on the basis of population patterns and the incidence of crime. However, allocating resources in this manner gave priority to cities over rural areas (United Nations, 1997c).

By February 1998, the HNP had become less dependent on MIPONUH because HNP had improved management capability and strengthened reporting relationships by building an effective cadre of commissariats and inspectors. This organizational improvement was supported by redeploying HNP officers across the country to improve the balance in police coverage between the capital and the provinces. However, during this period, the MIPONUH identified recurring human rights abuses by operational HNP officers and showed that a number of commissariats displayed poor leadership qualities (United Nations, 1998a).

Also during this period, the MIPONUH assisted the HNP in appointing a number of senior officers, refurbishing accommodation and communication facilities, and developing a number of quantitative performance benchmarks (United Nations, 1998a).

In August 1998, in conjunction with the MIPONUH, the HNP completed a qualitative study to examine its performance. The study identified consistent progress that had been made in certain areas and, in particular, some progress in the area of community policing at the rank-and-file level (United Nations, 1998g).

In February 1999, in conjunction with the United Nations Development Programme (UNDP), the MIPONUH developed a strategy paper for the Haitian government for 1999–2001. That paper outlined the objectives relating to governance and the rule of law. The strategy paper formed the basis for the MIPONUH and the HNP to develop a two-year program that was for technical assistance and that was designed to provide the fledgling police service with the expertise for training and institution building. The approach was to ensure that the

HNP had the capability to undertake basic policing after the MIPONUH was terminated (United Nations, 1999a).

Mission Achievements (Outcome)

In November 1997, the secretary-general of the UN noted that although the HNP had "made substantial strides forward [since the deployment of the first UN mission in September 1993], its development into a professional force continues to be slow and uneven" (United Nations, 1997c). The HNP was developing a greater capacity to maintain law and order, and its officers had a visible presence on the roads and in various communities (United Nations, 1998j). The secretary-general also noted that the HNP had "difficulty in dealing effectively" with banditry and drug trafficking (United Nations, 1997c).

By late 1998, the HNP had made considerable progress in improving its organizational and operational capability and had improved in respecting the legal rights of detainees in police stations. With assistance from the MIPONUH, the HNP leadership had displayed a commitment to developing and strengthening the force and had updated the official police development plan for the years 1998–2003 (United Nations, 1998j).

The HNP's capability to implement public works significantly improved. The HNP was able to undertake logistics operations and had successfully "planned and implemented a number of infrastructure projects," including the rehabilitation and construction of eight police stations in 1998 (United Nations, 1998j).

The UN reported that the HNP was "extremely fragile." The HNP had a weak investigative capacity, and police officer absenteeism was an extensive problem. The HNP did not have the "experience, professional skills, resources, and cohesion" of a "well-established police force" and still had a number of "instances of crime, corruption, and drug trafficking within the ranks" (United Nations, 1998j).

In November 1998, a "US Information Agency poll showed that 70% of those polled had confidence in the HNP as an institution—a truly extraordinary figure for a country with no tradition of civilian policing. By their presence and daily example, UN civilian police officers have had a positive effect on the conduct of police work in Haiti" (United Nations, 1998j).

The HNP also made progress in the respect for human rights, and there had been "a noticeable reduction in reports of ill treatment during arrests and interrogations" in early 1999 (United Nations, 1999a).

Ways the Mission Was Evaluated

In July 1998, a team of international consultants formally evaluated the UNDP Technical Assistance Project. Although critical in some areas, the report was largely positive. It concluded that "it is true both that the progress made in building the HNP over the past three years has been extraordinary but also that the HNP as an institution remains extremely fragile and without further development will collapse" (United Nations, 1998g).

The secretary-general noted in late 1998, that although the HNP's performance had improved and that training provided by the MIPONUH had been appropriate, "the development of an effective police force is a complex and lengthy task" and that "there will be a continuing need for international training of the HNP to strengthen the capacity of the force and consolidate the gains it has already achieved" (United Nations, 1998g).

Conclusion

The main task of MIPONUH was to assist the government of Haiti in professionalizing the HNP (United Nations, 2009d). In this regard, the mission "had placed special emphasis on assistance at the supervisory level and on training specialized police units" (United Nations, 2009o). The approach made limited progress in developing HNP's institutional capacity.

MIPONUH was succeeded by the new International Civilian Support Mission in Haiti (MICAH) on March 16, 2000. The establishment of MICAH was approved by the UN General Assembly in Resolution A/54/193 of December 17, 1999. The new mission's mandate was to consolidate the results achieved by MIPONUH and to further promote human rights and reinforce the institutional effectiveness of the Haitian police and the judiciary (United Nations, 2009o).

Case Study: United Nations Stabilization Mission in Haiti

Background to the Mission

The United Nations (UN) involvement in Haiti began in 1990 with the deployment of the United Nations Observer Group for the Verification of the Elections in Haiti (ONUVEH). The group observed the preparation for and the holding of elections in Haiti (United Nations, 2010d). A number of successive missions followed to develop the governance and the capacity of the Haitian National Police (HNP). The final mission, the United Nations Police Mission in Haiti (MIPONUH), was completed in March 2000.

A number of positive developments occurred during the successive missions, including the return of a level of democracy and some growth of civil society (United Nations, 2010d). However, "owing to the continuing political crisis and concomitant lack of stability in the country, serious reforms never" were accomplished leading to an armed conflict in February 2004 in the city of Gonaives (United Nations, 2010d).

Fighting quickly spread to other cities and "the insurgents took control of much of the northern part of the country" (United Nations, 2010d). Following the hostilities, the president of Haiti, Bertrand Aristide, departed Haiti for exile, and the UN Security Council declared that the "situation in Haiti constituted a threat to international peace and security" (United Nations, 2010d). On February 29, 2004, the UN Security Council adopted Resolution 1529 (United Nations, 2004ag), which established the Multinational Interim Force (MIF) and confirmed its "readiness to establish a follow-on United Nations stabilization force to support [the] continuation of a peaceful and constitutional political process and the maintenance of a secure and stable environment" (United Nations, 2010d).

During this "unrest, the HNP almost completely collapsed" (United Nations, 2004h). A large number of police stations were vandalized, burned, or seriously damaged, and equipment, records, and archives were looted or destroyed. Despite those problems, the HNP maintained a minimal law enforcement capability. A number of officers returned to work after several months of reduced or no activity, and they contributed to a protective detail for the interim president and prime minister. The HNP also maintained elements of an antiriot operational unit and a 250-strong judiciary police capacity (United Nations, 2004h).

Mandate of the Mission

On April 30, 2004, the UN Security Council adopted Resolution 1542 (United Nations, 2004ab), which established the United Nations Stabilization Mission in Haiti on June 1, 2004 (MINUSTAH) (United Nations, 2004z). The mission had an authorized strength of 1,622 civilian police, which included 872 advisers and six formed police units (FPUs) of 125 officers each (United Nations, 2004h). Police advisers were co-located with their HNP equivalent and provided advice and mentoring about management, training, and professional standards (United Nations, 2004h).

The mission's initial mandate was as follows:

- Provide support to the transitional government and to ensure a secure and stable environment that would allow the constitutional and political process in Haiti to take place.
- Assist the transitional government monitor, restructure, and reform the HNP to conform with democratic policing standards, including vetting and certifying its personnel, providing advice on training including gender training, and monitoring and mentoring members of the HNP.
- Assist the HNP with comprehensive and sustainable disarmament, demobilization, and reintegration (DDR) programs for all armed groups, including women and children associated with such groups, as well as weapons control and public security measures.
- Help restore and maintain the rule of law, public safety, and public order in Haiti by providing operational support to the HNP and the Haitian Coast Guard (United Nations, 2004aa; 2010d).
- Protect civilians under imminent threat of physical violence, within its capabilities and areas of deployment, without prejudice to the responsibilities of the transitional government and of police authorities (United Nations, 2004h; 2004ab).

The UN Security Council recommended that the mission be established initially for 24 months, during which time the mission would provide regular progress reports (United Nations, 2004h). Following the completion of this deployment, the Security Council "recommended that the Mission be authorised for subsequent periods of 12 months, with periodic reviews with respect to the appropriate mix of its different components and the priority assigned to its multiple areas of activity" (United Nations, 2004h).

By doing the following, the mission was to "assist in developing and enhancing in a sustainable fashion the overall law enforcement capacity of the HNP" (United Nations, 2004h):

- Assist the HNP academy to implement training programs.
- Mentor and provide on-the-job training at the main operational levels of the HNP.
- Transfer skills and proactively assist multi-tier management functions within the HNP.
- Develop and implement an effective, transparent, and accountable HNP oversight mechanism.
- Develop and implement vetting and certification programs in accordance with international standards.
- Support the implementation of a community-based policing program throughout the country.

The mission was to "build the public's confidence in the criminal justice sector by observing the HNP and advising and reporting on its activities regarding compliance with professional standards and human rights." The police component of the mission was also to assist in "civil disturbance management, land and marine border policing, judiciary, information gathering, immigration, customs, port authority, and related sectors of internal security, and in determining related infrastructure and logistical requirements" (United Nations, 2004h).

On June 22, 2005, the UN Security Council agreed to increase the authorized strength of the civilian police component of the mission by 275 personnel to a total of 1,897. The increase in the number of civilian police was to provide security "during the electoral period and subsequent political transition" (United Nations, 2005ac). On July 28, 2006, the authorized strength of the civilian police

was increased again to 1,951 personnel (United Nations, 2006q). Finally, the authorization increased to 2,091 personnel (which included 1,140 officers in nine FPUs) on August 22, 2007 (United Nations, 2007l; 2007w).

After the completion of the first two years, the mission was extended for 12 months every subsequent year (United Nations, 2006q; 2007l; 2009h). As of mid-2012, it continues.

Mission Deployment Environment

The HNP was the only official security agency in Haiti after the armed forces were disbanded by the United Nations Mission in Haiti (UNMIH) in 1995. In April 2004, the HNP comprised approximately 2,500 officers, while its authorized strength was 6,367. However, the secretary-general estimated "that the HNP would need a minimum of 10,000 officers, or [one] police officer for every 800 citizens, in order to meet Haiti's basic law-and-order requirements" for its 8.5 million inhabitants (United Nations, 2004h).

The HNP organization, as described by the United Nations (2004h), incorporated 189 countrywide operational police departments that were made up of the following:

- 10 commissariats de department
- 46 commissariats d'arrondissement
- 133 commissariats de commune

The HNP suffered from demoralization, erosion of professional standards, and a lack of resources. It was "plagued by heavy politicisation, corruption, and mismanagement," and the organization had lost its "credibility in the eyes of the Haitian population" because of its involvement in abuse, rape, and drug trafficking (United Nations, 2004h).

By April 2004, general police and traffic patrols were practically nonexistent. This situation was expected to improve with the deployment of the MIF and by the efforts of the HNP leadership "to bring back more HNP officers and to recruit new officers" (United Nations, 2004h).

A mission predeployment team consisting of eight civilian police officers arrived in Port-au-Prince to establish a headquarters; to conduct an assessment of the current structure; and to determine training, logistical, and administrative requirements of the HNP (United Nations, 2004h).

Actions of the Mission (Output)

On June 1, 2004, the civilian police component of MINUSTAH was deployed to Port-au-Prince. By August 17, 2004, 22 of those officers were deployed to Cap-Haïtien, 15 to Fort-Liberté, 16 to Gonaïves, 15 to Hinche, 19 to Jacmel, 14 to Jérémie, 17 to Les Cayes, and 8 to Port-de-Paix (United Nations, 2004p) and by November had "established operations in all 10 administrative districts in Haiti" (United Nations, 2004v). During the deployment phase, regional operational centers were established and were open 24 hours a day in those locations (United Nations, 2004q).

The approach taken by the mission was to undertake joint patrolling with the HNP and to deploy the MINUSTAH police advisers "at every decision-making level of HNP" and with "every special and regional unit" (United Nations, 2004q). Because of the increased security threat in the early phase of the mission, MINUSTAH civilian police focused "mainly on providing operational support" to the HNP rather than on the developmental and training needs of the HNP (United Nations, 2004v).

In July 2004, the MINUSTAH established a "special training team" to undertake an assessment of the training needs of the HNP and to develop a regional training implementation plan. This team also designed mechanisms to enable the HNP to respond to domestic violence, especially violence against women, in Port-au-Prince. The mission also assisted the HNP to develop a six-month training program that complied "with international policing and human rights standards" and with a "train-the-trainers" program that was delivered by "54 local police instructors" (United Nations, 2004q).

In February 2005, progress had been made in the deployment of civilian police personnel that enabled MINUSTAH to put a greater emphasis on the HNP's training and capacity building. The mission helped train 570 recruits, 285 existing HNP officers, and 121 senior management officers (United Nations, 2005f). The mission deployed 28 civilian police advisers to the HNP

police academy to help develop and implement a cadet training program (United Nations, 2005a). The final cadet training program consisted of two components: four months of residential duty and two months of station duty (United Nations, 2005f).

In May 2005, the mission negotiated a "memorandum of understanding with the HNP to institutionalize and strengthen the co-location programme" and deployed 14 advisers to develop the investigative capacity of special crime units (United Nations, 2005b). The mission also developed an HNP officer vetting program and began a "pilot project in one police station aimed at improving facilities in police stations [so that they could] receive women [who were] victims of violence" (United Nations, 2005n).

By September 2005, 1,546 officers had graduated from the HNP academy. The MINUSTAH had established a new curriculum that included "elements relating to child protection and HIV sensitization" and included an outreach training program. Also included in the training program were 410 MINUSTAH police officers who were to accompany and provide operational support to the HNP, as well as provide specialist in-service training at 46 police stations (United Nations, 2005w).

In September 2005, the MINUSTAH, in conjunction with the HNP and the Haitian Coalition for Child Rights, established a campaign to raise awareness of "all forms of violence against children, including sexual abuse and child prostitution" (United Nations, 2005w). In early 2006, a certification program and a project to register all serving HNP officers were implemented. All HNP officers were identified, and the serial numbers of their weapons were recorded during registration, which clarified the police capability and provided a baseline for future development (United Nations, 2006d).

All HNP officers and units were included in the certification program. Officers were issued a provisional certification that was valid for 12 months. The provisional certification was "renewable based on the officer's observance of the necessary standards" and "on [gaining] satisfactory results from [the] vetting" process (United Nations, 2006d). The program was designed to be completed in three phases that included individual officers, units, and the entire HNP organization (United Nations, 2006d). By mid-2006, 5,783 HNP serving officers and

Table 10.2. Composition of MINUSTAH Civilian Police Officers, May 2005 to August 2009

Date	Civilian Police			Formed Police Units			Grand Total
	Male	Female	Total	Male	Female	Total	
May 5, 2005	N/K	N/K	623	N/K	N/K	790	1,413
Sept. 9, 2005	N/K	N/K	602	N/K	N/K	869	1,471
Jan. 31, 2006	N/K	N/K	777	N/K	N/K	1,000	1,777
July 15, 2006	N/K	N/K	690	N/K	N/K	997	1,687
Dec. 10, 2006	N/K	N/K	747	N/K	N/K	995	1,742
Mar. 26, 2008	894	45	939	945	53	998	1,937
Feb. 25, 2009	822	65	887	1,090	44	1,134	2,021
Aug. 25, 2009	880	58	938	1,099	35	1,134	2,072
Feb. 22, 2010	768	60	828	1,321	28	1,349	2,177
Sept. 1, 2010	1,106	128	1,234	1,674	155	1,829	3,063

Source: Author (from various United Nations documents from 2005 to 2010).
Note: N/K = not known.

the serial numbers of their weapons had been registered (United Nations, 2006q).

During early 2006, the MINUSTAH police had completed renovation and rehabilitation work on 22 of the 50 police stations where MINUSTAH police officers and HNP personnel were co-located (United Nations, 2006d).

In late 2006, the MINUSTAH, in conjunction with the HNP, developed a seven-month recruit training curriculum that would be followed by three months of field training (United Nations, 2007l). All training materials were revised to include human rights standards in all aspects of basic police training (United Nations, 2006aa).

By 2009, the HNP, with the assistance of the MINUSTAH, had 9,247 active officers (United Nations, 2009c).

Mission Implementation (Model)

The UN Security Council initially authorized the mission civilian police strength at 1,622 (United Nations, 2004h). This strength was increased to 1,897 members within 12 months of the mission's start (United Nations, 2005ac) and was increased a further two times to 1,951 in 2006 (United Nations, 2006q) and finally to 2,091 in 2007 (United Nations, 2007l). Table 10.2 presents the total

number of civilian police by gender and the composition of the FPUs by gender for June 2005 to August 2009. Although the mission quickly deployed, it did not achieve the initial 2004 authorized strength until the end of 2005 and did not achieve the final 2007 authorized strength until late 2009.

To ensure that there was coordination and agreement on the ground when implementing MINUSTAH's tasks, the mission initiated and held regular meetings with officials from the Ministry of Justice, the Ministry of Interior, and the HNP to discuss where assistance was required to further stabilize the country. Those discussions included reforming, restructuring, developing, and professionalizing the HNP (United Nations, 2004q) and led to the introduction of the Interim Co-operation Framework Sectoral Round Table (ICFSRT) on police. The ICFSRT would "ensure co-ordination in the execution phase" and would establish a reporting regime for the results achieved (United Nations, 2004v).

In November 2004, the MINUSTAH signed a memorandum of understanding (MoU) with the Organization of American States (OAS) to establish a closer working relationship, to develop police training, and to plan for the elections. The MoU was to form a "basis for enhanced regional and international collaboration in supporting the electoral process" (United Nations, 2004v).

In early 2005, the MINUSTAH, in conjunction with the transitional government, developed the HNP Reform and Restructuring Plan (United Nations, 2005b), which provided the strategic direction for the civilian police component of the mission. The mission recognized that reforms of the HNP were "a long-term task, requiring dedicated attention, [and] organizational efforts and resources to root out corruption and counter the negative public image of the police" (United Nations, 2005m). The MINUSTAH and the transitional government were to identify a "provisional desired end state (size and standards) for the HNP and to develop a programme (timetable and resources)" for this objective (United Nations, 2005m). To assist in this process, the UN Security Council (United Nations, 2005m) authorized the deployment of a review team to travel to Haiti in April 2005 to assess and evaluate the following:

- Current situation of the HNP and the mechanisms for its reform and the creation of a credible, accountable, and respected police force
- Implementation of the MINUSTAH security mandate and the way ahead by taking into account the current capacity of the HNP and by enhancing the HNP's coordination with MINUSTAH
- Steps taken to implement a DDR program that addressed all illegal armed groups comprehensively, including the program's legal basis, and actions to be taken by the transitional government and measures that required immediate implementation, including the MINUSTAH

The Haitian conseil supérieur de la police nationale adopted the National Police Strategic Development Plan (NPSDP) for 2004–08 on March 15, 2005, which was developed in conjunction with the ICFSRT (United Nations, 2005n). The plan detailed specific "key objectives for the development of the police such as the creation of new senior posts, [the] adoption of a new organization chart, [the] training for senior officers, a comprehensive appraisal of the police force, and the strengthening of the National Penitentiary Authority" (United Nations, 2005n).

The NPSDP was a blueprint (United Nations, 2006aa) that determined that the HNP would build on an initial basic police capability of 7,000 officers (United Nations, 2006d), but it would eventually have 18,000 to 20,000 officers who would "implement the full range of security sector responsibilities in Haiti" (United Nations, 2006q). The NPSDP also noted that a major area in need of reform was the Office of the Inspector General (OIG) (United Nations, 2006d). The proposed OIG's first priority would be to "assist in ensuring professional values within the national police" (United Nations, 2006d). The second priority of the proposed OIG would include strengthening "key institutional capacities within the HNP" (United Nations, 2006q).

To support the implementation of the NPSDP, the mission adjusted its focus on changing management to concentrating on the HNP's vetting process at the station level (United Nations, 2006q).

To support the implementation of the NPSDP, the MINUSTAH developed a set of standard operating procedures (SOPs). Those procedures guided the operational activities of the military component and the FPUs of the police component that enhanced the existing Joint Operations Center and developed a missionwide Joint Mission Analysis Cell (JMAC) whose members were responsible for managing information. The SOPs provided a framework to better inform the decisions and plans of the mission (United Nations, 2005n). The JMAC was tasked to assist the MINUSTAH gather and analyze intelligence in field operations (United Nations, 2006d).

In October 2005, the MINUSTAH signed a MoU with the HNP to provide assistance in developing a reform plan. The plan was to enhance professionalism and technical skills and was to include vetting and certification of police officers. During this period, the MINUSTAH assisted the Haitian conseil supérieur de la police nationale in establishing a joint commission to investigate human rights abuses by the HNP (United Nations, 2005w).

During the earlier phase of the mission, the MINUSTAH civilian police did not have a criminal intelligence framework. The situation left the civilian police heavily reliant on information provided by the HNP or on information that was voluntarily given, "for a variety of reasons, by the public" (United Nations, 2006d).

In February 2006, a steering committee co-chaired by the MINUSTAH and the HNP was established to monitor the progress of implementing HNP reforms. The MINUSTAH, jointly with the HNP, established a planning team to assist this steering group. The planning team's task was "to identify areas for development, [to] coordinate and give direction to development initiatives, and to promote their implementation." The planning team also developed a model police station so that the project could establish a police presence in neglected areas and could renovate and equip police stations nationwide. This project included the co-location of MINUSTAH police advisers in 50 main police stations throughout Haiti (United Nations, 2006d).

In early 2007, the MINUSTAH provided the following operational support to the National Commission for Disarmament, Dismantlement, and Reintegration to develop and implement a number of community-based projects (United Nations, 2007l):

- Facilitate the return of former gang members to their communities.
- Reinforce the capacity of local communities to resolve conflicts peacefully.
- Promote a culture of peace.
- Assist victims of violence.
- Support the creation of temporary employment.

To provide a measurable implementation framework for the NPSDP, the MINUSTAH developed benchmarks and action plans for competency and performance evaluations, for staffing, for reallocation of office space and equipment, for technological improvements, and for technical and ethical training. The critical milestone for MINUSTAH in implementing the NPSDP was establishing a sustainable security structure that would let Haiti "respond effectively to potential threats within the country and along its land and maritime borders while respecting international standards and individual freedoms" (United Nations, 2008d).

To support the implementation framework over the two 12-month periods, October 2009 to October 2010 and October 2010 to October 2011, the MINUSTAH and the HNP developed these two comprehensive sets of Year Indicators of Progress (United Nations, 2009h):

October 2009 to October 2010

- Continue advances in maintaining security and stability in urban and rural areas, drawing on collaboration between international and Haitian security forces.
- Continue strengthening the HNP presence, with MINUSTAH support, along land and maritime borders and throughout the country.

- Continue progress in reaching the objectives that were established by the HNP reform plan by doing the following:
    - Graduate additional HNP members through promotions, permitting continued increase of overall staffing in accordance with reform plan timelines.
    - Continue vetting and certification.
    - Continue strengthening technical capabilities of Haitian judicial police.
    - Progress in developing coast guard capability.
    - Strengthen HNP administrative capacity and progress in training mid- and upper-level management.
    - Continue developing HNP infrastructures.
    - Prepare a follow-on development plan to the current HNP reform plan.
- Give full and expeditious consideration to the Presidential Commission on Security recommendations, and reach broad agreement on follow-up action.
- Progress in the public weapons registration program.

October 2010 to October 2011

- Make further progress in all areas that were outlined by the Haitian National Police Reform Plan, so that by the end of 2011, most key objectives of the HNP Reform Plan would be attained or within reach as follows:
    - HNP strength at 14,000 adequately trained and professional officers
    - HNP certification process complete
    - HNP capacity able to provide essential police services throughout the country
- Provide sustainable security along the land and maritime borders, drawing on international assistance and complementary bilateral activities as necessary.
- Approve further development planning for the HNP.
- Complete registration for approximately 31,000 weapons.

Mission Achievements (Outcome)

By February 2006, confidence had increased in the HNP to the level that 38,836 Haitian citizens had applied for admission to join the next class of police officers (United Nations, 2006d). While "criminal activities by armed groups, in particular kidnappings, had started to decline in the capital [during] January and February," gang violence remained "a serious destabilizing factor" (United Nations, 2006q).

In addition to the civilian police component of the mission, MINUSTAH began to reform and restructure the judicial and corrections systems with the aim of reducing the number of pretrial detentions, thus increasing the number of cases heard and increasing the number of correctional officers (Smith, Holt, and Durch, 2007).

The United Nations (2006q) reported that the needs of the country remained vast and the challenges immense, and the Haitian state had only a very limited capacity to address crime—in particular, gang and cross-border trafficking activities. The UN also reported that illicit trafficking in weapons and drugs remained an obstacle to successfully fighting crime, impunity, and corruption.

By March 2008, the Haitian macroeconomic indicators had improved, and the country experienced economic growth at a level that had not been possible for decades. Although the HNP consisted of 7,441 officers who were assuming purely policing duties, there were also 144 firefighters, 69 coast guard personnel, and 790 corrections officers (United Nations, 2008d). Those figures indicate the achievement of a police to population ratio of 1.366 to 1,000 (United Nations, 2009d).

A public opinion poll undertaken in late 2008 revealed that 58 percent of Haitians considered that there had been a positive change in the HNP. During 2009, more than 30,000 applications had been received to become HNP officers. Although progress had been made in reforming the HNP, it lacked the capacity to address the many threats to Haiti, including organized crime and drug trafficking, which were among the main threats to the country's governance, stability, and development (United Nations, 2009d).

Ways the Mission Was Evaluated

The 2005 review mission that assessed the MINUSTAH noted that although MINUSTAH had a clear mandate to help the transitional government monitor, restructure, and reform the police, "[I]t was unable to make marked progress in this important area because of the ambiguous attitude of the police regarding the need to undertake serious reforms" (United Nations, 2005m).

A second major issue for the mission was that it suffered from a lack of French-speaking members of the civilian police (United Nations, 2005m). The low number of civilian police who could speak French "hampered the ability of the Mission to implement its mandate" (United Nations, 2009d).

Conclusion

In September 2009,

> … the Presidential Commission on Public Security, in its report issued on 6 August 2009, recommend[ed] that, in addition to ongoing enhancement of police capacity, Haiti should re-establish an additional force with a military status. This body, with a suggested composition of 4,000 to 5,000 members, would assume a variety of tasks, several of which are currently being discharged by MINUSTAH or by the National Police, and could incorporate certain elements of the National Police. Its responsibilities would include the maintenance of security along Haiti's borders and, in rural areas, protecting the population against natural disasters, fighting illicit trafficking, [supporting] the police in cases of civil unrest, and [protecting] the environment. The political, practical, and financial dimensions of these recommendations are expected to give rise to extended political and public debate (United Nations, 2009h).

The major issues that the mission faced were the HNP's lack of professionalism and the inadequate timelines for developing and implementing the police officer certification process. The mission also lacked a strategic implementation plan (SIP) that would guide the HNP at the conclusion of the current reform plan. A SIP should contain sufficient detail to assist the mission to develop and implement reform strategies and should include a fiscally sustainable vision for the HNP (United Nations, 2009h).

The mission was ongoing as of June 2010.

Chapter 11

Kosovo

Map 11.1. Kosovo

Source: Courtesy of the University of Texas Libraries, The University of Texas at Austin.

Case Study: United Nations Interim Administration Mission in Kosovo

Background to the Mission

Kosovo, because of its geographical location between Serbia and Albania, has a long history of being invaded and of occupation. Kosovo was invaded in World Wars I and II and has had its borders revised on several occasions. As a result of those historical actions, interethnic tensions worsened throughout the 1980s (SANU, 1986).

Following the disintegration of Yugoslavia and the signing of the Dayton Agreement in 1995 that ended the war in Bosnia, the Kosovo Liberation Army (KLA), an ethnic Albanian guerrilla group, confronted the Serbian and Yugoslav security forces, which resulted in conflict and the beginning of the Kosovo War (Rogel, 2003). The nearly two-year war resulted in more than 1 million ethnic Albanians fleeing or being driven from Kosovo, with more than 11,000 people killed and 3,000 identified as missing (BBC News, 1999).

The Kosovo War was brought to an end in February 1999 with the drafting of the Rambouillet Accords. However, the Serbs found the terms of this accord unacceptable, and they refused to sign the draft. This action resulted in (a) an extensive North Atlantic Treaty Organization (NATO) bombing campaign of Yugoslavia, (b) the agreement by the Serbians to a foreign military presence within Kosovo, and (c) a withdrawal of Serbian troops (NATO, 2010c).

The Kosovo Force (KFOR), a NATO-led international military peacekeeping force responsible for establishing security in Kosovo, entered the country on June 12, 1999. Although KFOR comprised only military personnel, its mandate was to establish and maintain public safety and civil order (NATO, 2010b). However, KFOR's ability to maintain public safety and civil law and order was limited because of its concentration on establishing the mission and deploying personnel (United Nations, 1999h).

Mandate of the Mission

Parallel to the NATO establishment of KFOR, the United Nations (UN) adopted Resolution 1244 on June 10, 1999.

This resolution established the civilian United Nations Interim Administration Mission in Kosovo (UNMIK) for an initial period of 12 months (United Nations, 1999e). The resolution identified that an advance team would be deployed to Kosovo to develop and plan the mission. The first police officers within UNMIK were deployed on July 3, 1999, as liaisons to five locations in Kosovo (United Nations, 1999h).

The mission was to be comprehensive, involving not only police reform, but also government institution building. It included establishing an interim civilian administration led by the UN (United Nations, 2010l). The mandate adopted by the UN Security Council (2010l) tasked the UNMIK to do the following:

- Perform basic civilian administrative functions.
- Promote the establishment of substantial autonomy and self-government.
- Facilitate a political process to determine Kosovo's future status.
- Coordinate humanitarian and disaster relief of all international agencies.
- Support the reconstruction of key infrastructure.
- Maintain civil law and order.
- Promote human rights.
- Ensure the safe and unimpeded return of all refugees and displaced persons to their homes in Kosovo.

Although UNMIK was led by the UN, the mission comprised individual strategic pillars, each led by a different institution (United Nations, 2010l). The four pillars were as follows:

- Pillar 1—Humanitarian assistance led by the United Nations Office of the High Commissioner for Refugees
- Pillar 2—Civil administration led by the UN
- Pillar 3—Democratization and institutional building led by the Organisation for Security and Co-operation in Europe (OSCE)
- Pillar 4—Reconstruction and economic development led by the European Union (EU)

Pillar 1 included the control and oversight of police and justice activities. The UNMIK advisers were to increase police efforts to maintain law and order. They were to do so through better coordination of information and work and, in particular, by "an effective police and judicial response against destabilizing serious criminal activity." The mission was specifically tasked by the UN Security Council to "oversee the expansion of the Kosovo Police Service (KPS) from the present target goal of 4,000 to a total of 6,000 police officers by the end of 2002" (United Nations, 2010l). The secretary-general noted that the "two main goals will define UNMIK's law-and-order strategy in Kosovo: provision of interim law enforcement services, and the rapid development of a credible, professional and impartial Kosovo Police Service" (United Nations, 1999e).

To achieve those goals, the advance team developed a deployment plan that comprised three separate elements and located UNMIK police personnel to five Kosovo regions. As described by the United Nations (1999e), those elements included the following:

- Civilian police—1,800 officers
- Special units—10 formed police units (FPUs) of approximately 115 officers each
- Border police—205 officers

The advance team identified that the mission would evolve over time and would, therefore, require a three-phased approach to implement the following three elements (United Nations, 1999e):

- Phase 1: This was the stability and deployment phase. Because the UNMIK police had not been deployed, KFOR would maintain public safety and order until this responsibility could be transferred to the UNMIK. However, the UNMIK's civilian police would advise KFOR on policing matters.
- Phase 2: Once UNMIK was responsible for law and order, the UNMIK police would have executive authority and would carry out normal police duties. The UNMIK special units were responsible for public order and crowd control.

UNMIK was also to develop a professional KPS by doing the following:

a. Initiating on-the-job training
b. Advising and monitoring
c. Overseeing selection and screening of recruits
d. Developing an effective and transparent KPS command structure

- Phase 3: Once there were sufficient numbers of appropriately selected and trained KPS officers, the UNMIK would plan for the transfer of "responsibilities for law and order and border policing functions to the Kosovo Police Service."

Mission Deployment Environment

The Yugoslav army and the Serbian security forces began their withdrawal from Kosovo following the deployment of KFOR on June 12, 1999, which was completed by June 20, 1999. On June 21, 1999, the KLA signed an undertaking that established the process and scheduled the KLA's demilitarization (United Nations, 1999e).

The situation was tense but was settled with the KLA's moving back into all regions and large numbers of Kosovo Serbs departing for their homes in Serbia. The departure was prompted by an increase in the number of violent incidents, including killings and abductions, thus resulting in Kosovo Serbs deserting a number of cities (United Nations, 1999e).

The lack of security in the country was caused by (a) the absence of law-and-order institutions and agencies and (b) the lack of confidence in the justice process as crimes could not "be properly pursued." Criminals and criminal gangs exploited this void because the KFOR was still being deployed and the KFOR's ability to maintain law and order was limited (United Nations, 1999e).

Actions of the Mission (Output)

According to Jones, Wilson, Rathmell, and Riley (2005), the mission established comprehensive plans before beginning the reformation of the KPS. The plans identified the difficulty of coordinating the implementation of the reform program.

The UNMIK was deployed initially to the Pristina region before policing and law enforcement initiatives were undertaken in the other four regions. The Pristina region was given priority for deploying police officers because approximately one-third of all reported Kosovo crimes occurred there (United Nations, 1999f).

The UNMIK was responsible for establishing the local police, the KPS (United Nations, 2000d). However, a number of institutions, including the UNMIK, were involved in developing the KPS. For example, personnel from the OSCE, in conjunction with UNMIK, developed the civil law and the institution-building component, which included establishing and managing the KPS training school at Vučitrn (United Nations, 1999f).

A strategic plan was developed by UNMIK and OSCE to coordinate the training provided at the academy that was operated by the OSCE. The UNMIK delivered field training programs and planned to train and develop more than 3,500 KPS officers by January 2001 (United Nations, 2000d). To achieve that goal of 3,500 required developing a number of options, including the reduction of the time taken on the basic training course for KPS cadet officers and the development of plans "to recruit a significant number of former Kosovo police officers expelled by the Federal Government in 1989 and 1990" (United Nations, 1999j).

The deployment of UNMIK police was steady from September to December 1999. By the end of December, a presence had been established in 70 percent of Kosovo, and full law enforcement authority had been established in the Pristina and Prizren regions. However, UNMIK had assumed full investigative responsibility only in Mitrovica, Gnjilane, and Uroševac municipalities (United Nations, 1999j). By late December, the mission had assumed responsibility for managing 39 police stations, five border police stations, five regional headquarter facilities, and the main police headquarters (United Nations, 1999j).

The UNMIK, in conjunction with the KFOR, undertook joint foot and vehicle patrols, along with weapons and ordnance searches; established a joint operations center in Mitrovica (United Nations, 2000b); and introduced a comprehensive criminal intelligence structure and a protective persons unit (United Nations, 2000d; 2000i). UNMIK police also maintained a security presence in ethnic minority areas and enhanced the effectiveness of the delivery of policing services by implementing a number of community-based initiatives (United Nations, 2003m).

UNMIK's major priorities for strategic security policing were to solve serious crimes and to increase its capacity in countering terrorism and organized crime (United Nations, 2001b). To assist in the institutional development of these areas of crime, according to the United Nations (2002a), the UNMIK police and the Joint Interim Administrative Structure (JIAS) Department of Judicial Affairs formed a single structure to provide focus, centrality, and coordination and to establish the following five specialized units:

- Central intelligence
- Kosovo organized crime bureau
- Sensitive information and operations unit
- Legal policy
- Victim advocacy and assistance unit

Mission Implementation (Model)

The mission to Kosovo "proved to be one of the most complex international community missions of modern times" (United Nations, 2010j). The blueprint for the UNMIK mandate was contained in the UN Security Council Resolution 1244, which was passed on June 10, 1999 (United Nations, 1999h). To achieve this mandate, the UNMIK operated as a transitional administration, thereby performing a spectrum of essential functions and services, including law and order. A regional structure with five regional administrators and 30 municipal administrators was also established by the mission (United Nations, 2010j).

Two objectives defined the UNMIK's law-and-order strategy: the "provision of interim law enforcement services, and the rapid development of a credible, professional, and impartial KPS." To achieve those objectives, the UNMIK police component was given executive authority. Moreover, civilian police officers, FPUs, and border police were deployed to five Kosovo regions (United Nations, 1999e).

The slowness in deploying police advisers severely constrained the effectiveness of the UNMIK throughout the first year. The first FPUs did not begin to deploy until mid-2000, and it was not until May 2000 that the mission police component reached 75 percent of its authorized strength.

Table 11.1. UNMIK Civilian Police Staff Numbers, September 1999 to March 2009

Year	Month	UNMIK Civilian Police Officers[a]
1999	September	1,100
	December	1,817
2000	March	2,361
	May	3,626
	September	4,000
	December	4,400
2001	March	4,445
	June	4,387
	October	4,375
	December	4,465
2002	June	4,524
	October	4,274
2003	March	4,389
	June	4,067
	September	3,727
	December	3,735
2004	March	3,248
	June	3,524
	October	3,611
2005	January	3,451
	December	2,143
2006	May	2,106
	August	1,990
	October	1,895
2007	February	1,984
	June	1,997
	August	1,993
	November	2,011
2008	March	2,006
	June	2,056
	October	1,880
2009	March	49

Source: Author (from United Nations documents).

Note: a. From September 2000 through March 2009, the figures comprise advisers and members of formed police units (FPUs).

Table 11.1 presents the total number of UNMIK civilian police officers deployed from September 1999 to March 2009. The table shows how the police component of the mission changed since the reform of the local police began in 1999. The numbers of personnel deployed in the police component of the mission remained reasonably constant from late-2000 until mid-2003 and then again in early 2004 until late 2005. The number of officers began to decrease after 2005.

To implement the mandate as described by the United Nations (1999e), the police component of the UNMIK comprised three integrated phases:

- Phase I—KFOR is responsible for public safety and order until the civilian police presence is able to take over the responsibility.
- Phase II—UNMIK civilian police undertake normal police duties with executive authority.
- Phase III—Law enforcement and border policing functions are transferred to the KPS.

The UNMIK began developing and reforming the KPS immediately upon deployment. The KPS was restructured in accord with international standards of democratic policing, and recruits were screened and their backgrounds checked. The KPS was to be ethnically representative of the population. To achieve this goal, the UNMIK undertook background screening of recruit applicants and assessing the performance of the applicants (United Nations, 1999e). Table 11.2 presents the composition of the KPS from October 2002 to March 2009 and demonstrates that although there had been an increase in the total number of KPS officers, the percentage of Kosovo Serbians deployed remained stable, and the percentage of other ethnicities and women employed decreased.

UNMIK developed and implemented an institution-building component of the KPS, which included delivering on-the-job training, providing advice and monitoring (United Nations, 1999e), and improving the awareness of human rights (United Nations, 2000i). To ensure that an interface was developed between the UNMIK police and the public, the UNMIK trained a cadre of local community liaison officers (United Nations, 1999a), who would be based at every police station in Kosovo and

Table 11.2. Composition of Kosovo Police Service, October 2002 to March 2009

Date		Total	Kosovo Albanians		Kosovo Serbians		Other Ethnicity		Men		Women	
Year	Month		%	No.	%	No.	%	No.	%	No.	%	No.
2002	October	5,240	85.23	4,184	8.11	498	6.67	558	84.34	4,419	15.66	821
2003	March	5,247	84.09	4,407	9.20	473	6.67	367	84.60	4,460	15.00	787
	June	5,207	84.26	4,387	9.51	495	6.24	325	84.71	4,411	15.29	796
	October	5,769	84.36	4,867	9.41	543	6.23	359	82.40	4,904	17.60	865
	December	5,704	84.60	4,823	9.30	529	6.20	352	85.20	4,860	14.80	844
2004	June	5,983	84.50	5,054	9.50	567	6.00	362	85.20	5,100	14.80	883
	October	6,282	84.50	5,309	9.40	593	6.00	380	85.60	5,382	14.30	900
2005	January	6,254	84.60	5,290	9.40	585	6.00	379	85.80	5,365	14.20	889
	December	6,864	84.50	5,800	9.67	664	5.83	400	86.10	5,910	13.90	954
2006	May	6,826	84.52	5,769	9.65	659	5.83	398	86.21	5,885	13.90	941
	August	7,249	84.05	6,093	10.17	737	5.78	419	86.33	6,258	13.67	991
	October	7,185	83.94	6,031	10.30	740	5.76	414	86.40	6,208	13.60	977
2007	February	7,215	83.99	6,060	10.31	744	5.70	411	86.44	6,237	13.56	978
	August	7,200	84.31	6,070	10.04	723	5.65	407	86.36	6,218	13.64	982
	November	7,160	84.37	6,041	10.00	716	5.63	403	86.41	6,187	13.59	973
2008	March	7,106	84.45	6,001	9.96	708	5.59	397	86.48	6,145	13.52	961
	June	7,076	84.51	5,980	9.92	702	5.57	394	86.48	6,119	13.52	957
	October	7,043	84.48	5,950	10.00	704	5.52	389	86.57	6,097	13.43	946
2009	March	7,070	84.60	5,981	9.92	701	5.49	388	86.66	6,127	13.34	943

Source: Author (from various United Nations documents).

who would concentrate on building links with vulnerable minority communities (United Nations, 2000i).

Under the mandate, KFOR was responsible for demilitarizing the Kosovo forces. The major initiative of the demobilization was to incorporate suitably qualified KLA members into the proposed Kosovo Protection Corps (KPC). In fact, the KPC was to consist of up to 3,000 active and 2,000 reserve members and was not to have any role in law enforcement or the maintenance of law and order. The KPC was to be used only for civil emergencies, for search-and-rescue missions, for demining projects, and for rebuilding infrastructure and housing (United Nations, 1999j).

In mid-2000, UNMIK developed a strategic plan to focus on the mission's planning. The resulting plan provided a framework to identify forthcoming tasks that would ensure effective coordination between the mis-

sion's components (and with KFOR) and the procedures that had been developed to address key policy and operational issues (United Nations, 2000d).

The UNMIK also established a special task force that designed a number of programs to target ethnic violence. The task force comprised staff members from UNMIK and KFOR who implemented the program in conjunction with the information coordination group (United Nations, 2000g). The task force's responses included "the provision of military and police patrols" and "personal protection for high-risk individuals" (United Nations, 2000i).

In September 2000, the UNMIK established three new regional police training centers and developed a training program for future KPS supervisors. A procedure was also designed to transfer the responsibilities of the KPS academy to the KPS (United Nations, 2000i).

By the end of 2001, UNMIK had trained 32 senior KPS commanders (United Nations, 2001d). The UNMIK also began to reform the KPS into a full-spectrum law enforcement agency. The reform process was based on the "lessons learned to date and developments on the ground" and on the following four phases that would be evaluated (United Nations, 2000i):

- Transfer of patrol responsibilities
- Transition of tactical functions, whereby members of the KPS become first-line supervisors
- Transition of operational functions, whereby members of the KPS assume mid-level management positions
- Strategic transition, whereby members of the KPS assume senior management positions

To strengthen and coordinate the fight against crime, the UNMIK and the Department of Judicial Affairs were combined in May 2001. According to the United Nations (2001d), those institutions were to achieve the following four objectives:

- Maintain effective international control and oversight over police and justice activities during the medium term, which would enable the effective transition of those agencies to the control of Kosovo communities.
- Increase the short-term effect of law-and-order efforts through enhanced coordination of information.
- Enable effective police and judicial response against destabilizing serious criminal activity in Kosovo.
- Establish an unbiased judicial process through initial international participation and reform of the judicial system.

In mid-2002, UNMIK developed a number of strategic performance benchmarks that would provide direction and a vision for both of the provisional institutions and the UNMIK. The performance benchmarks were for measuring progress and building capacity in the provisional Kosovo institutions and for stimulating the planning processes (United Nations, 2002e).

During 2003, the UNMIK began the transfer of the management and the responsibility of individual police stations (United Nations, 2003e). By the end of 2003,

10 police stations had been transferred to the KPS; by mid-2008, a total of 22 police stations had been transferred. Transferring responsibility for law enforcement to the KPS was strengthened by the signing of a memorandum of understanding (MoU) with Montenegro that would aid in combating organized crime (United Nations, 2004b). The MoU also established a local crime prevention council in each municipality (United Nations, 2004u) and deployed a further 300 community policing officers to areas that were populated by vulnerable minority communities (United Nations, 2005d).

By 2006, the UNMIK police component was concentrating principally on mentoring and monitoring the KPS because the KPS had assumed further operational functions. The mission also helped with the introduction of a regulation that established the framework and the guiding principles of the KPS. The new regulation created the Police Inspectorate and the Kosovo Academy for Public Service Education and Development and provided "a sound legal and ethical basis for a transitioned" service (United Nations, 2006b).

Mission Achievements (Outcome)

The UNMIK took direct action to tackle two primary security threats to Kosovo. The mission implemented several organizational units within the police and justice pillar whose focus was primarily on security. The mission also established ways to share information across country borders. The information sharing included cooperative agreements with Serbia, Albania, and the Former Yugoslav Republic of Macedonia (Jones et al., 2005).

At the beginning of the UNMIK deployment in 2000, the KPS was the only functioning public service institution that was multiethnic in Kosovo (United Nations, 2000d). By the end of 2008, the KPS comprised 7,124 officers, had a rank structure in place (United Nations, 2002e), and was a respected and trusted police service (United Nations, 2008r). The KPS also commanded and managed 33 police stations, all special and tactical squads, and five out of the six regional police headquarters across Kosovo (United Nations, 2008r).

The UNMIK helped introduce and promulgate a regulation that established the new Ministries of Justice and

Table 11.3. Number of Returning Internally and Externally Displaced Persons to Kosovo, 2000 to 2007

Year	2000	2001	2002	2003	2004	2005	2006	2007	Total
Number	1,906	1,453	2,754	3,801	2,469	2,126	1,627	1,685	17,821

Source: Adapted from United Nations (2008r).

Internal Affairs (United Nations, 2006b). The UNMIK also provided assistance in drafting the regulation that codified the framework and the guiding principles of the KPS, thus establishing "concrete guarantees for minorities" (United Nations, 2006j).

The KPS established municipal and local public safety committees in 13 of the 17 communities (United Nations, 2007d) that were to work alongside the police. A number of police substations were opened to increase the level of decentralization that would create stronger relations with local communities (United Nations, 2006j). The establishment of the community liaison framework was supported by the implementation of the Kosovo police inspectorate in late 2006 (United Nations, 2006y), which assumed responsibility for the audit and inspection elements of the KPS and "for investigating all complaints" against the service (United Nations, 2007s).

In late 2006, the KPS, in conjunction with the Ministry of Internal Affairs and the Ministry of Justice, documented its strategic action and financial management plans for 2007–11 (United Nations, 2006y). This move created a stable management environment for the service. At this time, the KPS finalized its chain of command for civil emergencies, changed the name of the Kosovo Police Service School to the Kosovo Centre for Public Safety Education and Development, and created an independent professional standards board (United Nations, 2007i).

Reforming the KPS created a stable environment that allowed democratic institutions to be developed, helped national elections to be held, and enabled internally (IDP) and externally (EDP) displaced persons to return to their respective communities (United Nations, 2008r). Table 11.3 identifies the number of returning

IDPs and EDPs for each year from 2000 to 2007, as well as the total number for the entire period.

Ways the Mission Was Evaluated

The first evaluation of the KPS reform was undertaken in May 2004 following the violence that occurred in March of the same year. The evaluation focused "on the schedule for transition of station command from UNMIK police to [the] KPS, the increase in the final target number of KPS special police units from three to five, the procurement of basic anti-riot equipment for all police stations, and the provision of anti-riot training for all KPS members" (United Nations, 2004m).

Following the evaluation, the UNMIK revised the transfer of police stations to the KPS, a change that was included in the transition plan to "ensure that stations that performed well would transition to KPS control earlier than those where significant problems were [being] experienced." The plan retained the existing transition process and ensured that all stations and regional headquarters were transferred to KPS control by mid-2006 (United Nations, 2004m).

In June 2008, the secretary-general noted that the mission had made progress in completing the tasks contained in the mandate, "since the inception of the Mission in 1999, the scope of activities that it has performed has been reduced significantly." The secretary-general also noted that "without careful management, recent developments and future emerging realities on the ground could lead to increasing tension between the Kosovo communities and [could] contribute to friction between UNMIK and other actors, local and international, in Kosovo." For those reasons, a review of the mission was undertaken to ensure that it was suitably structured to address current and emerging operational requirements in Kosovo (United Nations, 2008h).

Conclusion

The UNMIK was significantly different from previous UN civilian police missions (Jones et al., 2005; Greener, 2009; Bayley and Perito, 2010). The police component of the mission was to provide temporary policing services and to establish and develop a professional, impartial, and independent local police. UNMIK was the first UN mission to include an armed executive police component in a region where there was no host government (Dwan, 2002; Bayley and Perito, 2010). Furthermore, the UN had faced a sweeping undertaking that was unprecedented in both scope and structural complexity. No other mission had invited other multilateral organizations to become full partners under UN leadership (United Nations, 2010l).

The slow arrival of UN police contingents at the beginning of the mission created a situation where the UN was unable to restore order and establish the rule of law. The situation initially undermined the international mission and encouraged extremists to engage in ethnic violence (Bayley and Perito, 2010).

Bayley and Perito (2010) claim that lessons can be learned from the mission to Kosovo. Future missions need to be comprehensive and to include police, courts, and prisons. Those three components of the justice sector should be established at the beginning of the mission to ensure that order is restored and that public security is created.

Chapter 12

Liberia

Map 12.1. Liberia

Source: Courtesy of the University of Texas Libraries, The University of Texas at Austin.

Case Study: United Nations Mission in Liberia

Background to the Mission

Liberia has suffered two distinct and different civil wars: the first from 1989 to 1996 and the second from 1997 to 2003, which led to 200,000 civilian deaths, to 1 million refugees, and to a complete breakdown of law and order (United Nations Mission in Liberia, 2010).

1989 to 1996

On December 24, 1989, a militia group, the National Patriotic Front of Liberia (NPFL), led by Charles Taylor, an ex-Liberian government minister who was accused of embezzlement, invaded Liberia and confronted government forces (United Nations Mission in Liberia, 2010). The NPFL later split into two groups: the original NPFL and a second group, the Independent National Patriotic Front of Liberia (INPFL), which was led by Prince Johnson.

The Liberian Army retaliated severely against the Liberian civilian population, "attacking unarmed civilians and burning villages" (United Nations Mission in Liberia, 2010), which caused a large number of persons to be displaced, with many leaving the country for Guinea and Côte d'Ivoire.

By late 1990, the INPFL controlled the capital city of Monrovia, and the NPFL controlled the remainder of the country (United Nations Mission in Liberia, 2010).

The civil war continued until the Economic Community of West African States (ECOWAS) brokered a peace agreement in Cotonou, Benin, on July 25, 1993. This agreement followed a number of unsuccessful peace agreements. Following the signing of the Cotonou Agreement, the United Nations (UN) established the Observer Mission in Liberia (UNOMIL), whose mandate it was to assist with the implementation and compliance of the agreement by all parties (United Nations Mission in Liberia, 2010).

The Cotonou Agreement broke down because of delays in its implementation, and fighting resumed between the NPFL and the INPFL. In late 1995, a supplementary agreement was negotiated, which led to a cease-fire and to Charles Taylor's being elected president (United Nations Mission in Liberia, 2010).

1997 to 2003

Following the election of Charles Taylor as president in July 1997, the civil war slowed but did not end. Violence and fighting continued and a new militia was formed: the Liberians for Reconciliation and Democracy (LURD). Their aim was to destabilize the government and to gain control of the local diamond fields. Those confrontations led to the Second Liberian Civil War (United Nations Mission in Liberia, 2010).

In November 1997, the UN established the Peace-Building Support Office in Liberia (UNOL). Its task was to help the Liberian government consolidate peace following the July 1997 elections. However, the UNOL was not able to achieve its mandate because of the fighting and "the inability of the Government and opposition party leaders to resolve their differences over key issues of governance" (United Nations Mission in Liberia, 2010).

The Second Liberian Civil War eventually ended in July 2003 when the United States intervened by sending in the U.S. Marines.

During the period of 1989–2003, the Liberian National Police (LNP) was alleged "to have functioned more as an instrument of repression than as an enforcer of law and order" (United Nations, 2003c). Furthermore, the LNP was identified as being corrupt and incompetent, and it did not have the confidence of the public. The situation was compounded by the Taylor government's disregard for the rule of law and by the breakdown of supporting judicial institutions (United Nations, 2003c).

The signing of the Accra Comprehensive Peace Agreement (CPA) in 2003 called for reforming and restructuring the LNP, having an interim police force maintain law and order, and eventually deploying a newly trained national police force. The CPA also identified that the UN was "to monitor the activities of the interim police force, assist in the maintenance of law and order, and help to develop and implement police training programmes, including gender training" (United Nations, 2003c).

Mandate of the Mission

The United Nations Mission in Liberia (UNMIL) was established by UN Security Council Resolution 1509, which was adopted on September 19, 2003. The mission was to support the implementation of a cease-fire agreement and the peace process and to assist "in national security reform" (United Nations, 2003r). The reform would include monitoring and restructuring the police force of Liberia to ensure that it complied with democratic policing principles and developed a police training program (United Nations, 2003r; 2010p). The resolution authorized "the deployment of a United Nations peacekeeping operation with a troop strength of up to 15,000, including 250 military observers, 160 staff officers, up to 875 UN police officers, and an additional five armed formed units each comprising 120 officers" (United Nations, 2003c; 2003r).

The mission was established under Chapter VII of the Charter of the United Nations and was authorized for an initial period of 12 months from October 1, 2003, following the transfer of authority from the forces of the ECOWAS-led mission in Liberia (ECOMIL) to UNMIL (United Nations, 2003r). The ECOMIL mission was to act as liaison with ECOWAS and was to provide the "maintenance of law and order throughout Liberia." It was designed to be a "multidimensional operation composed of political, military, civilian police, criminal justice, civil affairs, human rights, gender, child protection, disarmament, demobilization and reintegration, public information, and support components, as well as an electoral component in due course" (United Nations, 2003c). Mission personnel were to be co-located with their counterparts in local national institutions (United Nations, 2003c).

To ensure that the process to reform the LNP was transparent, credible, and efficient, UNMIL established a technical committee that was to "develop a plan for restructuring and reorganizing the Liberian national police." It also was to assist in determining "the composition, selection, and vetting of would-be members of the interim police force" (United Nations, 2003c). As discussed by the United Nations (2003c), the committee would "focus on areas of potential reform," including the following:

- Have the police restructure and revision the legal framework governing the police.
- Establish the criteria for the selection and vetting of new and former police officers.
- Assess infrastructure and logistical needs and planning for renovations or repairs.

- Develop an office to coordinate international assistance to the police service.

The deployment plan for the UNMIL civilian police component identified that personnel would be "gradually deployed in phases to provide advice and operational support to the interim police force and to help restructure, train, and advise in the development of a professional" LNP (United Nations, 2003c). The concept of operations for the civilian police component, as discussed in the United Nations (2003c), consisted of the following four phases:

- Phase 1—October to December 2003. The focus of this phase was on determining the mission action plans and establishing the foundations for the deployment of the core civilian police component that would assist the interim police force in law-and-order functions. Two formed police units (FPUs) were also deployed during this phase to stabilize the law-and-order situation in and around the capital city of Monrovia.
- Phase 2—December 2003 to February 2004. This phase consisted of deploying additional civilian police advisers, trainers, and an additional three FPUs in the remaining three regional headquarters. Reconstitution and rehabilitation initiatives were to begin during this phase.
- Phase 3—March 2004 to the end of the mission. This phase consisted of training and developing the LNP with a focus on coordinating and integrating all capacity development efforts.
- Phase 4—Following the end of the mission. UN civilian police were to retain a limited number of core advisers during the final period to help local police carry on the reform and capacity enhancement initiatives.

The five FPUs were to be stationed in Monrovia and were to support the LNP in high-end law enforcement, including crowd control. The deployment of the FPUs would allow the LNP to concentrate on fast-track training initiatives. As described by the United Nations (2003c; 2003n), the FPUs were mandated to do the following:

- Support the interim police force in its law-and-order functions in several major population areas.
- Assist the interim police force in addressing civil disorder problems.

- Assist in developing local structure and capacity to meet such challenges in the future.
- Support the protection of civilian lives and property in areas of deployment.

The mandate of the UNMIL identified the tasks that were to be given priority by the civilian police component. According to United Nations (2003c), the tasks included the following:

- Assist in restructuring the police service, including vetting and certifying interim law enforcement officers.
- Reactivate the police academy, and help develop general and thematic police training programs, including mentoring and on-the-job training.
- Advise, report, and follow up on the activities of interim police force members regarding their compliance with professional standards and human rights obligations.
- Assist in the social reintegration of the disarmed and demobilized combatants into civil society through mutual confidence-building initiatives of community policing practices.
- Assist in overall enhancement of the law enforcement capacity, including border policing, customs, immigrations, port authority, and other related sectors of the internal security.

The civil affairs component of UNMIL was to act as a liaison with the civilian police component of the mission. As described by the United Nations (2003c), the UNMIL civil affairs component was to do the following:

- Assist the national transitional government extend and consolidate state authority throughout the country.
- Provide advice and assistance to the national transitional government in planning for elections.
- Assist and build the capacity of civil society organizations.
- Assist in formulating programs to reintegrate and to reconcile victims and perpetrators of the war.
- Assist the civilian police in reforming and restructuring the local police and promoting the participation of women in the local police force and in auditing the performance of the police and other agencies involved in maintaining law and order.

- Coordinate the activities of a committee that is charged with investigating and reporting on the conduct of personnel throughout the mission area.
- Deliver induction training for all civilian and military staff members of the mission.

The secretary-general of the UN noted that the police component of the mission was to be decentralized, with civilian police being "stationed in regional offices and numerous other locations throughout Liberia" (United Nations, 2003k) and with teams of civilian police officers "deployed in all four sectors of UNMIL and at the Mission's headquarters in Monrovia" (United Nations, 2003n). The civilian police component of the mission was to "be responsible for conducting an assessment of Liberia's law enforcement system and its overall structure, as well as developing and implementing a programme for the restructuring of the LNP" (United Nations, 2003n).

The UNMIL mandate was renewed annually on the anniversary of its expiration; as of June 2010, the mission was ongoing. In mid-2006, the UN Security Council reviewed the mission's mandate by authorizing an increase in the size of the mission's police component by 125 officers (United Nations, 2006ab) and identified four new tasks that were to be given priority. The UNMIL civilian police component, according to the United Nations (2006e), was to do the following:

- Maintain a stable and secure environment.
- Assist the government to complete the reintegration and rehabilitation program for ex-combatants.
- Facilitate the completion of the return and resettlement of refugees and internally displaced persons.
- Accelerate the training and institutional development of the LNP and other security agencies, including demobilizing the former police.

A second review of the mission's mandate was undertaken because of increasing challenges throughout the country that related to the maintenance of law and order. In early 2008, the UN Security Council authorized an increase from five to seven FPUs, which represented an increase from 605 to 845 personnel (United Nations, 2008k).

Mission Deployment Environment

The UN Security Council established a multidisciplinary mission assessment team that arrived in Liberia on August 21, 2003. The team was made up of representatives from a number of UN departments and agencies and of personnel from the World Bank (United Nations, 2003c).

The assessment team identified that—although the security situation in Liberia had improved—it remained highly unstable, with large numbers of armed groups including the NPFL, INPFL, and LURD operating throughout the country. Those armed groups moved unimpeded in and out of Liberia and the neighboring countries of Côte d'Ivoire, Guinea, and Sierra Leone and contributed to the entire subregion's instability (United Nations, 2003c). The instability was compounded by widespread population displacement, poverty, high unemployment, and a proliferation of small arms.

Control of the country was divided. The Liberian government controlled the greater Monrovia area and the center of the country. The LURD rebel movement, estimated to have 5,000 fighters, primarily controlled western Liberia. The Movement for Democracy in Liberia (MODEL), with between 1,500 and 3,000 fighters, controlled the eastern parts of the country (United Nations, 2003c).

Because of the prolonged civil war and the government's disregard for the rule of law, the Liberian justice institutions "suffered an almost complete breakdown" and the LNP "functioned more as an instrument of repression than as an enforcer of law and order" (United Nations, 2003c).

Actions of the Mission (Output)

The primary services undertaken by the UNMIL civilian police included community policing, "responding to calls, investigating crimes and attending crime scenes, demonstrating respect for human rights," and administering police records. UNMIL also concentrated on reestablishing "police services in areas where police were forced to leave because of the civil conflict" (United Nations, 2004g). They also provided advice to the transitional government when establishing the Seaport Police, the Special Security Service, and 12 other statutory law enforcement agencies (United Nations, 2005b).

In late 2003, UNMIL was instrumental in establishing an emergency response system, "dial 911," which was used successfully in preventing mob violence and as a crime reporting system. By late 2003, UNMIL had also conducted a number of serious crime investigations with the LNP (United Nations, 2004g).

On December 15, 2003, UNMIL launched Operation Restore Calm. Police officers were deployed to areas of Monrovia identified as being particularly afflicted by violent crimes. On January 12, 2004, a training program was launched for LNP officers who were to police Monrovia pending the formation of a new, restructured LNP. The mission also developed a number of thematic courses to increase the capacity of the LNP in criminal investigations and in riot control and to enhance general safety and security (United Nations, 2004g).

The UNMIL police component was to register the Liberian law enforcement personnel, and by May 1, 2004, 3,492 members of the LNP had finished the process. The registration program was completed in September 2004 (United Nations, 2004j).

On July 12, 2004, the LNP Academy reopened, and training began for the first class of 132 cadets. The UNMIL helped the LNP develop the new recruit course, which consisted of a three-month program of classroom and field training (United Nations, 2004s).

In March 2005, the UNMIL developed a plan to deploy LNP officers to the interior of the country where there was a minimal police presence. A new LNP organizational structure was implemented in March 2005, which included deploying LNP commanders to five regional LNP centers (United Nations, 2005j). To address the shortfall in midlevel supervisors and senior leadership in the LNP, UNMIL developed a basic management course and a senior leadership qualification program in 2006.

Mission Implementation (Model)

On September 19, 2003, the UNMIL civilian police force was deployed following the adoption of the mandate included in UN Security Council Resolution 1509 (United Nations 2003r). However, the mission did not reach its authorized strength until May 2004. Table 12.1 presents

Table 12.1. UNMIL Civilian Police Staff Numbers, December 2003 to February 2010

Year	Month	Total Civilian Police Officers
2003	December	158[a]
2004	March	278
	May	720
	August	1,090
	December	1,104
2005	March	1,059
	August	1,090
	December	1,088
2006	March	1,016
	June	1,051
	September	1,056
	December	1,098
2007	March	1,201
	August	1,177
2008	March	1,194
	August	1,092
2009	February	1,225[b]
	August	1,343[c]
2010	February	2,164[d]

Source: Author (from various United Nations documents dated 2003 to 2010).

Notes: a. Includes 120 officers in formed police units (FPUs).

b. Includes 722 officers in FPUs.

c. Includes 855 officers in FPUs.

d. Includes 844 officers in FPUs.

the total number of UNMIL civilian police staff members from December 2003 to February 2010.

In May 2004, the UNMIL established a Rule of Law Implementation Committee to "ensure a holistic approach in supporting the reform of Liberia's security sector" and "to coordinate the reform of the police, the judiciary, and correctional institutions" (United Nations, 2004j). The committee developed a strategy to reform and restructure the Liberian police and proposed a new name for the Liberian Police Service (LPS).

The UNMIL civilian police also established a recruitment drive that was for the new police service and that emphasized the need for an ethnic and gender balance. All new recruits were to complete a three-month training program at the Liberian Police Service Training Centre and a six-month, on-the-job training program. Upon completion of on-the-job training, the candidates returned to the academy for final testing (United Nations, 2004j).

In March 2005, the UNMIL—in conjunction with the UN missions in Sierra Leone and Côte d'Ivoire and the United Nations Office for West Africa—established an inter-mission working group to enhance cooperation in sharing information and formulating joint strategies. The working group focused on facilitating lessons learned, on sharing information, and on "developing long-term strategies in support of the peace processes in the three regions and [on] coordinating joint activities" (United Nations, 2005g).

In March 2006, the UNMIL civilian police component changed their existing operational police reform approach of the LPS to one of providing mentoring, monitoring, and technical advice on general institutional police development and specifically on election security (United Nations, 2005j, 2006e). UNMIL provided assistance to the LPS and other national Liberian security agencies in developing a deployment plan (United Nations, 2005j). The deployment plan covered police patrol and assignment to personal protection duties (United Nations, 2005s). However, the transitional government was slow to implement the police reforms (United Nations, 2005j).

To assist with the new LPS, UNMIL advised the government about the appointments of a new director of police and a number of deputy and assistant directors. The appointments of new LPS senior executives led to redeploying several senior police officials who had been appointed under the previous administration and had been trained by the UN police (United Nations, 2006k).

In June 2006, UNMIL developed a number of benchmarks to guide Phase I of the consolidation, drawdown, and withdrawal of the UNMIL. The benchmarks comprised four major areas and included security, governance and the rule of law, economic revitalization, and infrastructure and basic services. Completing the benchmarks was critical to determine what the pace and timing of the mission's drawdown and eventual withdrawal would be. The benchmarks were primarily long-term tasks and were indictors of progress for the period 2006 and 2007. As described by the United Nations (2006t), the three components that were to be achieved of those benchmark areas were as follows:

1. Armed Forces of Liberia Training and Deployment
   - Training commences for Armed Forces of Liberia.
   - Ministry of Defense is fully staffed.
   - A concept of operations is produced by Armed Forces of Liberia.
   - First Armed Forces of Liberia battalion is operational.
2. LPS Training and Deployment
   - Deactivation of LPS personnel is completed.
   - The 3,500 LPS personnel are recruited and trained.
   - The LPS support unit is trained and equipped.
   - All county police stations are fully staffed and operational.
3. National Security Strategy and Architecture
   - National security review is completed.
   - National security strategy is produced and adopted, and implementation begins.
   - National Security Council and local structures are in place and functioning.

On January 20, 2007, a joint initiative of the Liberian government and UNMIL, which was funded by the Netherlands, was launched to recruit qualified women into the LPS. The initiative included an educational support program for female police candidates and aimed to improve the educational qualifications of women who were under the age of 35 and who were interested in joining the police force. Successful applicants of the program attended an intensive three-month program to achieve a high school equivalency diploma (United Nations, 2007e).

In January 2006, UNMIL refocused its strategic goals on consolidating peace and on helping Liberia attain a steady state of security with police and armed forces that are able to stand on their own. The narrowing of the UNMIL strategic direction was a response to the tasks remaining and the challenges emerging that were straining the mission's limited resources (United Nations, 2007j).

In early 2008, UNMIL helped the National Security Council develop a national security strategy and operational plan. The strategy focused on coordinating infor-

mation among law enforcement and security agencies and on strengthening community and police cooperation through sharing information. Also, in early 2008, UNMIL developed a number of performance benchmarks for Phase 2 of the consolidation, drawdown, and withdrawal of the mission. As described by the United Nations (2008c), the Phase 2 benchmarks that pertained to the LPS included the following:

- Complete the nationwide implementation of administrative operational and operating procedures.
- Establish an oversight mechanism for the 500-member Emergency Response Unit.
- Improve human resource quality through officer competency validation and fitness certification by UN police (integrity and skill based) accepted by the inspector general of police and the Ministry of Justice.
- Improve operational capacity through police infrastructure enhancement, logistics support, and equipment provision at county police stations to ensure support for sustained LPS deployments and enhanced operational capacity.
- Realign the security coverage of the LPS county police station by deploying personnel in identified high-threat areas.

Implementation of the Phase 2 benchmarks was set in the context that the UNMIL civilian police component would increasingly focus on offering strategic advice and expertise in specialized fields to the LPS and would reduce the operational support to the LPS's regular activities. The consolidation and drawdown plan also "provided for a three-year implementation timeframe with built-in hold and review periods to assess the security situation and core benchmarks, as well as to adjust the pace or depth of the troop and police adjustments, as necessary" (United Nations, 2008k).

Mission Achievements (Outcomes)

The early deployment of the UNMIL civilian police and their patrol methods in all of the districts in Liberia greatly increased the mission's capacity to consolidate stability in the country's interior. Those rapid deployments improved law and order and "in the extension of State authority, improve[d] the free circulation of people and allow[ed] for the resumption of the disarmament, demobilization, reintegration and repatriation process" (United Nations, 2004g).

However, even with those improvements, the law and order and the security situation remained fragile through early 2006. Exacerbating the situation were the armed robberies by criminal gangs, the slow reintegration of ex-combatants, and the slow restructuring and reform of the police service (United Nations, 2006e; 2006t).

In early 2007, the government of Liberia decided to increase the size of the Police Quick Reaction Force from 500 members to 4,000 members. A larger quick reaction force ensured that the police had "the capacity to respond quickly, efficiently, and robustly to major breaches of internal security" (United Nations, 2007e).

In mid-2007, the government developed a new national security strategy and architecture, which defined the respective roles of the LPS and other law enforcement agencies, including the Armed Forces of Liberia. The new strategy included a provision for a national policymaking and crisis management capacity as well as an intelligence gathering agency. This structure was to ensure that Liberia's security sector could anticipate and address security threats before they materialized (United Nations, 2007j).

By mid-2008, UNMIL made appreciable progress in reforming and restructuring the LNP. UNMIL's progress included (a) providing the LNP with equipment and infrastructure and deploying into the counties and (b) providing basic training for 3,661 officers. However, a number of challenges remained in the development of the LPS, especially in relation to the LPS's operational capacity (United Nations, 2008k).

In early 2009, UNMIL, in conjunction with the government, developed a national security strategy, which involved all security and law enforcement agencies and included a detailed implementation matrix. The new security strategy provided a road map for security sector reform and formed the basis of a five-year strategic plan for the LNP. The police strategic plan included a comprehensive development framework and a support program to facilitate its implementation (United Nations, 2009b).

Ways the Mission Was Evaluated

In early 2006, a UN assessment mission identified that it was too early to draw down UNMIL. This view was sup-

ported by the government to guarantee peace and stability in the country. However, the UN assessment mission recognized that as several of the initial tasks assigned to UNMIL were completed, the size and configuration of the mission needed to be reviewed (United Nations, 2006e).

A second UN assessment mission that visited Liberia in early 2007 identified that any proposed drawdown of UNMIL civilian police should be linked to the progress made in achieving the mission's mandate. According to the United Nations (2007j), the assessment mission proposed that the following five core benchmarks should be achieved before a drawdown began:

- Complete the basic training of 3,500 LPS personnel by July 2007.
- Complete police operating procedures by December 2008.
- Complete the formation of the 500-member Police Quick Reaction Unit by July 2009.
- Equip police personnel and their deployment to the counties, as well as build police infrastructure by December 2010.
- Finalize the national security strategy and architecture and its implementation throughout the country by December 2008.

The second assessment mission also recommended that the UNMIL civilian police component gradually reduce in size from 498 police advisers in seven stages between April 2008 and December 2010. The assessment mission recommended that police advisers with specialist policing skills—especially in forensics, criminal investigation, management, intelligence, operations, organized crime, professional standards, drug enforcement, airport security, and protection of women and children—be deployed to the mission. The deployment would be during routine rotations so as to provide the national police force with advanced training and appropriate mentoring (United Nations, 2007j).

Conclusion

To help with the implementation of a comprehensive security framework, the government made progress on several reform agendas, including fighting against corruption, reforming public financial management, and developing overall strategies for strengthening the LNP and the rule of law sector (United Nations, 2009b). However, as late as mid-2008, the LPS continued to struggle to achieve a level of sustained operational effectiveness that would enable them, independently of UNMIL, to provide a quality and an efficient service (United Nations, 2008k). Although the LPS had increased in size and a number of police stations had been refurbished in the counties and their presence had increased in the counties, the LPS was weak and lacked capacity (United Nations, 2008k).

The presence of the LPS outside the capital remained limited because of severe logistical and infrastructure limitations. The LPS also remained constrained by in-dividual competencies, especially in regard to "management capacity and specialised skills." The situation was exacerbated by weak LPS "command and control structures, including the capacity to plan and execute operational activities" and experienced "continued problems of misconduct and discipline" (United Nations, 2009b).

As a result of those challenges, the mission's preliminary assessment found that its police component needed to remain at its current strength for the short term. The mission would continue to provide operational support and advice, with an increased emphasis on patrol supervision, station command, community policing, and emergency response unit support. The mission would also give technical advice to the leadership of the LNP leadership (United Nations, 2009b).

Chapter 13

Palestinian Territories

Map 13.1. Palestinian Territories (Israel)
Source: Courtesy of the University of Texas Libraries, The University of Texas at Austin.

Case Study: European Union Police Co-ordinating Office for Palestinian Police Support

Background to the Mission

In April 2005, following a diplomatic exchange between the European Union (EU) and the Palestinian prime minister, the European Council established the European Union Co-ordinating Office for Palestinian Police Support (EU COPPS). The EU COPPS police advisers provided guidance to the chief of the Palestinian Civil Police and senior management about organizational reform and structure and about operational issues. Members of the mission acted as liaisons between the Palestinians and international stakeholders and coordinated and monitored donor assistance (European Union Co-ordinating Office for Palestinian Police Support, 2006).

In July 2005, the EU foreign ministers agreed that the EU COPPS should take the form of a European Security and Defence Policy (ESDP) mission and build upon the efforts of the European Union Co-ordinating Office for Palestinian Police Support (European Union Co-ordinating Office for Palestinian Police Support, 2006). This agreement led to the transition of EU COPPS to the European Union Police Co-ordinating Office for Palestinian Police Support (EUPOL COPPS) (European Union Co-ordinating Office for Palestinian Police Support, 2006).

Mandate of the Mission

On June 18, 2005, the Council of the European Union adopted Joint Action 2005/797/CFSP, which established EUPOL COPPS (Council of the European Union, 2005d). The mission was established initially for three years from January 1, 2006, and was to support the Palestinian Civil Police (PCP) to increase the level of safety and security as well as to enforce the rule of law (Council of the European Union, 2005b). The mandate of the mission was extended in 2008 for a further three years expiring on December 31, 2010 (Council of the European Union, 2008c).

The EUPOL COPPS mission was included in the framework of the ESDP (Council of the European Union, 2005a) and was to assist "the Palestinian Authority in complying with its Road Map obligations, in particular, with regard to security and institution building." Support included providing advice on "consolidating the Palestinian security organisations into three services and reporting to an empowered Palestinian Minister of Interior." The mission was to be complementary to the existing international development efforts and was to "seek coherence and co-ordination with the capacity-building actions of the Community, notably in the domain of criminal justice" (Council of the European Union, 2005d).

The focus of EUPOL COPPS was to be long term, and its aim was to "contribute to the establishment of sustainable and effective policing arrangements under Palestinian ownership and in accordance with best international standards. The Mission was to cooperate with the Community's institution building programme as well as other international efforts in the wider context of the Security Sector including Criminal Justice Reform" (Council of the European Union, 2005a; 2005d). Specifically, the Council of the European Union (2005a; 2005d) suggested that the mission was to do the following:

- Assist the PCP in implementing the Police Development Program by advising and mentoring the PCP while focusing on senior officials at district, headquarters, and ministerial levels.
- Coordinate and facilitate EU and member state assistance and, where requested, international assistance to the PCP.
- Advise on police-related criminal justice elements.

The mission was based in Ramallah and was made up of 33 unarmed officers and civilian experts who were seconded from EU member states. These personnel did not have executive authority (Council of the European Union, 2005a; European Union, 2010a).

Mission Deployment Environment

In 2002, the United States, the EU, the Russia Federation, and the United Nations (UN) agreed to assist

Israel and the Palestinians in developing a peace agreement. The peace agreement process led to developing a road map to form an independent Palestinian state. To help implement the road map and to help the parties comply with their obligations, the EU established the European Union Coordinating Office for Palestinian Police Support in early 2005 (Council of the European Union, 2005a).

The PCP is the only law enforcement agency within the Palestinian Authority and consisted of 18,700 officers, 12,100 of which were deployed in Gaza and 6,600 in the West Bank (European Union Co-ordinating Office for Palestinian Police Support, 2006). Those figures include 3,000 Public Order Police (POP) in Gaza and 1,000 POP in the West Bank (European Union Co-ordinating Office for Palestinian Police Support, 2006). The PCP structure comprises 10 district headquarters, with Ramallah serving as the main central command, and 78 police facilities in the West Bank (Palestine Ministry of Interior, 2008).

Following the deployment of the EU COPPS in April 2005, the mission police advisers in conjunction with the PCP developed the Palestinian Civil Police Development Programme 2005–08 (PCPDP) (European Union Co-ordinating Office for Palestinian Police Support, 2006). The PCPDP was designed to act as a blueprint to develop the PCP over the following three years, and its primary objective was to establish a "transparent and accountable police organisation with a clearly identified role" (European Union Co-ordinating Office for Palestinian Police Support, 2006). The PCPDP was to operate within a sound legal framework, be capable of delivering an effective and robust policing service, and be responsive to the needs of society. It must also be able to manage its human and physical resources (European Union Co-ordinating Office for Palestinian Police Support, 2006).

The PCPDP consisted of two principal components: a transformational plan and an operational plan. The transformational plan presented a reform of the PCP that included "fundamental organisational changes" that would need to be implemented over the long term. The operational plan included operational capacity and performance measurements that could be implemented in the short term (European Union Co-ordinating Office for Palestinian Police Support, 2006).

Actions of the Mission (Output)

The EUPOL COPPS advisers were stationed in Ramallah and were primarily tasked to support the Palestinian Authority to establish sustainable and effective policing arrangements (European Union, 2009b).

The EUPOL COPPS initially developed and delivered basic and specialist police training to the PCP (European Union, 2009b). The mission also delivered rehabilitation or in-service training and courses to the PCP that included advanced crime scene analysis, antinarcotics training, management training, and motorcycle techniques (European Union Co-ordinating Office for Palestinian Police Support, 2009). The mission's mandate was extended until 2010 and its scope was enlarged to include capacity building and transforming the PCP (European Union Co-ordinating Office for Palestinian Police Support, 2008).

The EUPOL COPPS provided advice to the PCP on operational issues and on "longer term transformational [organizational] change." The mission's approach also included the mentoring of senior PCP officers at the district and headquarters levels (European Union, 2009b).

Mission Implementation (Model)

The EUPOL COPPS consisted of 33 civilian police officers who advised and mentored members of the PCP at all levels (Palestine Ministry of Interior, 2008). To achieve this assistance, the Council of the European Union (2005b) describes the mission as comprising the following four elements:

1. Head of mission or police commissioner
2. Advisory section
3. Program coordination section
4. Administration section

The EUPOL COPPS, in conjunction with the PCP, established the Programme Steering Committee (PSCO) that would provide the framework "to transform the PCP into an effective, efficient, capable, and credible police service within three years" and to implement the strategies identified in the PCPDP (Palestine Ministry of Interior, 2008). To provide a structure for the implementation of the PCPDP strategies, the PCPDP included the following seven Foundations for Police Reform:

1. Criminal investigation
2. PCP criminal justice
3. Information technology and communications
4. Specialized policing
5. Transportation
6. Training and capacity building
7. Infrastructure

To ensure that the implementation of the PCPDP strategies and the seven Foundations for Police Reform could be measured, the Palestine Ministry of the Interior (2008) described the following objectives that PSCO developed for the period from 2008 to 2010:

- Connect: complete internal connectivity and community access.
- Train: conduct core and specialty training resulting in a professional and modern police force.
- Build: achieve sustainable operational capacity through priority infrastructure.
- Equip: provide the right tools for basic to complex policing solutions.
- Mobilize: complete mobilization that enables first-response capacity.

In 2009, the EUPOL COPPS reviewed the PCP's training program. That review focused on the organizational structure, processes, equipment, and infrastructure. Drawing on the results of the review, the EUPOL COPPS in conjunction with the PCP developed a training curriculum, which was based on a community civilian policing model and on best international policing standards (European Union Co-ordinating Office for Palestinian Police Support, 2009).

Mission Achievements (Outcomes)

According to the European Union (2010a), by the end of 2009, the main achievements of the mission were as follows:

- Support to the PCP for immediate operational priorities and longer-term transformational change as described in the Palestinian Civil Police Development Programme
- Advice to and mentoring of the PCP, specifically senior officials at district and headquarters level
- Coordination and facilitation of financial assistance
- Advice, program planning, and project facilitation for the Palestinian Criminal Justice Sector

As described by the European Union Co-ordinating Office for Palestinian Police Support (2008), the mission also assisted with the following:

- Purchase equipment and furniture, and refurbish 38 police stations in the West Bank.
- Provide PCP training in public order.
- Establish the Jericho Police Training Centre.
- Establish the Explosive Ordnance Disposal Unit and the Criminal Investigation Department.

Ways the Mission Was Evaluated

The mission does not appear to have been evaluated. However, in November 2009, the Council of the European Union noted that the mission had provided advice to the PCP on the civil policing model and on community policing (European Union, 2010a).

Conclusion

The approach of the EUPOL COPPS police component was comprehensive, especially in regard to creating a secure environment for the Palestinian public. However, the EUPOL COPPS is a police-centered program and did not take into account the complete Palestinian criminal justice system. For this reason, the mission plans to expand the rule of law section in the renewed mission mandate with 20 additional staff members (European Union Co-ordinating Office for Palestinian Police Support, 2006).

Chapter 14

Sierra Leone

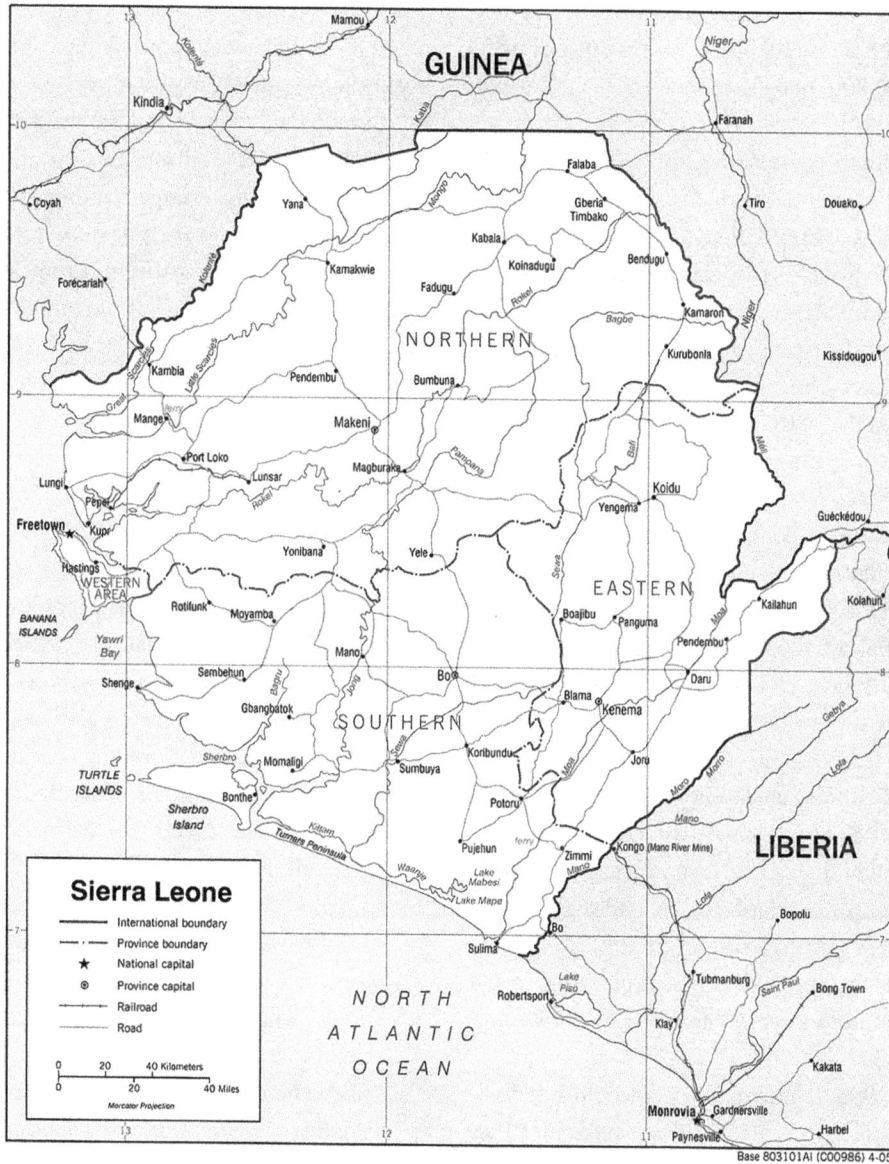

Map 14.1. Sierra Leone
Source: Courtesy of the University of Texas Libraries, The University of Texas at Austin.

Case Study: United Nations Observers Mission in Sierra Leone

Background to the Mission

The internal conflict in Sierra Leone began in March 1991 when the Revolutionary United Front (RUF) launched a violent campaign to overthrow the Sierra Leonean government (United Nations, 2010h). Those actions caused approximately 100,000 people to flee to neighboring countries. The Sierra Leone Army attempted, with support from the Military Observer Group (ECOMOG) of the Economic Community of West African States (ECOWAS), to subdue the RUF and to defend the government (United Nations, 2010h). However, on April 29, 1992, the Sierra Leone Army launched a successful military coup, which destabilized the civil government and established a military junta called the National Provisional Ruling Council (NPRC) (United Nations, 2010h).

Following the coup, the civil war between the NPRC and the RUF continued unabated. In November 1994, the head of the state of Sierra Leone requested that the United Nations (UN) facilitate negotiations between the government and the RUF. On December 15, 1994, in response to the Sierra Leone request, the UN sent an exploratory mission to Sierra Leone to initiate talks. During the mission, the team noted the serious deterioration of the country's situation as a result of the three-year conflict. About 10 percent of Sierra Leone's population had taken refuge in neighboring countries, and at least 30 percent of the population was internally displaced. Vital infrastructure had been destroyed, and three-fourths of the national budget was spent on defense (United Nations, 2010h).

In response to the findings of the exploratory mission, the UN appointed a special envoy to Sierra Leone (United Nations, 2010h).

In February 1996, parliamentary and presidential elections were held, but the RUF did not recognize the results because it did not participate in the elections. Negotiations between the government and the RUF continued, and a peace agreement, known as the Abidjan Accord, was signed between the government and the RUF in November 1996. However, the agreement was disrupted by another military coup in May 1997. Following that coup, the army joined with the RUF to form a ruling junta (United Nations, 2010h).

In October 1997, a peace plan and cease-fire were negotiated by ECOWAS in Conakry (United Nations, 2010h). However, the plan was never implemented because the junta failed to support a number of its provisions.

ECOMOG ousted the military junta in March 1998 and reinstated a democratically elected government. Following the establishment of a civil government, a number of RUF leaders were apprehended or killed during confrontations with government forces.

During the civil war and the military and ruling junta periods, the reputation and the capability of the Sierra Leone police suffered. A large number of police officers had collaborated with the junta or were "forced to flee, leaving much of the country without a police service" (United Nations, 1998l). Because of the public's poor perception of the police and the police's relationship with the public, the government was compelled to comprehensively restructure the police (United Nations, 1998m).

Mandate of the Mission

On July 13, 1998, the UN Security Council adopted Resolution 1181 (United Nations, 1998m), which established the United Nations Observers Mission in Sierra Leone (UNOMSIL) (United Nations, 1998e). The mission was made up of 10 military liaison officers and five civilian police advisers. As described by the United Nations (1998l), the objective of the mandate was to accomplish the following:

- Advise—in coordination with other international efforts, the government of Sierra Leone, and the local police officials—about (a) improving police practice, (b) training, (c) taking care of re-equipment and recruitment, (d) meeting the need to respect internationally accepted standards of policing in democratic societies, (e) planning the reform and restructure of the Sierra Leone police force, and (f) monitoring progress.
- Report on violations of international humanitarian law and human rights in Sierra Leone, and—in con-

sultation with the relevant UN agencies—assist the government of Sierra Leone in its efforts to address the country's human rights needs.

The primary role of the civilian police advisers was to help the government restore confidence in the Sierra Leone Police Force (SLPF) and to advise about police recruitment, practice, training, and resources needs (United Nations, 1998f; 1999b). The UNOMSIL civilian police were to "work closely with a team of police advisers deployed at the request of Governments from Commonwealth countries" (United Nations, 1998f). According to the United Nations (1999b), the civilian police were to also advise the government about the following:

- Respecting internationally accepted standards of policing in democratic societies
- Planning the reform and restructuring of the SLPF
- Monitoring the progress in the SLPF's reform and restructuring

Mission Deployment Environment

As a result of the prolonged civil war, the SLPF was basically nonexistent. A large number of police had abandoned their posts or had been killed, and numerous police stations were destroyed or vandalized. The SLPF did not have the capacity to provide any leadership or to plan strategically, and it had not undertaken any form of training since the civil war began (United Nations, 1998i).

Although the SLPF had increased in size since 1996, it suffered from "inadequate logistical support," a lack of equipment, and low morale because of "unattractive salaries and poor conditions of service." The major problem was the lack of vehicles that would ensure mobilization (United Nations, 1998i).

The lack of an effective police organization was exacerbated by the breakdown in the entire justice system. Courts operated only in Freetown and in three other cities, and the detention facilities were in poor condition (United Nations, 1998i).

Actions of the Mission (Output)

The UNOMSIL civilian police advisors acted as liaisons with the UNOMSIL Human Rights Unit and the Commonwealth Police Development Task Force for Sierra Leone (CPDTF) to provide advice and assistance to the government in police training, in police procedures within a democratic society, and in the need for the police to respect internationally accepted standards of policing (United Nations, 1998c, 1998d, 1998i).

To assist the mission in fulfilling its mandate, civilian police advisers visited a number of different police regional headquarters, divisional headquarters, departments, courts, police stations, and posts. During those visits, police advisers assessed the SLPF's work methods and their logistical and training needs. The preliminary findings and recommendations from the visits were presented in a report to the Sierra Leone government (United Nations, 1998i).

To improve the administrative effectiveness of the SLPF, the UNOMSIL civilian police restructured the departments of human resources, personnel development, and finance. The restructuring was designed to improve the service and to streamline "logistical accountability, operations, and crime management"; it also included providing assistance with personnel selection and training (United Nations, 1998l).

To improve operational policing, UNOMSIL civilian police provided advice on developing and introducing a decentralized training program and officer refresher training and on documenting training manuals (United Nations, 1998l).

Mission Implementation (Model)

The UNOMSIL was made up of five civilian police officers and, for the term of the mission, acted as liaisons with the CPDTF to ensure that the SLPF's development was coordinated (United Nations, 1998f; 1998l). During the period from 1999 to 2001, the mission helped the government develop principles and priorities of the SLPF reform and the strategic development plan (United Nations, 1998i).

To assist the government in implementing the strategic development plan, the UNOMSIL civilian police advisers, in conjunction with the CPDTF, introduced a number of pilot projects to "improve communications and equipment and to introduce effective and efficient policing based on local needs and community involvement" (United Nations, 1998l).

Mission Achievements (Outcomes)

The UNOMSIL police advisers helped the government make considerable progress in the reform and the reconstitution of a functioning police presence in the capital (United Nations, 1999c). However, the January 1999 rebel attack on Freetown resulted in the killings of more than 200 police officers and in the destruction of police equipment and infrastructure including the Criminal Investigation Department Headquarters and all its files, records, and documentation (United Nations, 1999b).

Ways the Mission Was Evaluated

The secretary-general of the UN noted in mid-1999 that although progress in reforming and restructuring the SLPF was considerable, "resource constraints present[ed] serious obstacles to the effective and fast implementation of reform" (United Nations, 1998i) and to the reversal of the extensive "damage and the collapse of the police structure in most parts" of Sierra Leone, which would "require substantial external assistance" (United Nations, 1999c).

Conclusion

Although UNOMSIL was a small mission with a specific mandate, it was able to—with the assistance of the CPDTF—lay the groundwork and make significant inroads into creating a structure for reforming the SLPF. UNOMSIL was terminated on October 22, 1999, when the UN Security Council authorized deployment of a new and significantly larger peacekeeping operation— the United Nations Mission in Sierra Leone (UNAMSIL). Upon the termination of the UNOMSIL mandate, the UN Security Council directed that UNAMSIL would take over the substantive civilian and military components of that mission (United Nations, 2010h).

Case Study: United Nations Mission in Sierra Leone

Background to the Mission

On July 13, 1998, the UN Security Council established the United Nations Observers Mission in Sierra Leone (UNOMSIL) for an initial period of six months, which was subsequently extended until October 22, 1999 (United Nations, 2010g). The primary role of the police component of the mission was to assist the government in restoring the public's confidence in the Sierra Leone Police Force (SLPF) and to advise the government about police recruitment, practice, training, and resourcing needs (United Nations, 1998f; 1999b).

Conflict between the government and the rebels continued during the presence of UNOMSIL and on July 7, 1999, both sides signed an agreement in Lomé to end hostilities and to form a government of national unity. The agreement expanded the role of the UNOMSIL (United Nations, 2010g).

Mandate of the Mission

On October 22, 1999, the UN Security Council adopted Resolution 1270, which established the United Nations Mission in Sierra Leone (UNAMSIL) for an initial period of six months. The mission was to have an authorized strength of 6,000 military personnel and was to include six civilian police advisers (United Nations, 1999o).

The mandate of the mission, as described by the United Nations (1999o), was to accomplish the following:

- Cooperate with the government of Sierra Leone and the other parties regarding the peace agreement and its implementation.
- Assist the government of Sierra Leone in implementing the disarmament, demobilization, and reintegration plan.

- Establish a presence at key locations throughout the territory of Sierra Leone, including the disarmament reception centers and demobilization centers.
- Encourage the parties to create confidence-building mechanisms and to support the functioning of those mechanisms.
- Facilitate the delivery of humanitarian aid.
- Provide support, as requested, to the elections, which were to be held in accordance with the present constitution of Sierra Leone.

The mission's mandate was subsequently expanded with the UN Security Council's adoption of Resolution 1289 on February 7, 2000. That resolution called for the mission to help coordinate and assist the Sierra Leone law enforcement authorities in the discharge of their responsibilities (United Nations, 2000j). The mandate was expanded again in March 2001 to include assisting the government of Sierra Leone extend its authority, restore law and order, and stabilize the situation progressively through the country (United Nations, 2000f; 2001l).

As a result of the lack of stability and the increasingly violent security environment within Sierra Leone, on September 17, 2004, the mission was to start the following (United Nations, 2004ae):

- Support the Sierra Leone armed forces and police (a) in patrolling the border and the diamond-mining areas in the north of the country, including offering support in joint planning and joint operations, where appropriate, and (b) in monitoring the growing capacity of the Sierra Leone security sector.
- Support the SLPF in maintaining internal security, including security for the Special Court for Sierra Leone.
- Assist the SLPF with its recruiting, training, and mentoring program, which was designed to further strengthen the capacity and the resources of the SLPF.

The UN Security Council, in assigning those tasks to the mission, expressed its intention to regularly review the UNAMSIL's presence in Sierra Leone against the benchmark of the ability of the Sierra Leone armed forces and police to effectively "maintain security and stability" across the country (United Nations, 2004ae).

The mission's mandate was extended in six monthly increments and was finally completed on December 31, 2005 (United Nations, 2005l). When each mandate expired, the authorized strength of the civilian police component was increased; in March 2004, it reached the maximum number of 80 officers (United Nations, 2004z).

On August 31, 2005, the UN Security Council adopted Resolution 1620, which established the United Nations Integrated Office in Sierra Leone (UNIOSIL) for an initial period of 12 months beginning January 1, 2006 (United Nations, 2005ae). The mandate for the civilian police component of the mission was to develop "the independence and capacity of the justice system and the capacity of the police and corrections system" (United Nations, 2005l) and to provide advice that would strengthen the rule of law. The mission was to be made up of 20 civilian police advisers who were to "provide specialized training and advice to the Sierra Leone police, monitor the performance of police personnel, conduct in-service and train-the-trainers courses, [and] coach senior and mid-level managers" (United Nations, 2005l).

Mission Deployment Environment

The SLPF had been severely shaken during the late 1998 RUF offensive, known ominously as "Operation No Living Thing" (Dobbins et al., 2005). Hundreds of police officers were killed, and a large number of police stations were destroyed in the course of the January 1999 assault on Freetown.

Following the transition from UNOMSIL to UNAMSIL, the SLPF still lacked the necessary personnel, facilities, and equipment to fulfill essential tasks. The major problem was that the SLPF did not have the facilities to deliver training or to facilitate restructuring, because the national police training school was destroyed during the rebel offensive in January 1999 (United Nations, 2000c).

Because of the fragile security situation, progress in developing and restructuring the SLPF was slow. But the development process improved when stable security conditions were established (United Nations, 2000f).

Table 14.1. UNAMSIL Civilian Police Staff Numbers, November 1999 to November 2005

Year	Month	Number of UNAMSIL Civilian Police Officers
1999	November	6
2000	January	60
	July	37
2002	March	87
	September	170
2004	December	90
2005	November	30

Source: Author (from various United Nations documents).

Actions of the Mission (Output)

UNAMSIL civilian police, in conjunction with advisers from the Commonwealth Community Safety and Security Project (CCSSP) developed and launched a program that covered "all facets of police operations, including [at] the strategic and supervisory level, [and] assistance to patrol officers, as well as traffic and criminal investigation[s]" (United Nations, 2001j). The program was piloted in the country's Western Area and was principally "aimed at enhancing the effectiveness of the local police" (United Nations, 2001j).

In early 2002, the UNAMSIL police component was increased by 30 staff members who were to perform election-related tasks. The UNAMSIL police election advisers developed an electoral training program for SLPF and aided the SLPF in carrying out their election-related security duties (United Nations, 2002c).

The UNAMSIL police advisers, in conjunction with the CCSSP advisers, developed a number of training manuals and delivered training to the SLPF recruits, to trainers, and to other specialists. The UNAMSIL police advisers also delivered "workshops in various areas of policing, including professional standards and ethics, human rights, basic computer skills, Community Policing, family support, and handling of suspects" (United Nations, 2003i).

To meet the personnel requirements, UNAMSIL increased the capacity of the Police Training School in Hastings by renovating and rebuilding a number of buildings (United Nations, 2003i; 2003o). Those enhancements increased the capacity of the "training school from 200 to 300 cadets per intake" (United Nations, 2003h).

The UNAMSIL police developed a number of manuals to provide the framework that would ensure that the UNAMSIL mentoring process of the SLPF was transparent and met with democratic policing standards. The UNAMSIL police advisers also provided assistance to the SLPF to "enhance its [professional] policing standards" by providing advice on "human rights, police ethics, the rights of women and children, and the handling of suspects" (United Nations, 2003o).

Mission Implementation (Model)

In July 2000, the UNAMSIL police component consisted of 37 advisers who were deployed to Freetown, Lungi, Bo, Moyamba, Kenema, the Crime Investigation Department, the Elections Commission, the Joint Co-ordination Committee, and the Police Training School (United Nations, 2000e). Those UNAMSIL police advisers focused principally on developing training courses and on the "promotion of community policing both in Freetown and in the South, where the effectiveness of the Sierra Leone Police Force [was] gradually being restored" (United Nations, 2000h). Table 14.1 presents the total number of UNAMSIL civilian police officers deployed from November 1999 to November 2005.

The UNAMSIL police advisers, with the assistance of the CCSSP, developed plans that were based on the work completed by the UNOMSIL, which was to restructure and to strengthen the SLPF. Those plans detailed the methods that would be implemented to improve the SLPF service conditions, to monitor SLPF officer conduct, and to oversee SLPF structural and personnel changes (United Nations, 2000c).

To improve the security environment, the UNAMSIL retrained more than 100 members of the armed Special Security Division (SSD) of the SLPF. The retrained SSD members were deployed in Bo and Kenema to provide protection for their unarmed colleagues (United Nations, 2000c).

In March 2001, the UNAMSIL, with assistance from the CCSSP, opened a new regional police training school in Kenema in the Eastern Province (United Nations, 2001a). The mission police component also supported the SLPF members who were deployed to a number of rural area cities, including Kambia, Lunsar, Magburaka, and Makeni (United Nations, 2001f). The SLPF and the UNAMSIL prepared a detailed deployment plan to ensure that the SLPF members were deployed to every district by the end of January 2002 (United Nations, 2001h).

In September 2001, the UNAMSIL helped the government establish the National Recovery Committee, which was to "coordinate the extensive activities with all stakeholders and [to] set priorities for humanitarian action and the rehabilitation of government infrastructure in newly accessible areas" (United Nations, 2001g). The committee also developed a benchmark to measure the Sierra Leone police's progress in restoring state authority in newly accessible areas (United Nations, 2001g).

In September 2002, the government designed a strategic plan to develop the SLPF. The plan included a number of specific target areas including (a) the recruitment of new cadets and their training, (b) the training for trainers and for serving personnel, (c) the provision of necessary equipment, and (d) the development of police infrastructure (United Nations, 2002h).

In late 2002, the UNAMSIL police advisers—in conjunction with the CCSSP—developed and implemented the Local Needs Policing Concept (United Nations, 2003b). During this period, the UNAMSIL provided assistance to the SLPF in reviewing its staffing levels (United Nations, 2002l) and in developing a risk-based deployment plan. That plan was aimed at reinforcing the SLPF presence in areas that would be vacated by the UNAMSIL drawdown, which was to be "guided by progress in the implementation of the key security benchmark," all of which affected the capacity development of the Sierra Leone police and army (United Nations, 2003b).

On September 24, 2002, the UN Security Council adopted Resolution 1436 (United Nations, 2002o), which authorized an increase in the civilian police component of the UNAMSIL to 170 officers (United Nations, 2003h). The increased number of personnel was deployed to provide training to new recruits and to serve

SLPF personnel. UNAMSIL civilian police were also deployed to 17 police stations across the country so they could provide mentoring to the SLPF in basic policing skills (United Nations, 2003h).

The headquarters staff of the civilian police component was responsible for providing strategic advice, for dealing with cross-border issues, for policing diamond mines, and for providing airport security. The headquarters staff also provided specialized unit advisers that dealt with intelligence, the International Criminal Police Organization (Interpol), community policing, family support, and the driving school. In December 2004, the UNAMSIL civilian police component was decreased by 80 officers (United Nations, 2004l).

By late 2004, the primary responsibility for security was transferred from UNAMSIL to the SLPF (United Nations, 2004w). The UNAMSIL acted as a liaison with the other two UN missions in the region—the United Nations Mission in Liberia and the United Nations Operation in Côte d'Ivoire—to share information and lessons learned, as well as "to assist in the reform and the restructuring of [their respective] national police services" (United Nations, 2005g).

In early 2005, the UNAMSIL reviewed the progress that had been made in reaching the benchmarks that had been set in the mandate. The team noted that the government of Sierra Leone had moved toward "accomplishing the benchmarks for stabilization in the country and for the withdrawal of the residual UNAMSIL presence" (United Nations, 2005l).

Mission Achievements (Outcomes)

The UNAMSIL, in conjunction with the CCSSP, assisted the Sierra Leone government to increase the size and capacity of the SLPF by "recruiting and training new cadets, improving their policing skills, and planning for their deployment, in conjunction with the drawdown of UNAMSIL" (United Nations, 2003b). Table 14.2 presents the number of new SLPF recruits trained, the number of serving officers trained in basic policing, and the total number of officers deployed between December 2000 and December 2005. The table identifies the rapid increase in the total number of officers in the SLPF and

Table 14.2. Total Number of SLPF Officers, Number of New SLPF Recruits Trained, and Number of Serving Officers Trained, December 2000 to December 2005

Year	Month	Total Number of SLPF Officers in Reporting Period	Number of New SLPF Recruits Completing Training	Number of Serving SLPF Officers Completing In-Service Training[a]
2000	December	N/K	N/K	1,500
2001	January	6,500	N/K	N/K
2003	March	6,053	N/K	N/K
	September	6,241	384	N/K
2004	February	7,115	980	4,000
	September	7,903	897	N/K
	December	7,700	N/K	N/K
2005	April	8,200	N/K	N/K
	September	8,532	750	3,400
	December	9,500	N/K	600

Source: Author (from various United Nations documents dated 2000 to 2005).

Notes: N/K= not known.

a. Number of officers completing training in the reporting period.

the large number of serving officers who completed basic policing skills courses during this period.

By December 2005, the SLPF members were deployed throughout the country and had established 75 police stations and 112 police posts (United Nations, 2005b). The establishment of those stations and posts was a critical element in providing security for establishing the grounds for governance and for providing stabilization (United Nations, 2001f).

By the end of 2005, the SLPF had the skills, capacity, and ability to train the remaining police personnel to bring its strength to the authorized target of 9,500 by 2006. The SLPF was also able "to deal effectively with localized internal threats" (United Nations, 2005v). The SLPF lacked a communications and a logistics capability, and it would be challenged, "particularly in the districts, in the event of a countrywide crisis" (United Nations, 2005v).

Ways the Mission Was Evaluated

In June 2002, the secretary-general of the UN said that the SLPF was now a much improved force as a result of

the training provided by the UN civilian police and by the commonwealth police training team (United Nations, 2002g). The SLPF was able to improve its capability because of the leadership and the provision of new equipment provided by donors (United Nations, 2002h).

In March 2004, the secretary-general of the UN noted that the SLPF had been able to build on its skills and that remarkable gains had been made with the assistance of the UNAMSIL. However, the SLPF was not yet fully capable of handling serious widespread public disturbances, particularly in Freetown and in the diamond-mining areas where unemployed youths and ex-combatants were concentrated. The SLPF was also limited in its ability to strengthen its infrastructure and presence in the strategic areas of the country, because of a lack of police stations in those areas (United Nations, 2004f).

By the end of 2005, public confidence in the SLPF had increased, and members of the SLPF had the ability to "acquit themselves satisfactorily since [the] UNAMSIL [had] transferred security primacy to them last year" (United Nations, 2005v; 2005y). The secretary-general of the UN also noted that "the short-term indicators regarding internal security are positive, with little probability of a return to civil conflict, while criminal activities [were] expected to remain at a manageable level" (United Nations, 2005y).

Conclusion

According to Dobbins et al. (2005), UNAMSIL went through two distinct phases. The first phase was marked by failure, mainly from reliance on poorly trained, ill-equipped, and unprepared military units. The second phase remedied those deficiencies with limited success.

UNAMSIL has been identified as a success story in peacekeeping and may serve as a prototype for the new emphasis the UN places on building peace. This success story, as demonstrated by the United Nations (2010g), features the following accomplishments.

Over the course of its mandate, the mission disarmed tens of thousands of ex-fighters, assisted in holding national elections, helped in rebuilding the country's police force, and contributed toward rehabilitating the infrastructure and bringing government services to local communities.

UNAMSIL was not always foreseen to succeed. At one point in May 2000, the mission nearly collapsed when the rebel RUF kidnapped hundreds of peacekeepers and renounced the cease-fire in a move that endangered the credibility of UN peacekeeping.

UNAMSIL completed most of the tasks assigned to it by the UN Security Council. UNAMSIL helped the government restore its authority and social services in areas previously controlled by rebels, trained thousands of police personnel, and constructed or reconstructed dozens of police stations.

Following the completion of the UNAMSIL mandate, the UN established UNIOSIL, which was to help consolidate peace in the country. Its mandate was to cement UNAMSIL's gains and to help the government (a) strengthen human rights, (b) realize the UN's Millennium Development Goals, (c) improve transparency, and (d) hold free and fair elections in 2007 (United Nations, 2010g).

Chapter 15

Sudan and Darfur

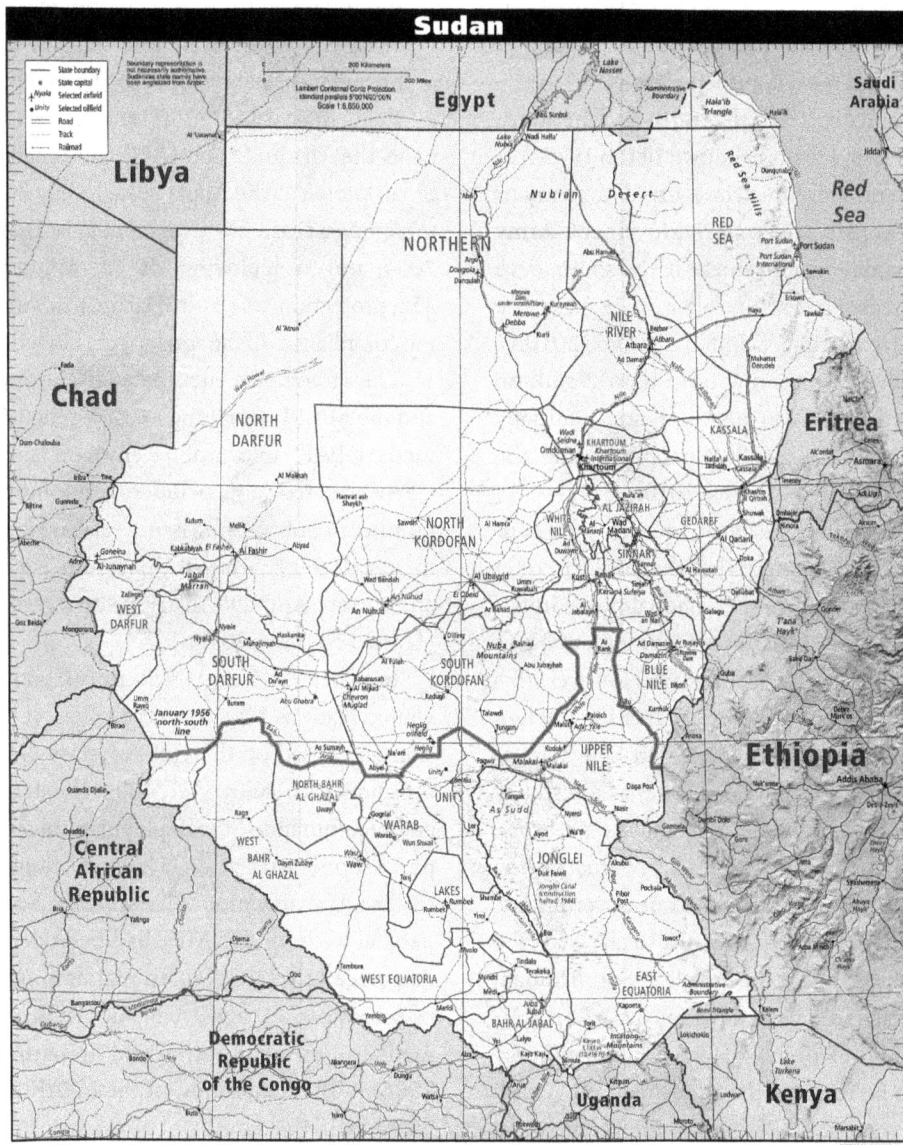

Map 15.1. Sudan
Source: Courtesy of the University of Texas Libraries, The University of Texas at Austin.

Case Study: United Nations Mission in Sudan

Background to the Mission

Since gaining independence from the United Kingdom and the Republic of Egypt on January 1, 1956, Sudan has experienced civil war for more than 43 years (United Nations, 2010n). Because of the war, the country is one of the world's poorest and most deprived nations.

The current conflict between the north and the south began in 1983, following the breakdown of the 1972 Addis Ababa Agreement. Since that time, the "Government and the Sudan People's Liberation Movement/Army (SPLM/A), the main rebel movement in the south, have fought over resources, power, the role of religion in the state, and self-determination" (United Nations, 2010n). Those conflicts have resulted in more than 2 million people being killed, 4 million people being internally displaced, and more than 600,000 people fleeing the country as refugees (United Nations, 2010n).

In 1993, because of the devastation caused by the conflict in Sudan and the possibility that the conflict could spread to neighboring countries, a regional peace initiative, under the guidance of the Inter-Governmental Authority on Development (IGAD) began. However, this initiative took until July 2002 to come to fruition—when the UN secretary-general visited the Sudan. The Machakos Protocol was signed on July 20, 2002, as a result of the visit. The parties reached an "agreement on a broad framework, setting forth the principles of governance, the transitional process, and the structures of government" (United Nations, 2010n). The protocol also clarified "the right to self-determination for the people of South Sudan, and on state and religion" (United Nations, 2010n).

The Machakos Protocol provided the foundation for two agreements to be reached: the Agreement on Wealth Sharing and the Protocol on Power Sharing (United Nations, 2010n). The Machakos Protocol enabled the United Nations (UN) Security Council to adopt Resolution 1547 (United Nations, 2004ad), which established the United Nations Advance Mission in the Sudan (UNAMIS) (United Nations, 2010n). This "special political mission" was mandated to "facilitate contacts with the parties concerned and to prepare for the introduction of an envisaged United Nations peace support operation" (United Nations, 2010n). The mandate was extended by UN Security Council Resolution 1556 (United Nations 2004ai) in "response to the escalating crisis in Darfur" (United Nations, 2010n).

The UNAMIS asserted that the population did not trust the Sudanese national police and that the police did not undertake active patrolling. As a result, there was a "need for a substantial civilian police component [of any proposed mission] to assist with monitoring and capacity-building" of the Sudanese national police (United Nations, 2004r).

Following years of effort to seek a solution to the Darfur issue, the African Union (AU) coordinated peace negotiations, known as the Abuja talks, in July 2004. The talks led to signing a cease-fire agreement in N'Djamena on April 8, 2004, and to deploying "60 AU military observers and 310 protection troops in Darfur to monitor and observe the compliance" of the agreement (United Nations, 2010n).

The agreements culminated in the Sudan government and the SPLM/A signing a Comprehensive Peace Agreement (CPAK) in Nairobi, Kenya, on January 9, 2005. The CPAK created and included a resolution process for a number of outstanding issues relating to security arrangements, power sharing in Khartoum, southern autonomy, and a more equitable distribution of economic resources (United Nations, 2010n).

In March 2005, the UN Security Council established the United Nations Mission in the Sudan (UNMIS). The mission was based on the UN Secretary-General's Report to the council on January 31, 2005, (United Nations, 2005c) and recommended the deployment of a multidimensional peace support operation (United Nations, 2010n).

The African Union Mission in the Sudan (AUMIS), in parallel with the UNMIS, had been deployed to the Sudan since July 18, 2005. To maintain security during the transition period of the UNMIS, AUMIS required an immediate increase in authorized strength (United Nations, 2006p). The finalization of the CPAK created new tasks for AUMIS that could not be undertaken safely within its current strength. The new tasks included the following (United Nations, 2006p):

- The establishment and patrolling of demilitarized zones around camps for internally displaced persons

- The establishment and patrolling of buffer zones
- The patrolling of humanitarian supply routes and nomadic migration routes
- A rapid cycle of investigating and reporting cases of cease-fire violations
- The deployment in camps of displaced persons and in areas of civilian control, plus monitoring of security in those camps
- The protection of women and children and the provision of training and capacity-building knowledge to the community police

The AU agreed to an increase in the "authorised strength of [AUMIS] of 6,171 military personnel and 1,560 civilian police," which was to coincide with the deployment of UNMIS (United Nations, 2010n).

The mandate and the tasks of UNMIS were expanded by the UN Security Council Resolution 1706 (United Nations, 2006ad) on August 31, 2006. The mandate authorized an increase in strength to 17,300 military personnel, 3,300 civilian police, and 16 formed police units (FPUs). Following the adoption of Resolution 1706, UNMIS could not deploy to Darfur because the Sudan government opposed a peacekeeping operation that was undertaken solely by the UN. To resolve this issue, the UN began to strengthen the AUMIS in phases and established a joint AU and UN peacekeeping operation in Darfur. The mission was named the United Nations and African Union Mission in Darfur (UNAMID) (United Nations, 2010n).

Mandate of the Mission

When the UN Security Council established UNAMIS on June 11, 2004, for an initial period of three months, the mission, according to the United Nations (2004ad), was to coordinate support for capacity building and was to monitor and assist in the following areas:

- Police and rule-of-law institutions
- Human rights and child protection

Following the deployment of UNAMIS, the United Nations Security Council (on March 24, 2005) adopted Resolution 1590, which established UNMIS (United Nations, 2005aa). The mission was for an initial period of six months and was to consist of 10,000 military personnel and up to 715 civilian police personnel. The mission's mandate, according to the United Nations (2005c; 2005aa), was to include the following:

- Assist the parties to implement the CPAK.
- Restructure the police service in Sudan consistent with democratic policing to develop a police training and evaluation program and to otherwise assist in training police.
- Promote the rule of law, including an independent judiciary, and protect human rights of all people of Sudan through a comprehensive and coordinated strategy to combat impunity and to contribute to long-term peace and stability.
- Assist in developing and consolidating the national legal framework.

The tasks of the UNMIS, as described by the United Nations (2010n), were as follows:

- Support the implementation of the CPAK.
- Facilitate and coordinate the voluntary return of refugees and internally displaced persons.
- Provide humanitarian assistance.
- Assist in demining operations.
- Contribute toward international efforts to protect and promote human rights in the Sudan.

The principal objective of the civilian police component of UNMIS was to help develop a transparent police service, as the Machakos Protocol and other agreements describe (United Nations, 2005c). The mission was to support peace and security sector reform strategies. Moreover, according to the United Nations (2005c), it would comprise the following four broad areas of engagement:

- Good offices of political support for the peace process, which would be addressed by the special representative
- Security, which would be addressed by the military
- Governance and assistance, which would be addressed by civilian police, rule of law, human rights, civil affairs, electoral assistance, and gender components (humanitarian and development assistance

would be addressed by components for disarmament, demobilization, and reintegration; humanitarian coordination; protection; recovery, return, and reintegration; and mine action)

- Peace support operation

The structure of the mission was to include the following (United Nations, 2005c):

- Establish civilian police headquarters in Khartoum, headed by a police commissioner and supported by a core staff of 34.
- Establish headquarters in Juba for forward operations, headed by a deputy police commissioner and supported by a core staff of 54.
- Establish sector headquarters that would be a liaison with provincial commanders to develop plans that would deploy additional advisers and monitors.
- Expand monitoring functions throughout the mission area of operations.
- Deploy additional trainers and mentors to expedite training and to assist local southern Sudan police in their recruitment and selection processes.

The secretary-general of the UN delivered a report on AUMIS and the expanded mandate of the AUMIS to the UN Security Council on July 28, 2006. The mandate was expanded to complement the UNMIS mandate and to help implement the CPAK (United Nations, 2006p). The expanded mandate consisted of the following two main pillars (United Nations, 2006ad):

1. Assist the Sudanese national police—in coordination with bilateral and multilateral assistance programs—in restructuring reforms and developing institutions in training and building capacity of the police; in implementing community policing; and in monitoring the Sudanese police performance through mentoring, co-location, and joint patrols.
2. Assist the Sudanese national police in monitoring and in verifying the redeployment and disengagement provisions of the Darfur Peace Agreement, including actively providing security and patrols in demilitarized and buffer zones, and in deploying police, including FPUs, in areas where internally dis-

placed persons are concentrated, along key routes of migration, and other vital points.

On August 31, 2006, because of the security situation in the Sudan, the UN Security Council adopted Resolution 1706, which expanded the UNMIS mandate to include Darfur and to increase the authorized strength of UNMIS to 17,300 military personnel, 3,300 civilian police, and 16 FPUs. The council also agreed to regularly review the strength and structure of UNMIS (United Nations, 2006ad).

The new resolution expanded the mandate of the mission to help in "restructuring the police service in the Sudan consistent with democratic policing, to develop a police training and evaluation programme, and to otherwise assist in the training of civilian police" (United Nations, 2006ae). In the Darfur, the mission was to do the following:

> To assist in addressing regional security issues in close liaison with international efforts to improve the security situation in the neighbouring regions along the borders between the Sudan and Chad and between the Sudan and the Central African Republic, including through the establishment of a multidimensional presence consisting of political, humanitarian, military, and civilian police liaison officers in key locations in Chad, including in internally displaced persons and refugee camps and, if necessary, in the Central African Republic, and to contribute to the implementation of the Agreement between the Sudan and Chad signed on 26 July 2006 (United Nations, 2006ae).

Following the changes in the mandate, the UN Security Council (on September 22, 2006) adopted Resolution 1709, which extended the deployment of the UNMIS until October 8, 2006, "with the intention to renew it for further periods" (United Nations, 2006ae). The mission was ongoing as of June 2010.

As mentioned earlier, the Sudanese government opposed a peacekeeping operation that was solely by the UN. Thus, the UN Security Council adopted Resolution 1769 (United Nations 2007v) on July 31, 2007, authorizing the establishment of the United Nations African Union Hybrid Operation in Darfur (UNAMID) (United Nations, 2010n).

Mission Deployment Environment

In most of the Sudan, the functioning police were described as being paramilitary and hierarchical and as lacking in transparency and accountability (United Nations, 2005c). In January 2005, the Sudanese police were located in five areas in the south and comprised approximately 17,000 former government police and a developing police force that had derived from the Sudan People's Liberation Army (United Nations, 2005c).

The secretary-general of the UN noted that the existing Sudanese police forces needed to be restructured if they were to reach international professional democratic standards of operation and to meet the "challenges of the post-war environment" (United Nations, 2005c). Police capability could be increased through training and monitoring, which would also increase security in the Darfur and would "facilitate the delivery of humanitarian relief" (United Nations, 2004r).

To increase the level of security in the Darfur region, the Sudanese government deployed 4,000 police on July 15, 2004, to all areas where internally displaced persons were susceptible to attacks (United Nations, 2004r). The government advised the United Nations about this change on August 30, 2004. In addition, the government also advised the United Nations that an additional 500 police would be deployed by the end of July and that a further 2,000 police "would be deployed into areas identified in accordance with the Plan of Action" (United Nations, 2004r). However, local people claimed that police in Darfur lacked discipline and that Janjaweed (rebels) had been recruited into the police (United Nations, 2004r).

The events in Darfur increased the lack of trust and confidence in the central government and the police. Any proposed UN police mission that would assist in the transfer of the Sudanese police needed to be large and needed to take a comprehensive change-management approach. The UN mission would need to be made up of senior police officers who could effectively command self-contained units and of other officers who could do the majority of researching, monitoring, mentoring, inspecting, and training, along with administrative duties (United Nations, 2005c).

In April 2005, the AUMIS consisted of 6,171 military personnel and 1,560 civilian police. On October 20, 2004, the AU extended the mandate of the AUMIS until September 30, 2006. The mandate was expanded to include monitoring and observing the Sudanese police's compliance with the agreement, which would contribute to a secure environment for delivering humanitarian aid and for returning refugees and internally displaced persons to their home areas (United Nations, 2006p).

Actions of the Mission (Output)

The civilian police component of the UNMIS provided advice and assistance to the existing police and the SPLM/A police force in its transition from a military-style police force to a more community-based model. To achieve this transformation, UNMIS monitored members of the local police and gained a "detailed picture of their activities, and establish[ed] a baseline of available resources and needs." This approach allowed the UNMIS to be directly involved in the training program and in the design of capacity development programs "within the wider context of security sector reform" (United Nations, 2005c).

To achieve the mandate, the UNMIS police staff was co-located with the Sudanese police in police stations, and a strategic plan was prepared to develop and train the police (United Nations, 2005z). The mission fostered strong internal relationships that enabled the mission to act as a liaison between the military and the police components and that provided a managed approach to the reforming, restructuring, and rebuilding of the local police capacity (United Nations, 2006p). To ensure that both of the missions in Sudan were well organized, the UNMIS provided 33 police advisers to the AUMIS. Those advisers assisted the AUMIS with "logistics, operations, investigations, personnel, information technology, command and control, and other expertise" (United Nations, 2006v).

The provision of UNMIS police advisers to the AUMIS became known as the "light support package" and eventually culminated in a hybrid UNAMID, which involved both military and civilian police personnel. This new UN and AU mission designed a two-phase approach to resolve several outstanding issues (United Nations, 2007a).

The first phase of the new approach was implementing the light support package and deploying the personnel involved. The second phase involved designing and imple-

Table 15.1. UNMIS Civilian Police Staff Numbers, September 2005 to January 2010

Date	Number of Female Police Officers	Number of Male Police Officers	Total Number of Civilian Police Officers
September 2005	9	77	86
August 2006	41	625	666
December 2006	45	597	642
April 2007	47	606	653
October 2008	46	547	593
January 2010	85	604	689

Source: Author (from various United Nations documents).

menting the "heavy support package." This latter phase consisted of a "range of force enablers" that included the deployment of three FPUs (United Nations, 2007a).

During this period, UNMIS continued to make progress on its assigned tasks, and it established the police development committee (PDC) that enabled the community policing training program to be widened to include the southern transit camps for internally displaced persons. In northern Sudan, the UNMIS designed and delivered a number of training courses for the local police (United Nations, 2007a).

In mid-2008, UNMIS developed the Joint Integrated Police Unit for Abyei. A 10-day, basic police training course was delivered to both the regular police from the northern and southern regions and to the government police personnel as part of this initiative. The mission also trained 1,700 government police officers in forensics, crime investigation, gender issues, computers, explosives awareness, and community policing. In addition, the mission trained 100 government women police officers in Khartoum about issues of gender, child protection, and domestic violence. UNMIS trained 2,104 Southern Sudan Police Service (SSPS) officers in airport security, community policing, computers, criminal investigation, traffic, and special operations (United Nations, 2008n).

The SSPS was able to finalize its annual budget and streamline its payroll systems with assistance from the UNMIS. By implementing those strategies and developing train-the-trainers courses, the mission was able to extend the community police training program to the Dar

es Salaam, Wad al-Bashir, and Jebel Aulia camps in Khartoum. "This [extension] bridged the gap between the internally displaced person community and the police and promoted security and safety in communities of internally displaced persons" (United Nations, 2009j).

Mission Implementation (Model)

The authorized strength allowed in Resolution 1706 (United Nations, 2006ad) was a "minimum option" for achieving the mandate, according to the secretary-general of the UN. The authorized strength would allow a minimum presence for a "deployment in more than 100 locations, covering about 80 percent of the population" (United Nations, 2006p). By August 2007, the UNMIS co-located at 6 of the 10 state police commands and at 36 local police stations, and the UNMIS assisted the SSPS in developing its command and communications structures (United Nations, 2007k).

During May 2005, the AUMIS reached a total strength of 2,674 personnel, which included 460 civilian police. However, the AUMIS civilian police were 355 officers short of the authorized strength that was agreed on by the AU in October 2004 (United Nations, 2005q).

Table 15.1 presents the total number of UNMIS civilian police deployed and their gender during September 2005 through January 2010. The table illustrates that the mission did not reach its authorized strength of civilian police personnel during this period. The gap in deployment in both of the missions was mainly because police officers from the donor countries were not available and because of logistics in deploying officers from within the country (United Nations, 2005q).

Although the UNMIS consisted of only 86 civilian police officers, by September 2005, the contingent had established a forward headquarters in Juba and a presence in six sectors: Torit, Aweil, Bentiu, Melut, Bor, and Abyei (United Nations, 2005aa; 2006f). The mission had also prepared a strategic plan to develop and to train police officers to ensure that the bilateral and multilateral assistance program was coordinated and that a network of police stations was established in southern Sudan (United Nations, 2005aa).

In conjunction with the United Nations Development Programme (UNDP), the mission trained 700 senior officers in police management and held an executive workshop for 17 officers of the rank of major-general or brigadier (United Nations, 2006f). UNMIS trained police officers on "rule of law principles and the criminal justice chain" (United Nations, 2006s). UNMIS also delivered a new UN police training package that would improve local capacity and compliance with democratic policing principles and international best practices. The training package focused on basic police and crisis response skills and was designed to "strengthen the credibility of the police as an alternative to the military in maintaining law and order" (United Nations, 2007k).

By mid-2009, UNMIS had trained approximately 6,500 Sudan government police and SSPS officers in various aspects of policing and had prepared 202 SSPS officers so that they could take responsibility for the delivery of basic police training. UNMIS, jointly with the SSPS, developed a basic training curriculum for in-service personnel and new recruits (United Nations, 2009j).

As civilian police staff numbers increased and the mission needed to be capable of providing security, the UNMIS needed "to have a multidimensional presence in key locations in Chad, including in the camps for internally displaced persons and refugees and, if necessary, in the Central African Republic" (United Nations, 2006p). Deploying UNMIS civilian police to those areas would enable the police to act as liaisons with the local authorities and would provide an opportunity to monitor "major developments in the border area and to coordinate activities where appropriate" (United Nations, 2006p).

With assistance from the UNMIS, the SSPS established the PDC in May 2006 to form policy and to coordinate capacity-building efforts. The PDC, with UNMIS assistance, drafted a plan for community policing in Juba and drafted a code of conduct for the Sudan police. In conjunction with the UNMIS, the SSPS developed a police officer registration and an identity card system that was implemented in September 2006 (United Nations, 2006s).

From 2007 to 2010, the mission concentrated on training the local police. A UN training package included training in the areas of gender and child protection, human rights, and community policing. This training resulted in improvements in the Sudanese police's handling of public complaints and helping vulnerable persons and juveniles. UNMIS also delivered to local police train-the-trainers courses and specialist courses on (a) riot and crowd control, (b) VIP and close protection, (c) forensics, (d) community policing, (e) crime scene investigation, (f) human trafficking and organized crime, (g) human rights, and (h) advanced investigation (United Nations, 2009j).

Mission Achievements (Outcomes)

The mission initially faced a major problem: the governments of National Unity and of Southern Sudan resisted efforts to come together to address matters of common importance (United Nations, 2006f). However, the UNMIS was able to implement its co-location program with both the National Police and the SSPS and was able to develop and implement a program that registered and identified SSPS officers (United Nations, 2007f).

Then the UNMIS assisted the SSPS to establish an organizational structure and to design and implement a training curriculum and program (United Nations, 2007f).

By mid-2009, the mission completed the integration of the former SPLM/A personnel into the National Police Service of the government of the Sudan (United Nations, 2009j) and established an environment where the Sudanese government was able to draft and adopt legislation about criminal acts, criminal and civil procedure, and human rights. The Southern Sudan Land Act, Local Government Act, and Sudan People's Liberation Army

Act were adopted by the Southern Sudan Legislative Assembly (United Nations, 2009g).

Ways the Mission Was Evaluated

In December 2005, the African Union conducted an assessment mission of AUMIS with the input of a wide range of partners, including the UN (United Nations, 2006c). This assessment concluded that the AUMIS had a positive effect on the security and the humanitarian situations in Darfur. The assessment concluded that by taking a number of specific steps, the mission would further increase its effectiveness (United Nations, 2006c).

The secretary-general of the UN noted in reports to the UN Security Council in 2007 and in 2010, that although progress had been achieved in reforming and developing the National Police of Sudan and the SSPS, a number of geographical areas remained "administratively separate, with their own educational and police systems, which was in contravention of the Comprehensive Peace Agreement" (United Nations, 2007f). The secretary-general noted that because of the audacious conditions in Sudan, the SSPS faced serious challenges to logistics and communications in conducting its policing activities (United Nations, 2010f).

Conclusion

The mission encountered a number of problems. The mission was not able to reach its authorized strength because civilian police officers were not available from donor countries. When the mission did deploy officers, there were logistical problems in getting officers to their stations because of the harsh and challenging environment.

As a result of the deficiencies in the skills of those deployed, the mission was not able to implement a planning, reform, or training framework. This situation was exacerbated by the attitude of the SSPS. The continued absence of a police training strategy policy "or commitment to the training programme by the Southern Sudan Police Service and the Government of the Sudan police" posed "challenges to an effective police presence in the region" (United Nations, 2009j).

Case Study: United Nations and African Union Mission in Darfur

Background to the Mission

Because the government of Sudan objected to a peacekeeping effort in Darfur that would be solely by the United Nations (UN), the UN strengthened the African Union Mission in the Sudan (AUMIS) in phases, which allowed a joint African Union (AU) and UN peacekeeping operation to be established in Darfur. This operation, titled the United Nations and African Union Mission in Darfur (UNAMID), ran parallel with United Nations Mission in the Sudan (UNMIS) in the remaining regions of the Sudan (United Nations, 2010n).

In February 2007, 33 UNMIS civilian police joined the AUMIS as part of the first phase, or "light support package," in Darfur. When the second phase, or "heavy support package," was made final January 21, 2007, in Addis Ababa, the UN provided 721 civilian police personnel, 301 police advisers, and 3 formed police units (FPUs). The UN officers were to support the AUMIS by providing static security protection in the form of security guards in the displaced person camps, by assisting the implementation of the Darfur Peace Agreement, and by helping in administration and management (United Nations, 2007c).

The deployment of the three UN FPUs were to "complement AUMIS civilian police in performing" their tasks in the Darfur region (United Nations, 2007c). The deployment of the FPUs along with the light support package would help AUMIS develop an "integrated command and control structure and to increase the effectiveness and co-ordination of its operations" (United Nations, 2007h). The tasks of this combined operation included the following (United Nations, 2007c):

- Protect civilians and vulnerable communities under the threat of violence, as well as UN and AU personnel and facilities.
- Maintain a 24-hour presence in internally displaced person camps.
- Perform escort duties (collection of firewood, grass, and water).
- Conduct confidence-building patrols.

The light support package, according to the United Nations (2007h), consisted of equipment and personnel fully dedicated to AUMIS in the following four areas (United Nations, 2007h):

1. Logistical and materials support
2. Military staff support
3. Advisory support for civilian police, support for civilians in the areas of mine action, humanitarian liaison, public information, and support for the mission
4. Implementation support for the Darfur Peace Agreement

The AU and the UN deployed a joint quick review mission in Darfur on February 8–19, 2007, to assess how large a force would be required. The review suggested that because of emerging security trends, the hybrid force would need to be made up of 19,000–20,000 troops, as well as 3,772 police officers and 19 FPUs (United Nations, 2007h).

To assist with preparations for the transfer of authority from AUMIS to UNAMID, the UN and the AU established a multidisciplinary UNAMID transition team in El Fasher in August 2007. The planning team developed and implemented deployment plans for the transition (United Nations, 2007n).

Mandate of the Mission

On July 31, 2007, the UN Security Council adopted Resolution 1769 establishing in Darfur the AU and UN hybrid operation, UNAMID, for an initial period of 12 months (United Nations, 2007v). The mission was extended for two additional periods of 12 months, and its most recent mandate was due to expire on July 31, 2010 (United Nations, 2010n).

The original mandate authorized the deployment of 20,000 military personnel and 6,000 civilian police, thereby "making it one of the largest UN peacekeeping operations in history" (United Nations, 2010n).

The protection of civilians and displaced persons was part of the mandate of the UNAMID. The mission was to do the following (United Nations, 2010n):

- Contribute to security for humanitarian assistance.
- Monitor and verify the implementation of agreements.
- Assist in an inclusive political process.

- Contribute to the promotion of human rights and the rule of law.
- Monitor and report on the situation along the borders with Chad and the Central African Republic.

The UN Security Council authorized the mission "to take the necessary action, in the areas of deployment of its forces as it deems within its capabilities" in order to do the following (United Nations, 2010n):

- Protect UNAMID's personnel, facilities, installations, and equipment, and ensure the security and the freedom of movement of its own personnel and humanitarian workers.
- Support early and effective implementation of the Darfur Peace Agreement, and prevent the disruption of its implementation and armed attacks.
- Protect civilians.

The mission was to do the following (United Nations, 2010n):

- Contribute to a secure environment for economic reconstruction and development, as well as the sustainable return of internally displaced persons and refugees to their homes.
- Promote respect for and protection of human rights and fundamental freedoms in Darfur.
- Promote the rule of law in Darfur by providing support for strengthening an independent judiciary and a prison system and by providing assistance in developing and consolidating the legal framework, in consultation with relevant Sudanese authorities.
- Monitor and report on the security situation at the Sudan's borders with Chad and the Central African Republic.

For the mission to achieve those operational tasks, UNAMID staff members acted as liaisons with the national and local authorities in regard to the following (United Nations, 2007b; 2010q):

1. Security
   a. Promote the reestablishment of confidence, deter violence, and assist in monitoring and verifying the implementation of the redeployment and

disengagement provisions of the Darfur Peace Agreement, which included actively providing security and robust patrolling of redeployment and buffer zones. Accomplish the security by monitoring the withdrawal of long-range weapons and by deploying hybrid police, including FPUs, in areas where internally displaced persons were concentrated, in the demilitarized and buffer zones, along key routes of migration, and in other vital areas, including the provisions set out in the Darfur Peace Agreement.

b. Monitor through proactive patrolling the parties' policing activities in camps for internally displaced persons, demilitarized and buffer zones, and areas of control.

c. Support—in coordination with the parties as outlined in the Darfur Peace Agreement—the establishment and the training of community police in camps for internally displaced persons, support the government for having the Sudan police in Darfur learn capacity-building in accordance with international standards of human rights and accountability, and support the institutional development of the police.

d. Support the efforts of the government of Sudan and the police so that public order is maintained, and support efforts to increase the capacity of Sudanese law enforcement through specialized training and joint operations.

2. Rule of law, governance, and human rights

a. Support the parties that signed the Darfur Peace Agreement to restructure.

b. Build the capacity of the police service in Darfur through monitoring, training, mentoring, using co-locations, and having joint patrols.

During the initial planning for UNAMID, the planners proposed that the civilian police component consist of 3,772 advisers and 19 FPUs and that the existing AUMIS civilian police and the UN light and heavy support packages would form the core of the mission. The main task of the FPUs was to help provide "protection for civilians and personnel and property of the operation, in collaboration with the military component of the operation" (United Nations, 2007h).

In November 2009, UNAMID developed a strategic work plan in consultation with the AU. The plan included priority area benchmarks to track progress and measure the implementation of the mission's mandate (United Nations, 2009h). The achievement of those four priority areas was necessary to realize the goal of a "political solution and sustained stability in Darfur" (United Nations, 2009f). The four priority areas are as follows (United Nations, 2009k):

- Achievement of a comprehensive political solution
- Achievement of a secure and stable environment
- Enhancement of the rule of law, strengthened governance, and human rights
- Achievement of a stabilized humanitarian situation

The mission was to achieve the following two priority area benchmarks from 2009 to 2011 (United Nations, 2009k):

1. Create a secure and stable environment. The mission will contribute to the restoration and upholding of a stable and secure environment throughout Darfur, in which civilians, in particular vulnerable groups, are protected and where displaced populations can choose whether they wished to return to their places of origin.

2. Enhance the rule of law, governance, and human rights benchmark. The mission will contribute to national and local authorities and security and justice institutions, will enforce and maintain the rule of law, and will govern on a nondiscriminatory basis in accordance with international human rights standards and principles of good governance throughout Darfur.

Mission Deployment Environment

To ensure that UNAMID was able to effectively operate on the day authority was transferred, a joint planning forum was held in Addis Ababa from July 30 to August 2, 2007. The forum agreed to send an advance unit of police and military to Darfur before the transfer of authority

(United Nations, 2007n). The deployment would include one FPU and 40 individual police officers, as well as military personnel.

Along with the joint planning, UNMIS co-located with AUMIS counterparts and acted as liaisons with the AUMIS to identify and address all issues related to the transition from the AUMIS to the UNAMID. To this end, the light support and the heavy support package officers in Darfur co-located with their AUMIS counterparts to facilitate the work (United Nations, 2007p).

Actions of the Mission (Output)

The mission took a more proactive posture, which included conducting patrols, by reaching out to internally displaced persons and by supporting the humanitarian community (United Nations, 2007r). To ensure that all mission civilian police officers understood the new approach, all personnel transferring from the AUMIS and all new UNAMID personnel were trained before taking up their positions (United Nations, 2008b).

In January 2008, UNAMID police implemented a three-phase plan for patrolling the camps for internally displaced persons. The new plan was designed so that patrolling would occur between 8 a.m. and 6 p.m. daily in nearly all locations, which would increase trust and confidence (United Nations, 2008f). Patrols were later increased to cover the period from midnight to 8 a.m., with a view to extending the coverage to a full 24 hours (United Nations, 2008g).

The UNAMID trained 277 Sudanese police from six camps in community policing to "support the maintenance of law and order" (United Nations, 2008g). A crime prevention and public relations initiative was launched on July 20, 2008, which included "visits with the leaders of the displaced and the distribution of literature to six such camps in Northern Darfur" (United Nations, 2008l).

Mission Implementation (Model)

The heavy support package provided for 721 civilian police personnel, which consisted of 301 police advisers and 3 FPUs whose task it was (a) to assist the AUMIS in static camp security protection for displaced persons, (b) to implement the Darfur Peace Agreement, and (c) to provide assistance in administration and management (United Nations, 2007c). Because of the change to the hybrid mission (UNAMID) and because of the security situation, the number of personnel deployed was changed to 3,772 advisers and 19 FPUs (United Nations, 2007h).

Table 15.2 presents the number of FPUs deployed by UNAMID, the composition of the FPUs, and the number of civilian police advisers from July 2007 to October 2009. The table illustrates that the mission never reached its authorized strength or the authorized number of FPUs.

The initial UN transfers and deployments to UNAMID were deployed to El Fasher, Nyala, and Geneina so they could assist in the SSPS's reformation. UNAMID was to strengthen the SSPS command and control structures, improve the SSPS's monitoring and reporting systems, and establish mechanisms for the SSPS to address gender-based violence (United Nations, 2007r).

In May 2008, UNAMID began building 82 community policing centers. Besides serving as local police stations, the centers were also used as office space by UNAMID civilian police advisers (United Nations, 2008g).

In August 2008, UNAMID police advisers "conducted a series of training and capacity-building workshops for 119 members of the rebel police forces, 90 sheikhs and *umdas* (tribal elders), and 295 internally displaced persons on the subjects of human rights, gender, and community-policing" (United Nations, 2008m). Police advisers also started a community program for community policing initiatives and investigations in sexual and gender-based violence in all three sectors. The program was developed to foster a closer partnership between the Sudanese police, the rebel movements, and the communities (United Nations, 2008o).

In late 2008, UNAMID commenced a number of "quick-impact" projects. Actions that would improve security and the lives of displaced persons were included in those projects. UNAMID developed standard operating procedures to ensure that the projects were successfully implemented (United Nations, 2009f).

To increase the security in and around the camps, UNAMID undertook confidence-building patrols, which

Table 15.2. UNAMID Civilian Police Staff Numbers, July 2007 to October 2009

Date	Number of Formed Police Units	Number of Staff in Formed Police Units	Number of Civilian Police Advisers[a]
July 2007[b]	N/A	N/A	686
December 2007[c]	N/A	N/A	33
January 2008	1	140	1,510
March 2008	1	140	1,600
July 2008	1	140	1,728
October 2008	1	140	1,948
February 2009	5	699	1,940
May 2009	7	975	1,902
October 2009	11	1,697	2,752

Source: Author (from various United Nations documents).
Notes: N/K= not known.
    a. Does not include number of police officers in FPUs.
    b. Number of UNMIS police advisers.
    c. The light support package, which was developed jointly with the African Union.

placed an emphasis on facilitating humanitarian access and protecting convoys. UNAMID police advisers undertook monitoring, farming, and firewood patrols, and they visited community policing centers and government police stations throughout Darfur (United Nations, 2008o).

Mission Achievements (Outcomes)

This mission faces a number of logistical and political challenges and has had personnel deployed only since July 2007. As a result of the short time frame, the mission has not achieved the majority of the tasks identified in its mandate.

The mission, in the short time that it has been on the ground, has established some sense of security, which has allowed a form of normalcy to return to the country.

Ways the Mission Was Evaluated

The United Nations Department of Peacekeeping Operations undertook a formal evaluation between April 26 and May 7, 2009. The evaluation reviewed the operational objectives of UNAMID's military, civilian police, and civilian component, and it examined the challenges and constraints of the mission (African Press Organization, 2009).

The evaluation was intended to provide best practices and lessons learned in all areas of mission activity. The assessment team hopes to use those lessons in future UN missions (African Press Organization, 2009).

Conclusion

UNAMID was a large joint UN and AU mission that appears to have made progress in stabilizing Sudan and Darfur and in achieving its mandate. Stabilization of the country has been assisted by the opening of 82 community policing centers and by the start of training the SSPS in policing duties.

UNAMID also appears to have been successful in using large numbers of FPUs to provide high-level policing and to provide a sense of security.

The mission was ongoing as of June 2010.

Case Study: European Union Support to the African Union Mission to Sudan and Darfur

Background to the Mission

In June 2005, the African Union (AU) expanded the authorized strength of the African Union Mission in Sudan (AUMIS) to 6,171 military and 1,560 civilian police personnel. To assist the AU with managing of the increased number of personnel, the European Union (EU) deployed a political adviser, a military adviser, and a police adviser, "to the ad hoc Co-ordination Cell (ACC) established in Addis Ababa" (Council of the European Union, 2005b).

The EU mission was to provide effective and timely support to AUMIS (Council of the European Union, 2006c). Support was given to the EU by the police advisers in the ACC on the police component of the EU's action (Council of the European Union, 2005b). The EU support to the civil police component of AUMIS included planning and providing technical assistance to all AUMIS levels of command. The support included providing military observers, training African troops and observers, and advising about strategic and tactical transportation (Council of the European Union, 2006c).

Mandate of the Mission

On July 20, 2005, the Council of the European Union adopted a joint action that established the EU civilian-military action and that would support the AU's enhanced mission to Sudan and Darfur (EU AMIS). The mandate of the mission was for two and a half years, concluding on December 31, 2007. At the end of the mission, EU AMIS would then transfer to the UNAMID (Council of the European Union, 2005c).

The support action was addressed to the AU and its political, military, and police efforts to ease the crisis in Darfur. The aim of EU AMIS was to ensure effective and timely EU assistance to the AU's enhanced AUMIS mission and to provide police assistance and training (Council of the European Union, 2005c).

The tasks of the EU AMIS support action included the following (Council of the European Union, 2005c):

- Support the AUMIS police chain of command by providing the AU with highly experienced senior police advisers at all levels of the chain of command.
- Support the training of UNMIS civilian police (CIVPOL) personnel by providing for in-mission instruction by EU trainers.
- Support the development of a police unit within the secretariat of the AU.

Mission Deployment Environment

The AUMIS was first deployed to Sudan in May 2004 to monitor the 2004 humanitarian cease-fire agreement and other subsequent agreements. Specifically, AUMIS was "to assist in confidence-building and to contribute to a secure environment for the delivery of humanitarian aid and the return of refugees and internally displaced persons, thereby contributing to overall security in Darfur" (European Union Council Secretariat, 2008).

The AUMIS was subsequently expanded, and in October 2004, the mandate expanded to include providing assistance to the northern and the southern police (European Union Council Secretariat, 2008). The presence of AUMIS brought a sense of security to the civilian population in the camp areas and helped to achieve "a semblance of stability in parts of Darfur" (Appiah-Mensah, 2006, p. 19). However, a combination of structural conditions, a set of misguided politics, and a lack of AU management and practical peacekeeping experience seriously hampered the operation's overall effectiveness (Franke, 2009).

Actions of the Mission (Output)

The EU AMIS support action principally provided support and assistance to AUMIS as described in the following (European Council Secretariat, 2005a):

- It supported the CIVPOL component of AUMIS and the AUMIS CIVPOL chain of command. This action was undertaken by deploying 16 EU police officers to all levels throughout the chain of command of the local police. The deployment placed senior police advisers to the AU in Addis Ababa, to the office of the AUMIS head of mission in Khartoum, to the office of the police commissioner in El Fasher, to the three regional headquarters, and to the eight sector headquarters.

- It supported the training of CIVPOL personnel. Three in-mission training courses were designed and delivered by EU trainers to all categories of AUMIS CIVPOL personnel. The courses targeted senior command staff management, trainers, and postdeployment CIVPOL personnel.

- It supported the development of a police unit within the secretariat of the AU. Because the EU AMIS provided support to develop a police unit within the AU secretariat, the secretariat, in turn, assisted the AU in developing its longer-term capacity to plan and conduct police operations.

Mission Implementation (Model)

Since January 2004, the EU has assisted the AU in its endeavor to help stabilize Darfur. This assistance included financial, personnel, and political support to the ceasefire negotiations and "planning, technical, financial, and equipment support to AUMIS I and AUMIS II" (European Union Council Secretariat, 2006).

The EU AMIS support action was made up of 29 police officer advisers who were deployed to the AU headquarters in Addis Ababa, to the AUMIS headquarters in Khartoum, to the AUMIS forward headquarters in El Fasher, and to several AUMIS sector sites (European Union Council Secretariat, 2006). As part of the EU support action, police advisers supported the AUMIS CIVPOL by advising senior staff, by providing training to CIVPOL personnel, and by developing a police unit in the AU Secretariat (European Union Council Secretariat, 2008).

Mission Achievements (Outcomes)

Despite the decrease in violence, EU AMIS was unable to bring total peace to the Darfur. This finding was mainly because of the AU's lack of capacity and lack of peacekeeping experience (Franke, 2009). EU AMIS also lacked strategic coordination and was unable to implement a program in conjunction with the UN and the North Atlantic Treaty Organization.

The EU provided a consolidated package of civilian and military measures to support AUMIS. The supporting action of the EU continued until the end of December 2007 when the mandate of the AU mission ended and AUMIS was handed over to UNAMID, the joint AU and UN peacekeeping operation in Darfur. This move was in accordance with UN Security Council Resolution 1769 (United Nations, 2007v; European Union Council Secretariat, 2008).

Ways the Mission Was Evaluated

AUMIS had a positive effect on security in Darfur, but its ability to protect civilians was limited by capacity, insufficient resources, and political constraints. The main problem was that the EU AMIS was incapable of implementing the mandate (Behrens, 2006). The AUMIS lacked the logistical facilities to deploy troops and basic equipment that would have enabled members of the force to undertake their tasks effectively. Other problems included weak command and control capabilities and a lack of experience in dealing with asymmetric and guerrilla warfare (Behrens, 2006).

Conclusion

The EU AMIS was a successful small bridging mission between two very large and challenging missions (UNMIS/AUMIS and UNAMID). Although total peace was not achieved and the security situation remains less than desirable, the mission was successful in achieving the tasks that were identified in its mandate.

Chapter 16

Timor-Leste (East Timor)

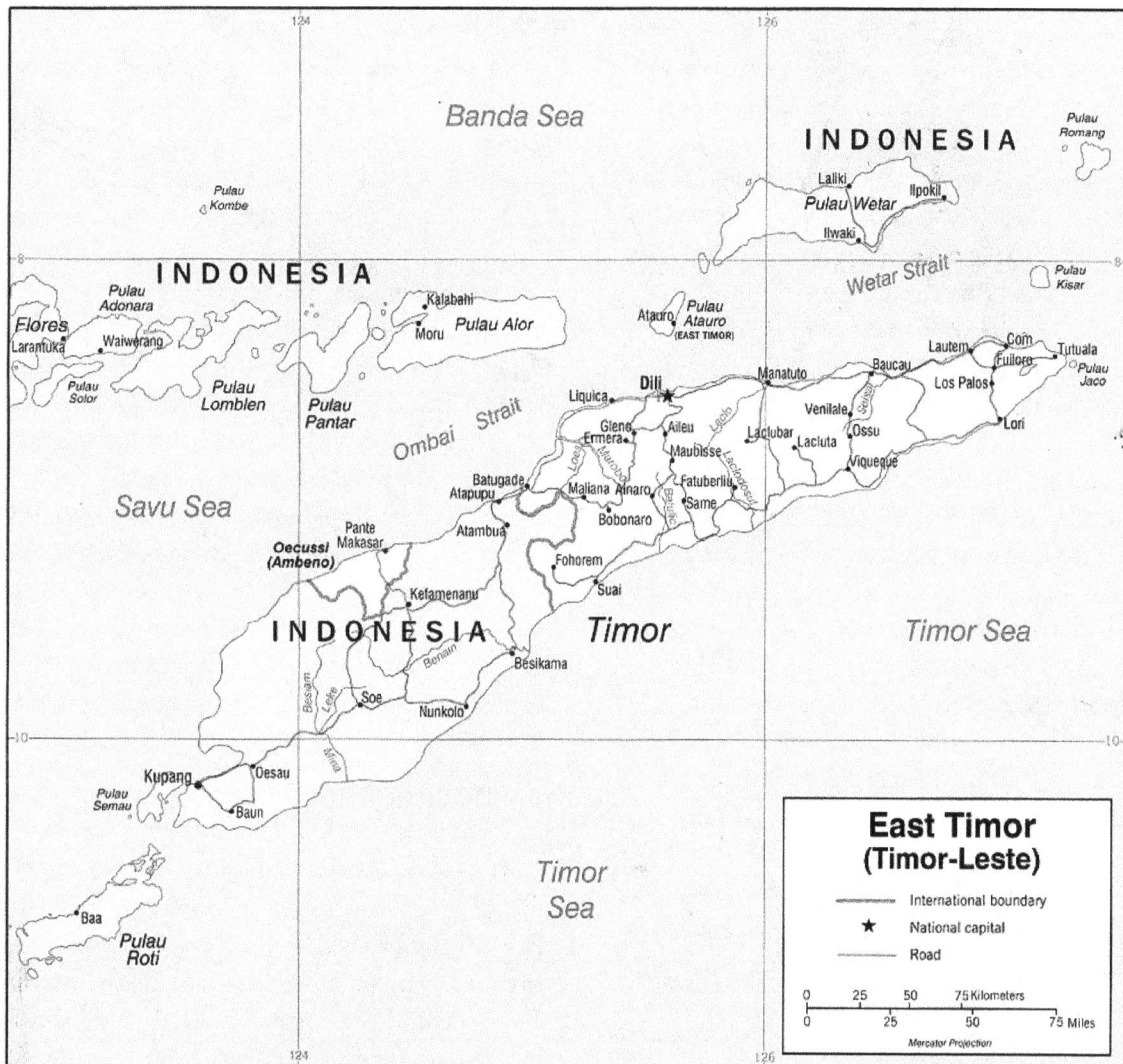

Map 16.1. Timor-Leste (East Timor)
Source: Courtesy of the University of Texas Libraries, The University of Texas at Austin.

There have been five separate United Nations (UN) missions to Timor-Leste since June 1999. The first two missions were before the Timor-Leste Declaration of Independence in May 2002, and the final three missions were subsequent to the country's independence. The five missions were these:

1. The United Nations Mission in East Timor (UNAMET) (June to October 1999) was a political mission that was mandated to organize and to conduct a popular consultation. The referendum would ascertain whether the East Timorese people would accept a special autonomy within Indonesia or whether they would reject a proposal that would lead to East Timor's separation from Indonesia.

2. The United Nations Transitional Administration in East Timor (UNTAET) (October 1999 to May 2002) was a peacekeeping operation that was established after the East Timorese rejected the special autonomy option. UNTAET exercised administrative authority over East Timor during the transition to independence.

3. The United Nations Mission of Support in East Timor (UNMISET) (May 2002 to May 2005) was also a peacekeeping mission. It was mandated to provide assistance to the newly independent East Timor until East Timor authorities had taken over all operational responsibilities. The mission was also to enable the new nation to become self-sufficient.

4. When UNMISET completed its mandate, a new political mission, titled the United Nations Office in Timor-Leste (UNOTIL) (May 2005 to August 2006), was established to support the development of critical state institutions and the police and to provide training in democratic governance and human rights (United Nations, 2010i).

5. The United Nations Integrated Mission in Timor-Leste (UNMIT) (August 2006 to present) was established following the political, humanitarian, and security crisis that the country suffered in April–June 2006.

Case Study: United Nations Mission in East Timor

Background to the Mission

On June 11, 1999, the UN Security Council adopted Resolution 1246, which established UNAMET (United Nations, 1999i). UNAMET was to be completed by August 31, 1999, but was extended until November 30, 1999 (United Nations, 1999m). The mission's mandate was to organize and to conduct the East Timor Autonomy Referendum about the future of East Timor, and the mission consisted of 280 police officer advisers and 50 military liaison officers (United Nations, 1999i). UNAMET was to oversee the transition period after the referendum and before the outcome's implementation (United Nations, 2010o).

Following the vote for independence in the autonomy referendum, which was held on August 30, 1999, the Timorese pro-Indonesian integration militia launched a campaign of violence. This turmoil resulted in establishing and deploying the United Nations International Force for East Timor (INTERFET), which was a multinational peacekeeping intervention task force that was mandated to address the humanitarian and security crisis following the referendum. Deployed from September 20, 1999, until the end of February 2000, the mission was to restore peace and security to East Timor, to protect and support the UN mission, and to facilitate humanitarian assistance operations until a UN peacekeeping force could be approved and deployed in the area (United Nations, 1999n).

Mandate of the Mission

UNTAET was established on October 12, 1999, when the UN Security Council adopted Resolution 1272 (United Nations, 1999p). UNTAET had the overall responsibility for the administration of East Timor and was empowered to exercise all legislative and executive authority, including the administration of justice (United Nations, 1999n). The mission's mandate was to do the following (United Nations, 1999p; 2010r):

• Provide security and maintain law and order throughout the territory of East Timor.

- Establish an effective administration.
- Assist in the development of civil and social services.
- Ensure the coordination and delivery of humanitarian assistance, rehabilitation, and development assistance.
- Support capacity building for self-government.
- Assist in the establishment of conditions for sustainable development.

The UNTAET mandate included the provision of governance and administration and was to include a civilian police element of up to 1,640 officers (United Nations, 1999p). The mission was to be completed by January 31, 2001 (United Nations, 1999p), but was extended by Resolution 1338 until January 31, 2002 (United Nations, 2001k).

Mission Deployment Environment

Following the announcement of the autonomy referendum results on August 30, 1999, the pro-Indonesian militias, with support from the Indonesian security forces, launched a campaign of violence, looting, and arson across the country. The Indonesian authorities did not respond effectively to the violence despite their clear commitment to the May 5, 1999, agreement. (The "Agreement between the Republic of Indonesia and the Portuguese Republic on the Question of East Timor" is available at http://www.asahi-net.or.jp/~ak4a-mtn/documents/unagreement99.html.)

Shortly after the outbreak of the violence, the Indonesian Armed Forces and the police began to withdraw from the country, eventually leaving completely. The withdrawal resulted in a large number of East Timorese being killed and in more than 500,000 people being displaced from their homes. Approximately half of the people left the country; in some cases, they left by force. As a consequence of those actions, UNAMET reestablished its headquarters in Dili on September 28, 1999, and began to restore the mission's logistical capacity and to redeploy staff members.

Actions of the Mission (Output)

The responsibility for providing civilian policing in East Timor was transferred from the INTERFET to the UNTAET in February 2000. The transfer was completed by February 28, 2000, and was conducted in four phases (United Nations, 2000a):

- Phase 1—the eastern sector (Baucau)
- Phase 2—the Oecussi sector
- Phase 3—the central sector (Dili-Same)
- Phase 4—the western sector

The UNTAET civilian police consisted of 1,485 officers (United Nations, 2001h) who were deployed in all 13 districts (United Nations, 2000a). This civilian police component included general duties and investigation capabilities, and it had a rapid reaction unit that was trained in crowd control (United Nations, 2001a).

The UNTAET police had the dual role of maintaining law and order and of training the East Timor Police Service (ETPS) (United Nations, 2001h). The UNTAET developed a selection criterion for new recruits of the ETPS and developed a basic training program that was for new recruits and that included three months at the academy and six months of field training (United Nations, 2000a). The UNTAET also mentored ETPS senior officers and developed specialized and refresher courses that were for members of management and that would enable their promotion (United Nations, 2001h).

Mission Implementation (Model)

The executive law enforcement powers of the UNTAET civilian police was unprecedented and required diplomatic command and control frameworks. The UNTAET had full responsibility for an incident, but the ETPS would assume operational command only upon transfer of the executive authority by the UN (United Nations, 2001h).

In late 2001, the role of UNTAET civilian police changed from one of providing basic patrolling and law enforcement to one of mentoring, managing, and administering the ETPS. The change in the role of UNTAET was in response to the ETPS's undeveloped infrastructure and minimum logistical and administrative capability (United Nations, 2001h).

Individual officers, specialized police units, and police districts were vetted and certified as part of the capacity development approach taken by the UNTAET. As each police district met the certification requirements, executive responsibility was transferred from the UNTAET to the ETPS. A timetable for the transfer was developed that was "based upon a survey of population distribution, crime statistics, complexity of tasks to be performed, and the level of training of East Timorese officers" (United Nations, 2002b).

The UNTAET developed recruit, refresher, and management training programs that included modules in democratic policing, ethics, human rights, and community policing (United Nations, 2001b). However, because of the lack of resources (United Nations, 2002b), the recruitment, training, and capacity building of the ETPS took much longer than anticipated (United Nations, 2002d).

The UNTAET drafted a plan to transfer responsibility for developing the ETPS from UNTAET to UNMISET (United Nations, 2002d). Four phases were included in the plan that would ensure that the ETPS would consist of approximately 1,800 officers (United Nations, 2002b) and that full executive responsibility for policing would be attained by January 2004 (United Nations, 2002d). The transfer plan also included downsizing the civilian police component of the UNMISET to 100 officers by January 2004. UNMISET was the follow-on mission to UNTAET (United Nations, 2002d).

Mission Achievements (Outcomes)

The ETPS was formally established on March 27, 2000, (United Nations, 2002d) and by early 2002 consisted of 1,453 officers, of which about 300 were female (United Nations, 2002d). The ETPS also included local officers in middle management, administration, and investigations and 126 officers at the command level (United Nations, 2002b).

The government developed a strategic vision for the ETPS that would ultimately consist of 2,600 officers, including 180 officers who had specialized training in crowd management (United Nations, 2002b) and who would also have the responsibility for border and immigration security (United Nations, 2002d).

Ways the Mission Was Evaluated

In mid-2002, the secretary-general of the UN noted that during the implementation of the mandate of UNTAET, significant progress had been made toward establishing a professional, efficient, and sustainable ETPS that operated in accordance with international standards and that the police training college was capable of providing basic training to cadets (United Nations, 2002d).

The secretary-general noted that the ETPS was on track to achieve its target number of personnel. He also noted that the ETPS would include officers who would be deployed to cover border and immigration security (United Nations, 2002d).

Conclusion

The UNTAET made progress in achieving its mandate, mainly because it heeded lessons learned from earlier missions. To ensure success, the police component was given executive authority, and disarmament, demobilization, and re-integration were implemented early in the mission. There were a number of familiar shortcomings in their performance. The mission was slow in deploying the police component and failed to prepare for the outbreak of violence following the autonomy referendum.

According to Durch (2006) and Greener (2009), much of the criticism that UNTAET received could be directly attributed to the lack of predeployment planning and mission preparation. Although the lack of planning was attributable to inadequate resources within the UN Department of Peacekeeping Operations, the UN did not prepare an appropriate concept of operations at the time and failed to identify how the police component would cooperate with other components of the mission.

The deficiency in planning was carried through to the mission itself. The mission did not develop performance benchmarks, had no clear understanding of an "end state," and did not develop a strategic plan to prepare the nation for independence (Durch, 2006).

Case Study: United Nations Mission of Support in East Timor

Background to the Mission

The mandate that was approved for the United Nations Transitional Administration in East Timor (UNTAET) covered the period from October 12, 1999, to May 20,

2002. The mission was created to support East Timor during and after the referendum for independence and to support the interim government as it established the institutions that would aid the country's independence.

The UNTAET's mandate expired on May 20, 2002, when East Timor became independent. The UN Security Council identified that East Timor required assistance in the transition of authorities and institutions from the United Nations (UN) to the interim Timor-Leste government.

Mandate of the Mission

On May 17, 2002, the UN Security Council adopted Resolution 1410, which established the United Nations Mission of Support in East Timor (UNMISET) for an initial period of 12 months beginning May 20, 2002 (United Nations, 2002l). The mission was to consist of 1,250 civilian police officers, and its mandate comprised the following three parts (United Nations, 2002l; 2010f):

1. Provide assistance to core administrative structures that are critical to the viability and political stability of East Timor.
2. Provide interim law enforcement and public security, and assist in developing a new law enforcement agency in East Timor, the East Timor Police Service (ETPS).
3. Contribute to the maintenance of the external and internal security of East Timor.

The civilian police component of the mission was to "be gradually reduced and withdrawn according to the achievement of predefined conditions" (United Nations, 2002l).

The UN Security Council tasked UNMISET to develop and complete a mandated implementation plan that comprised the following three programs (United Nations, 2002l; 2010f):

1. Stability, Democracy, and Justice
2. Public and Internal Security and Law Enforcement
3. External Security and Border Control

The second program, Public and Internal Security and Law Enforcement, had the following two objectives (United Nations, 2002l):

1. To continue providing executive policing after independence

2. To support the development of the ETPS through training, co-location, and the timely and coordinated hand-over of responsibilities

On May 19, 2003, the UN Security Council adopted Resolution 1480, which extended UNMISET's mandate for another 12 months, until May 20, 2004 (United Nations, 2003q). The UNMISET's mandate was extended again on May 14, 2004, for six months, with a view to extending the mandate for a final six months, until May 20, 2005 (United Nations, 2004ab, 2004af).

On March 28, 2003, the UN Security Council adopted Resolution 379, which specified "the composition and strength of the police component of UNMISET and the schedule for its downsizing" (United Nations, 2003d). The resolution also specified that the mission include the following specific measures (United Nations, 2003p):

- An internationally formed unit for one year
- An additional training capacity in key areas specified in the special report of the UN secretary-general
- A greater emphasis on human rights and rule-of-law
- The retention of a greater monitoring and advisory presence in districts where policing authority had been handed over to the Timor-Leste Police Service (TLPS)
- A follow-up of the recommendations outlined in the November 2002 report of the joint assessment mission on policing
- The adjustment of planning for the gradual transfer of policing authority to the TLPS

The UN Security Council on May 19, 2003, and on April 29, 2004, "decided to reduce the size of the mission and revise its tasks" (United Nations, 2010c). The UNMISET's key priority was changed to include improving the overall capabilities of the TLPS. Its mandate was extended to include the following (United Nations, 2003q; 2004c; 2004i; 2004ab):

- Support for the public administration and justice system of Timor-Leste and for justice in the area of serious crimes
- Support for developing law enforcement in Timor-Leste
- Support for the security and stability of Timor-Leste

On April 28, 2005, the UN Security Council adopted Resolution 1599 that established a "one-year follow-on special political mission in Timor-Leste, the United Nations Office in Timor-Leste (UNOTIL)," which was to remain in Timor-Leste until May 20, 2006 (United Nations, 2005ab). UNOTIL's mandate included the following (United Nations, 2005ab):

- Support for developing critical state institutions through the provision of up to 45 civilian advisers
- Support for further development of the police through the provision of up to 40 police advisers and support for developing the border patrol unit (BPU) through the provision of up to 35 additional advisers, 15 of whom may be military advisers
- Provision of training in observance of democratic governance and human rights through deploying up to 10 human rights officers

Mission Deployment Environment

Although UNTAET had achieved some of the elements in its mandate, East Timor was still a new nation with weak institutions that required international support and assistance. Following the independence of East Timor on May 20, 2002, the UN Security Council established UNMISET to provide assistance to East Timor over two years until all operational responsibilities were fully devolved to the East Timor authorities.

In May 2002, the emerging institutions and security situation were still fragile, and the TLPS was not capable of maintaining public order. The ETPS reform project was to be completed by UNMISET, which was also to contribute to the maintenance of the country's external and internal security.

Actions of the Mission (Output)

At the time of Timor-Leste's independence, the TLPS comprised 2,258 officers. Six months later in November 2002, all of those officers had completed the three-month basic training course developed by UNTAET and "were on duty, co-located with their UN counterparts at

appropriate levels of command for on-the-job training" (United Nations, 2002j).

The UNMISET civilian police mentored and monitored the TLPS by "promoting self-sufficiency and sustainability of the service [and] by assisting it to define basic policies and standard operating procedures" (United Nations, 2004c).

By November 2002, "the UN civilian police [had] handed over policing responsibilities to the TLPS in the districts of Manatuto, Aileu, Manufahi, and Ainaro" (United Nations, 2002d). The TLPS, despite its lack of resources, had kept law and order and was without major incidents in those districts. All 13 police districts were to be transferred to TLPS responsibility by January 2004 (United Nations, 2002j).

By mid-2003, the TLPS was capable of maintaining the recruit training program, implementing officer promotion recommendations, and fulfilling executive management positions. The TLPS had also developed a rapid deployment group, comprising 500 highly trained and well-equipped officers, who were capable of responding to challenges posed by armed groups (United Nations, 2003f).

UNMISET assisted the TLPS by establishing an institution-strengthening committee to develop and improve policing policy and policing administrative and legislative measures (United Nations, 2003c). The committee's objectives included the following (United Nations, 2003f):

- Improve the TLPS capacity in policy and planning.
- Improve the relationships between the TLPS and other parts of the government.
- Implement standardization of police policies and procedures.
- Develop public recognition and understanding of the role of the TLPS.
- Expand the basic training curriculum for the TLPS recruits to six months starting in January 2004.
- Increase efficiency in training implementation.
- Integrate human rights into all police training.

In February 2004, UNMISET helped the TLPS develop specialist training courses in surveillance and intelligence and in supervision and management. Those courses emphasized respect for human rights and issues of professional standards (United Nations, 2004c).

UNMISET developed an in-service training module for all border patrol officers that focused on the handling of firearms and the use of force (United Nations, 2004i). UNMISET also delivered a number of train-the-trainers courses (United Nations, 2005e). Although the BPU comprised 300 officers and was responsible for all border points in the three border districts (United Nations, 2004i), the unit had not reached the "capacity to perform professional tasks at the desired level of proficiency and competence" (United Nations, 2005e).

During 2004, the government adopted legislation including a defense act, which clarified the roles of the TLPS and the armed forces (United Nations, 2004i). In late 2004, the TLPS established a police reserve unit for community policing and specialized patrols (United Nations, 2005e).

The major initiative in late 2004 was to increase TLPS's accountability. The initiative called for trained professional ethics officers to help investigate professional ethics complaints in four of the UNMISET districts. During this period, the UNMISET civilian police began implementing its exit strategy. An increase in the number of liaison meetings with the TLPS and an increase in the transfer of policing knowledge were included in the exit strategy (United Nations, 2005e).

To help the TLPS develop its capability in logistics and infrastructure, the UNMISET completed a needs analysis in early 2005. The UNMISET civilian police also helped the TLPS administration develop a new personnel database and mentored the capacity-building unit. During this period, the capacity-building unit drafted and reviewed the standard operating procedures of the TLPS (United Nations, 2005e).

Mission Implementation (Model)

In November 2002, the United Nations Joint Assessment Mission (UNJAM) visited Timor-Leste to complete an in-country review of the progress that had been made since its independence. The UNJAM documented a road map that included strategies that would be reflected in a development plan and would be upheld by national policies of internal security and law and order. The road map noted the "strengthening of the Timor-Leste police's ca-

pability for management reforms, as a foundation for sustainable institutional development, which would receive the earliest attention" (United Nations, 2003a).

In mid-2002, the UNTAET, in agreement with the transitional government, designed a development plan that detailed the transfer of policing from the UN to the TLPS. The plan included an evaluated milestone-based approach that reduced the size of the United Nations mission over a two-year period as the transfer of responsibility for executive policing was completed. The plan also identified a number of mechanisms that would ensure that the mission's activities were coordinated with the government. The transfer of responsibility was to be completed only as individual officers were certified and districts were accredited (United Nations, 2002d).

Mobile teams of UNMISET civilian police officers reviewed the performance of individual police stations to make sure that a district or unit and its staff members met capacity and integrity standards required to certify individual officers and to accredit organizational structures. The development plan envisioned that, after transferring all police districts to the TLPS, the role of UNMISET civilian police would change from advising about training and operations to providing technical advice (United Nations, 2002d).

During the transfer period, UNMISET continued to develop the TLPS's organizational capacity and integrity and to review its organizational structure. The government endorsed this structure as well as the TLPS police commissioner, who had assumed full executive responsibility over the police (United Nations, 2002d).

At its deployment, the UNMISET civilian police component consisted of personnel from the completed UNTAET mission. During its mandate, the UNMISET personnel decreased from 1,250 in May 2002 to 134 in May 2005. This gradual decrease in staff members for the period of May 2002 to May 2005 is presented in table 16.1.

In mid-2003, the UNMISET noted that the mission needed to adjust its downsizing program. This adjustment was necessary because of the local security environment and the longer-than-expected process to reform and restructure the TLPS. By adjusting the downsizing program, the mission would maintain its operational capacity to address civil disturbances and to improve its capability to develop the Timor-Leste police's ability to

Table 16.1. UNMISET Civilian Police Staff Numbers, May 2002 to May 2005

Year	Month	Total Civilian Police Officers
2002	May	1,250
	June	1,130
	July	1,010
	September	850
	November	800
2003	January	720
	May	560
	June	500
2004	February	319
	April	302
	October	150
2005	January	140
	May	134

Source: Author (from various United Nations documents).

respond to emerging weaknesses. The gradual transfer of policing authority to Timor-Leste was "adjusted to include safeguards and arrangements for command and control" (United Nations, 2003a).

The downsizing adjustment allowed changes to be made to the mission's reform program. The mission emphasized human rights and the rule of law in police training and a "monitoring and advisory presence in districts where policing authority" had been transferred to the TLPS (United Nations, 2003f). The new approach enabled further capacity development (United Nations, 2004i); contributed to strengthening the TLPS's effectiveness, professionalism, accountability, and responsiveness; and provided a foundation for the organization to better meet the challenges that were emerging (United Nations, 2003p). Police advisers were co-located with their TLPS counterparts, which ensured a framework that would further support the development of the TLPS operational capability (United Nations, 2004i).

In mid-2004, UNMISET police advisers further enhanced the development plan, according to results of a survey of national police officers (United Nations, 2004s).

The survey identified gaps in police capacity and enabled training programs to be delivered at the district and sub-district levels. The training programs would ensure the long-term sustainability of the police. Supported by Australia, China, Malaysia, Thailand, and the United Kingdom, the programs included specialized and middle- and senior-management courses (United Nations, 2004t).

By early 2005, 1,700 TLPS officers had completed the new training program. However, only half of those officers achieved the desired level of competence. To ensure that the TLPS officers were able to reach a level of basic competency and to consolidate the acquired skills, UNMISET police advisers developed a follow-up course that focused on investigation skills and forensic science. By the end of January 2005, 300 TLPS officers completed that course (United Nations, 2005e).

Mission Achievements (Outcomes)

UNMISET gradually handed over its executive authority for security to the government of Timor-Leste during its mandate period. UNMISET concentrated on developing the capacity of police services, establishing law and order and external security, and developing the skills and knowledge of TLPS officers.

The mission helped develop the capability of operational line functions in the areas where a lack of Timorese expertise could have had a serious effect on peace and stability in the country (United Nations, 2010c).

Ways the Mission Was Evaluated

In November 2004, the secretary-general of the UN noted that "despite notable advances achieved in the last months, Timor-Leste has not yet reached the critical threshold of self-sufficiency, mainly in key areas such as public administration, law enforcement, and security" (United Nations, 2004ah). The TLPS had made progress in its development, with officers "gradually improving their skills and gaining experience in many areas of policing" through the training and mentoring provided by UNMISET police advisers, but a number of problems remained (United Nations, 2004t).

The TLPS was "capable of carrying out regular daily policing operations" but was restrained by the lack of progress on "the promulgation of the Organic Law that defines the role" of the TLPS and by "the lack of professional knowledge and expertise, administrative management capability, lack of equipment, infrastructure, and logistic support" (United Nations, 2004t).

The UNMISET police advisers had also received reports of TLPS "misconduct, including excessive use of force, assaults, negligent use of firearms, and various human rights abuses" (United Nations, 2005e). The misconduct and the TLPS's apparent lack of "critical skills and proficiency, particularly in the areas of investigations, forensics, and logistics," had contributed to their lack of accountability and the public's poor perception of those police officers (United Nations, 2005e).

Conclusion

On May 20, 2005, UNMISET successfully concluded its mandate in Timor-Leste. It was succeeded by a small political mission—UNOTIL. This mission was established by the UN Security Council to ensure that the underpinnings of a viable state were firmly in place (United Nations, 2010c).

Internally, the TLPS continued to face a lack of respect for discipline and human rights. The situation was compounded by "the fact that neither the Inspectorate nor the Professional Ethics Office [was] sufficiently resourced, and they [were] therefore not able to undertake investigations into all reported incidents of violations" (United Nations, 2004t). Operationally, the TLPS faced difficult challenges, "including a lack of professional skills and values, policing experience, necessary equipment and infrastructure, and management and co-ordination capabilities" (United Nations, 2004t).

Case Study: United Nations Integrated Mission in Timor-Leste

Background to the Mission

The United Nations Integrated Mission in Timor-Leste (UNOTIL) developed and delivered in-service training to the Timor-Leste Police Service (TLPS) and to the border patrol unit (BPU). The mission's civilian police advisers trained 2,556 Timorese police officers in general policing and management. The mission also assisted the TLPS in developing training materials, rules, guidelines and procedures, and several critical operational and training manuals for the specialized police units (United Nations, 2006i).

In early 2006, UNOTIL determined that the TLPS did not have the skills or capability in several operational areas. The two major reasons that the TLPS was not able to undertake further development were as follows (United Nations, 2006i):

1. The TLPS command and control structure had not yet been fully institutionalized.
2. There was an acute shortage of logistical resources, particularly in transportation and communication.

The government of Timor-Leste realized the challenges ahead for the TLPS and requested that the United Nations (UN), upon completion of UNOTIL's mandate, establish a special political office in Timor-Leste to assist the government to carry out free and fair elections. This proposal was agreed to by the UN Security Council; on May 21, 2006, a small, integrated UN office was established for 12 months. The office was to include a small number of police advisers who were to assist and support the leadership of the Timorese National Police (known by the Portuguese initials PNTL). UNOTIL was to assist by "planning and preparing electoral-related security arrangements, as well as in the facilitation and the provision of training and providing other resource requirements that would adequately prepare the national police to perform their roles and responsibilities during the conduct of the 2007 elections" (United Nations, 2006i).

Mandate of the Mission

Following the political, humanitarian, and security crises that broke out in Timor-Leste in April and May 2006, the UN Security Council adopted Resolution 1704 on August 25, 2006. This resolution established the United Nations Integrated Mission in Timor-Leste (UNMIT), a multidimensional peacekeeping operation. The mission was established initially for six months, with intentions to renew it for additional periods. Also, the mission was to be made up of a civilian component that included up to 1,608 police personnel and an initial component of up to 34 military liaison and staff officers (United Nations, 2006ac).

The mission's mandate was subsequently extended on February 27, 2007, for 12 months (United Nations, 2007b) and again following attacks on the president and prime minister of Timor-Leste in Dili on February 11, 2008 (United Nations, 2008p). The mandate was extended for a further 12 months on February 26, 2010, by the adoption of Resolution 1916 (United Nations, 2010r).

The UNMIT approach was to be undertaken within the framework of an executive policing mandate. The mission was to have two main roles (United Nations, 2006i):

1. In the immediate interim phase, the mission would, as requested, support the government by maintaining law and order through the provision of executive policing as may be necessary throughout the country, including areas of return of internally displaced persons, and by initiating a phased reconstitution of the PNTL.
2. The mission would advise and support the government in the reforming, restructuring, and rebuilding of its police service and the Ministry of Interior.

Specifically, the UNMIT was mandated to support the government as follows (United Nations, 2006ac):

- Consolidate stability, enhance a culture of democratic governance, and facilitate political dialogue among Timorese stakeholders in their efforts to bring about a process of national reconciliation and to foster social cohesion.
- Assist with security tasks and establish a continuous presence in three border districts alongside armed UN police officers assigned to district police stations.
- Ensure the restoration and maintenance of public security in Timor-Leste through the provision of support to the PNTL.
- Assist with further training, institutional development, and strengthening of the PNTL as well as the Ministry of Interior.
- Assist with the planning and preparation of electoral-related security arrangements that would adequately prepare the PNTL for performing its roles and responsibilities during the 2007 elections.
- Provide support to the national police and assist in conducting a comprehensive review of the role and needs of the security sector.

The Timorese government requested that the mission immediately establish a UN police force in Timor-Leste to maintain law and order in Dili and elsewhere in the country and to reestablish confidence among the people until the PNTL was reorganized and restructured to act independently and professionally (United Nations, 2006l).

During the first stage of the mission, the reform and reorganization of the PNTL took priority and proceeded simultaneously with the provision of executive policing to bring about the institution's rapid recovery. The mission's executive policing role was to adopt a community-oriented approach and to engage with the government, the civil society, and the public at large (United Nations, 2006r).

To assist with developing the operational and administrative capacity of the PNTL, UNMIT civilian police were tasked to do the following (United Nations, 2006r):

- Rationalize the PNTL's organizational structure and operational capacity, especially in communications and information systems, fleet management and maintenance, budget and finance, power supply systems, and other critical logistical functions.
- Design and implement a comprehensive vetting and certification program.
- Contribute to specialized training programs in all relevant policing thematic areas, including human rights and leadership training schemes.
- Build a strong, on-the-job mentoring program for leadership positions.
- Promote the participation of women in the PNTL, both at headquarters and in the districts.
- Develop a merit-based appointment and promotion system.
- Strengthen the PNTL's operational independence, internal accountability structures, and procedures and external oversight mechanisms.
- Establish institutional means for coordination with the defense sector.

The UNMIT was also to assist the Ministry of Interior in developing capacity in policy analysis, planning, legislative drafting, budget development, procurement, inter-ministerial relations, and public information (United Nations, 2006r).

Mission Deployment Environment

Because of a series of events culminating in a political, humanitarian, and security crisis in Timor-Leste, the UN Security Council extended the UNOTIL's mandate to August 20, 2006. The institutional failures of both the PNTL and the F-FDTL (known by the Portuguese initials for the Timor-Leste Defense Force) were at the core of this crisis. The UN Security Council noted that although progress had been made since 2002 in some areas of Timorese policing capacity, the "Ministry of the Interior had not only neglected the institutional development of [the] PNTL but had failed to build the ministry's own capacity, particularly in the areas of policy development, planning, budget development, and legislative affairs. It was also noted that they regularly interfered in policing activities at all levels, including police operations and in personnel decisions" (United Nations, 2006r).

The interference by the Ministry of Interior, combined with the PNTL's administrative and organizational weaknesses, had "seriously affected the overall effectiveness, professionalism and credibility of the national police force" (United Nations, 2006r).

As a result of the crisis, the incoming international UN forces began securing key installations in the country on May 26, 2006. From June 26 until July 9, an assessment team was deployed to identify the tasks required to be undertaken by a post-UNOTIL mission and to develop recommendations for a future UN presence (United Nations, 2010i).

Actions of the Mission (Output)

The assessment team's analysis of the crisis identified that the difficulties in both the PNTL and F-FDTL were interconnected. The analysis called for taking a holistic approach to the security sector to coordinate reform ef-

forts in the areas of policing and defense if the crisis was to be effectively overcome. To assist in this approach, the UNMIT established a security sector support unit (a) that could offer advice about security sector governance, including police and defense reform; (b) that could link activities that were related to the mission security sector with those of partners; and (c) that could facilitate international assistance in this area (United Nations, 2006r). The unit also advised on the reform and development of the Ministry of Interior, the Ministry of Defense, and the F-FDTL (United Nations, 2006r).

The deployment of UNMIT was given priority "to help restore and maintain public order, particularly in Dili, as a precondition for the achievement of the other key elements" of the mission's mandate (United Nations, 2007b). However, the mission experienced challenges from the start of its deployment. Those challenges came from within the PNTL, and the PNTL questioned "the need for UNMIT police, as the national force did not disintegrate in the districts as it did in Dili" (United Nations, 2007m). This situation resulted in a number of PNTL officers resisting the mentoring and supervision given by the UNMIT. A revised and streamlined mentoring program that focused on core policing competencies was developed by UNMIT in conjunction with the PNTL to overcome the challenges. Individual PNTL officers were certified after they were vetted and completed the new core program (United Nations, 2008j).

As the security situation stabilized, the role of the UNMIT civilian police changed from one of interim law enforcement to one that provided support to the PNTL's reforming, restructuring, and rebuilding (United Nations, 2007m). The mission's role included "monitoring and reporting from all districts, while also being available to provide advice. It offered operational support and, in extremis, assumed interim law enforcement responsibilities, when required and requested" (United Nations, 2008j). The UNMIT civilian police also undertook proactive policing patrols and implemented a number of community policing initiatives (United Nations, 2009a).

In mid-2009, the UNMIT developed and delivered training in community-based policing and assisted the PNTL in developing plans for special events such as the popular consultation anniversary celebrations. The UNMIT then implemented the transfer of primary policing responsibilities to the PNTL, and four districts were handed over by September 2009 (United Nations, 2009i).

On May 13, 2009, the UNMIT and the Timor-Leste government established a joint technical assessment team. The team developed four benchmarks to assess a PNTL station or district before the station or district could resume responsibility for delivering police services (United Nations, 2009i). The four benchmarks were as follows (United Nations, 2009i):

1. The ability of the national police to respond appropriately to the security environment in a given district
2. The final certification of at least 80 percent of eligible officers in a given district or unit to resume primary policing responsibility
3. The availability of initial operational logistical requirements involving transportation and communications
4. The stability of the institution, which includes the ability to exercise command and control and to gain community acceptance, among other things

Mission Implementation (Model)

The initial UNMIT civilian police component consisted of 1,108 officers (United Nations, 2006r). Most officers were deployed in the capital, Dili, and the remaining officers were deployed at district headquarter stations and sublevel police stations (United Nations, 2006r). Table 16.2 presents the number of UNMIT civilian police officers on staff from August 2006 to August 2009. The figures do not include police officers deployed within the formed police units.

In December 2007, the UNMIT undertook an assessment of the PNTL that included its 13 police districts, PNTL headquarters and subordinate units, and PNTL specialized units. The assessment formed the foundation to develop a plan to reform, restructure, and rebuild the PNTL. The plan would cover the PNTL's capacity-building and institutional development needs. The plan was developed in close consultation with the government and the PNTL, and it was envisioned to be implemented over five years. (United Nations, 2007b).

The major issues facing the UNMIT were officer resistance to mentoring (United Nations, 2008a) and the ca-

Table 16.2. UNMIT Civilian Police Staff Numbers, August 2006 to August 2009

Year	Month	Number of Civilian Police Officers
2006	August	1,108
2007	February	1,313
	August	1,635
2009	January	1,510
	August	1,560

Source: Author (from various United Nations documents dated 2006 to 2009).

pacity of the PNTL to absorb reform and development. Implementation of the certification training program that had been developed by the UNMIT in conjunction with the PNTL had a very low pass rate: "only 44 of the first 88 officers who underwent six-month mentoring" reached the pass rate for final certification (United Nations, 2007m).

In consultation with the government, UNMIT established a security sector reform working group. That group was to draft and to oversee implementation of the police reform plan. The plan identified the program for "the reform, restructuring, and rebuilding" of the PNTL and noted that the UNMIT "transition from executive policing to a strictly mentoring and observation role [would] be phased [in in] accordance with the registration and certification programme for the national police" (United Nations, 2007m). The transfer of executive responsibility to the PNTL was to depend on the following three factors (United Nations, 2007m; 2008j):

1. Completion of the registration and certification program for the district and unit members
2. Achievement of the benchmarks and attainment of the performance targets in the reform, restructuring, and rebuilding plan
3. Conditions of the general law-and-order situation in Timor-Leste

The police reform plan envisioned the transfer of responsibility to be at the rate of one district every two months, starting with the Dili district . However, a major weakness slowed the transfer rate. The process took longer in rural stations and districts because of the low number of UNMIT police officers deployed in those districts, especially in remote areas (United Nations, 2008j).

In mid-March 2008, an expert assessment team visited the mission. The team developed a timetable for the national police to resume policing responsibilities, which was to be implemented in three phases and based on the following five criteria (United Nations, 2008i):

- The security environment
- The staffing levels of certified officers
- The availability of initial operational logistical requirements involving transportation and communications
- The institutional stability
- The mutual respect between the F-FDTL and the PNTL

Those medium-term strategy and benchmarks would cover the following four priority areas of the UNMIT mandate (United Nations, 2008i):

1. Review and reform the security sector.
2. Strengthen the rule of law.
3. Encourage economic and social development.
4. Promote a culture of democratic governance.

Further benchmarks would be developed by UNMIT in consultation with the government "to measure whether the necessary structures, institutions, and processes [were] in place to provide a solid basis for achieving sustainable stability and prosperity in Timor-Leste" (United Nations, 2008i). This comprehensive cooperative approach was to "lay the foundation for the long-term development of the national police and so must be approached in a deliberate manner to ensure the integrity and effectiveness of the process" (United Nations, 2009a).

The UNMIT civilian police monitored and tracked the progress that the PNTL made in achieving the benchmarks. The UNMIT police remained "available to advise and provide operational support," and would reassume "interim law enforcement, if required and requested" (United Nations, 2009a). However, in early 2009, in consultation with the government, further priority benchmarks were added to the process. The new benchmarks were as follows (United Nations, 2009a):

- Provide adequate capacity, systems processes, and resources within security sector institutions for each police unit to fulfill its respective role, including human rights obligations, with clear and transparent mechanisms that would ensure civil oversight.
- Conduct a comprehensive review of the future role and needs of the security sector and develop coordinated reform plans.
- Clearly define respective roles for the various institutions of the security sector.
- Establish clear and transparent mechanisms to ensure civil oversight.
- Complete all outstanding investigations, and establish effective mechanisms to enhance the functioning and integrity of the judiciary.
- Adhere to the rule of law through respect for constitutional rights and guarantees for all citizens, and adhere to strict ethical standards.
- Improve the quality of life; increase the employment opportunities, especially in rural areas and for youth; and improve the sustainable return and reintegration of internally displaced persons.

In mid-2009, the UNMIT and the PNTL developed a system to monitor the progress of the PNTL in the districts and units where it had resumed primary policing responsibilities. The monitoring would sustain the continual reform, restructuring, and rebuilding of the force. On February 10, 2009, this monitoring was supported by the announcement of a new organic or encompassing law, which introduced significant changes in the PNTL's organizational structure (United Nations, 2009i).

Mission Achievements (Outcomes)

Since its establishment, the UNMIT has been working with the government of Timor-Leste to develop its institutions and to increase its security and stability. The mission improved the overall situation in Timor-Leste, although the security situation and the political climate remain volatile.

The mission had stabilized the country to such a level that three rounds of presidential and parliamentary elections were held in June 2007, the results of which were widely accepted by the population.

However, there have been a number of attempts to destabilize the country, including an armed attack on the president and on the prime minister. Those incidents created a challenge for the state institutions. Yet, parliament was still able to function and the attacks did not precipitate a crisis that destabilized the whole country. Since the attacks, the country has remained calm, and the mission has been able to focus on coordinating the capacity development of the PNTL.

Ways the Mission Was Evaluated

In February 2007, the secretary-general of the UN noted that the UNMIT had made substantial progress toward implementing its mandated tasks for transitional law enforcement, police reform, elections, and good offices. The mission had followed an integrated approach and had focused on the immediate challenges in priority-mandated areas (United Nations, 2007b). However, the secretary-general warned that the "ultimate success of the police reform process [would] depend on the commitment of the national police and the [g]overnment" (United Nations, 2008i).

In a later report dated October 2, 2009, the secretary-general stated that "continued incremental progress" had been achieved toward "the priority benchmarks [which had been] developed to cover the four mandated priority areas of UNMIT: review and reform of the security sector, strengthening of the rule of law, promotion of a culture of democratic governance and dialogue, and economic and social development" (United Nations, 2009i). However, the secretary-general also observed that "despite the progress made in the resumption of primary policing responsibilities by the national police, much more needs to be done" (United Nations, 2009i).

Conclusion

The use of civilian police reform within peacekeeping in Timor-Leste is an excellent case study because the UNMIT was the fifth UN mission to be deployed to the country in seven years.

UNMIT faced a number of challenges from the beginning, especially from within the PNTL. Yet the fact that there have been four earlier missions in the country raises two questions. The first is that if the earlier missions achieved their mandates, why were subsequent missions required? Moreover, did the first mission not lay a sustainable foundation for the PNTL to be able to undertake policing on its own? The second question raised is this: did subsequent missions not achieve their mandates? Perhaps something was wrong with each mandate or the mandate's implementation. Or perhaps something was wrong with the evaluation of each mission. These concerns need to be addressed.

The large number of missions to Timor-Leste, a country whose institutions and security remain fragile, begs the question of whether the approach taken was appropriate in reforming the PNTL after the country gained independence in 2002.

The mission was ongoing as of June 2010.

Part III

Analysis and Steps for the Future

Chapter 17

Analysis of the 23 Missions

Introduction

The examination of the 23 case study missions within the 14 chapters in part II has enabled further interpretation and analysis of that information. The next stage of analysis is to apply the 39-question template that was developed following the initial literature review of the information that was presented in part II.

This approach does not prescribe mission success but allows each mission's success to be measured on an individual basis, depending on its political and operational context (Druckman and Stern, 1997). The method of analysis formed a basis of comparison for identifying any differences between and among the missions.

The 39 questions are aggregated under the following five main headings that were presented in table 1.5. Those headings identify the different stages of a mission and the actions taken during a mission:

- Police Mission Planning
- The Mission
- Local Police Capacity
- Policing Approach
- Program Evaluation

This process provides a platform from which lessons may be learned, and it enables the development of a new model for police reform within intervention missions.

Police Mission Planning

The research examined 23 peacekeeping missions that included a role for civilian police within their mandate and that either commenced or finished between 1999 and 2007. The full and short title of the mission, the country of the intervention, and the start and finish date for each of the 23 missions are presented in appendix A.

Figure 17.1 and table 17.1 demonstrate that 1999 to 2007 was a busy period for the United Nations (UN) and the European Union (EU), with a number of missions commencing or finishing while others were deployed for the complete period. Figure 17.1 shows the different durations of the missions and highlights that although the research covered an 8-year period, two missions have been deployed for more than 10 years. The duration of each mission and its mandating council are presented in table 17.1.

Half the EU missions were completed within three years, with the majority finishing within six years. However, the UN missions appear to have run for a longer period, with the majority of missions taking between two and seven years to complete. From 1999 to 2007, the average length of both UN and EU police missions was 4.6 years, and the most common length was between 2.0 to 3.0 years.

Figure 17.1. Start and Finish Dates for 23 Mission Case Studies

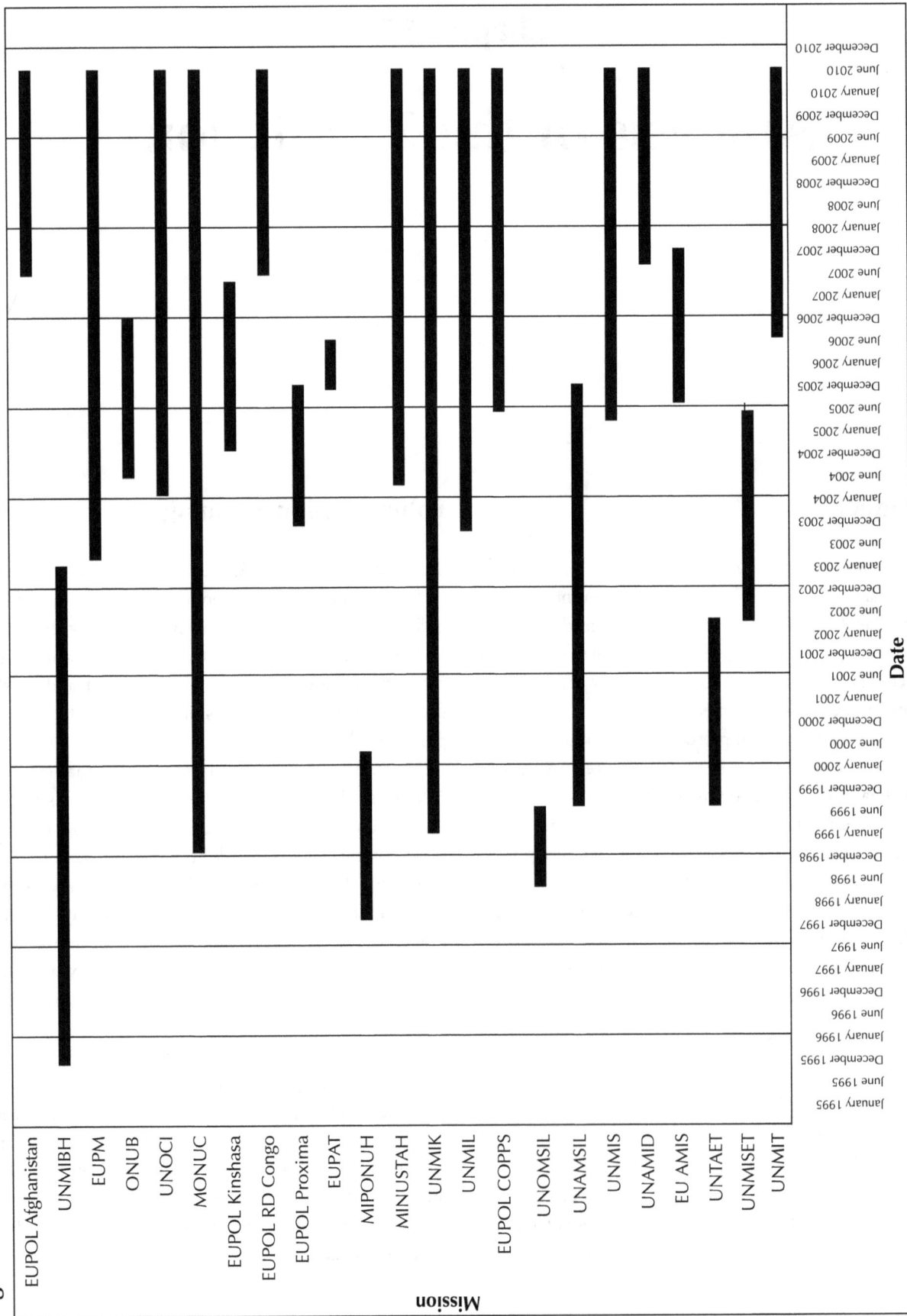

Source: Author.

Table 17.1. Duration of the Mission

Duration of Mission	Number	UN Missions	EU Missions
Less than 1 year	1	0	1
1 to 2 years	1	1	0
2 to 3 years	6	3	3
3 to 4 years	3	2	1
4 to 5 years	2	1	1
5 to 6 years	2	1	1
6 to 7 years	3	3	0
7 to 8 years	3	2	1
More than 10 years	2	2	0

Source: Author.

The mandates of the 23 missions outline five reasons that the missions were undertaken. The majority of both UN and EU missions were undertaken because of civil war or internal conflict. The mission identified in table 17.2.A as "foreign invasion" relates to EUPOL Afghanistan, and the three missions identified as "new state" all relate to Timor-Leste.

Of the 23 missions, 15 were mandated by the UN and 8 by the EU. Table 17.2.B presents an analysis of the missions by mandating council and by whether the missions were police only or were military and police. All the EU missions were police only except EU AMIS to Sudan and Darfur. The majority of the UN missions were joint military and police, with only 2 of the 15 being police only: MIPONUH and MINUSTAH in Haiti.

The function of each mission was specified within the mandate. Table 17.2.C presents the six different mission functions identified by the authorizing council. The first point is that there are a large number of UN "follow-on" missions and half the EU missions are to support and assist government or police or both. The second point is the difference in function between the UN and the EU missions. Half the functions of the EU missions were to support and assist the government and/or police, compared with only two UN missions naming this function as primary. This situation is reversed for the "reform institutions and/or police" function. Four UN missions consider this function primary, whereas only one EU mission includes this function in its mandate.

Table 17.2. Reason for, Form of, and Function of the Mission

A. Reason for the Mission

Reason	Total Missions	UN Missions	EU Missions
Civil war or internal conflict	17	10	7
Foreign invasion	1	0	1
Civil unrest	1	1	0
Weak state or coup	1	1	0
New state	3	3	0

B. Form of the Mission

Form of Mission	Number	UN Missions	EU Missions
Police only	9	2	7
Military and police	14	13	1

C. Function of the Mission

Identified Function	Total Missions	UN Missions	EU Missions
Follow-on mission	6	5	1
Support and assist government or police or both	6	2	4
Rule of law	3	2	1
Reform institutions or police or both	5	4	1
Monitor, mentor, and advise government or police or both	2	1	1
Protect civilians	1	1	0

Source: Author.

The other area that shows a clear difference between the UN and the EU missions is in their predeployment planning. As presented in table 17.3.A, predeployment planning of the mission was unable to be determined for most UN missions. This is not to say, however, that pre-

Table 17.3. Predeployment Plans

A. Police Involvement in Predeployment Planning

	Total Missions	UN Missions	EU Missions
Not indicated	14	12	2
Police were involved	9	3	6

B. Did Police Prepare a Predeployment Plan?

	Total Missions	UN Missions	EU Missions
Not indicated	12	11	1
Yes	11	4	7

Source: Author.

deployment planning was not undertaken; it just was not specified in the mandate. The three missions in which the UN did undertake predeployment planning were UNAMID, UNMIK, and UNOCI. Both UNAMID and UNMIK were multidisciplinary teams, and UNOCI was a police-only planning team. The usual practice of the EU was to state in the mandate that a predeployment planning team would be involved.

The involvement of police in the preparation or development of a predeployment plan clarifies this issue further. Table 17.3.B shows that 12 UN missions did not identify police as being involved in the predeployment planning. The number of UN missions that did not acknowledge preparing a predeployment plan decreased to 11. Four UN missions—MIPONUH, UNAMID, UNMIK, and UNMISET—prepared or developed predeployment plans. All eight EU missions except EU AMIS prepared predeployment plans.

All 23 missions included civilian police in their authorized strength. Five missions, four UN and one EU, did not state the type or form of the reform or capacity development of the local police to be undertaken. The mandates for most EU missions, in comparison to the UN missions, were specific in the type of reform to be undertaken.

Table 17.4.A shows that the UN missions were either mentoring or monitoring or were of a specific identified

Table 17.4. Reforms, Achievements, and Tasks Identified in the Mission Mandate

A. Type of Reform or Capacity Development of Local Police Specified in the Mission Mandate

Type of Reform	Total Missions	UN Missions	EU Missions
Not indicated	5	4	1
Mentoring and monitoring	6	2	4
Specific identified area(s)	7	4	3
Training and restructuring	4	4	0
Security sector reform	1	1	0

B. The Mission Principal Achievement Identified in the Mandate

Principal Achievement	Total Missions	UN Missions	EU Missions
Not indicated	1	1	0
Stabilize local situation or police	3	2	1
Implement specific agreement or plan	7	3	4
Restructure local police	3	2	1
Develop sustainable capacity of local police	3	2	1
Develop local police	4	3	1
Assist local police	2	2	0

C. The Mission Police Component Principal Task Identified in the Mandate

Principal Task	Total Missions	UN Missions	EU Missions
Institution building of local police	1	0	1
Mentor, monitor, and advise local police	2	0	2
Reform local police	10	7	3
Train local police	6	4	2
Advise or assist local police or both	4	4	0

Source: Author.

Table 17.5. Further Directions to Mission Police Component Identified in Mandate

Direction	Total Missions	UN Missions	EU Missions
Not indicated	14	10	4
Professionalize local police	2	0	2
Assist with implementing the mission	1	0	1
Focus on human rights	1	0	1
Include several specific objectives	3	3	0
Advise government or coordinate NGOs	2	2	0

Source: Author.

area. The category of specific identified area relates to an area of police reform that was designated within the mandate. Mandates generally become more specific upon renewal. As the UN undertakes new missions and as existing missions progress, the role of the police and what they are to achieve becomes more specific. Table 17.4.B demonstrates this point.

The mandates of all 23 missions indicated what the mission was to achieve, and all except UNTAET identified a primary goal to be achieved. The most common goal was the implementation of a specific agreement or plan, which is not surprising because the majority of peacekeeping missions are founded on the signing of a ceasefire or peace agreement. Those agreements are usually followed by a more specific national restructuring or development plan.

All the missions' mandates included a principal police task; however, all the identified goals were general and vague. The most common task to be achieved by the police component was to reform the local police. As shown in table 17.4.C, this achievement was the principal task for approximately half of both the UN and EU missions. Some mission mandates included a principal task, while other mandates added a second task.

To assist in the further interpretation of individual mission directives, the analysis examined the mandates of the missions to determine whether any other statements specified the mission direction or foundation. More than half the missions did not state any further direction other than the principal task. This finding was more frequent in UN missions than in EU missions.

A further five directives were included, and they have been presented in table 17.5. The EU directives differ from the UN directives in that the EU directives appear to be more strategic but more general in nature, whereas the UN directives are specific and task oriented.

Because all the principal achievements of the 23 missions related to improving or developing the local police, clarity was sought about whether the missions had strategic plans that detailed how the tasks were to be achieved. As displayed in table 17.6.A, approximately half the missions included strategic plans that had been developed by the police component. This figure was similar for both UN and EU missions.

Even if the police component had developed a strategic reform or capacity development plan in the missions, the analysis did not discount whether mission mandates included strategic aims. Table 17.6.B shows that eight missions did not identify a strategic aim: seven UN missions and one EU mission. Six of the seven UN missions had neither a strategic plan nor an aim (MINUSTAH, MIPONUH, MONUC, UNMISET, UNMIT, and UNTAET). However, one (UNAMSIL) had a strategic plan but did not have an aim.

EUPOL Afghanistan was the only EU mission that had neither an aim nor a strategic plan.

The number of missions identified as having strategic objectives decreases significantly from those identified as having a strategic plan or aim. As noted in table 17.6.C, only six missions had strategic objectives. Three missions were UN missions (UNAMID, UNMIS, and UNMIT), and three were EU missions (EUPOL COPPS, EUPOL Afghanistan, and EUPOL Kinshasa). All those missions were the last to be deployed in the 23 missions included in this research. This finding would suggest that both the UN and the EU are providing a clearer direction as to what they expect the individual mission to achieve. However, EU AMIS, which was deployed on July 20, 2007, did not state any specific strategic objectives.

Table 17.6. Strategic Plans, Aims, and Objectives of the Missions, plus Performance Measures

A. Missions in which Police Developed a Strategic Plan

	Total Missions	UN Missions	EU Missions
Not indicated	12	7	5
Yes	11	8	3

B. Strategic Aims of the Mission

Strategic Aim	Total Missions	UN Missions	EU Missions
Not indicated	8	7	1
Provide assistance and training to local police	3	2	1
Develop local police	2	1	1
Develop sustainable capacity of local police	3	1	2
Support local police	2	1	1
Follow international best practices	1	0	1
Establish rule of law	1	0	1
Provide security	1	1	0
Implement a specific agreement	1	1	0
Monitor and disarm, demobilize, and reintegrate (DDR)	1	1	0

C. Mission Mandates that Included Strategic Objectives

	Total Missions	UN Missions	EU Missions
Not indicated	17	12	5
Yes	6	3	3

D. Mission Mandates that Included Performance Measures or Framework

	Total Missions	UN Missions	EU Missions
Not indicated	19	14	5
Yes	4	3	1

Source: Author.

The issue of mission objectives is further clouded when attempting to determine whether the mission mandates included performance measures or a performance framework. Only four of the mission mandates included either performance measures or a framework; three of those missions were UN missions (MONUC, UNAMID, and UNMIT), and one was an EU mission (EUPOL COPPS). Although all four of the missions' performance measures were strategic and general in nature, none of the mandates specified how the quality of the performance measures in their individual mandates would be measured (see table 17.6.D).

Table 17.7 provides a summary of the four variables—strategic plan, strategic aim, objectives, and performance measures (see tables 17.6.A to 17.6.D)—that combine to make up the strategic framework for each of the 23 missions. Only two missions, EUPOL COPPS and UNAMID, have a comprehensive strategic framework comprising all four variables. Approximately half the 23 missions had a strategic plan or a strategic aim, and 8 had both.

The biggest deficiency in the strategic framework of missions is in setting performance measures and objectives. Only five missions included objectives in their mandate, and only four missions had performance measures.

Table 17.7. Summary of Missions' Strategic Framework

	Short Title	Strategic Plan	Strategic Aim	Objectives	Performance Measures
1.	EUPOL Afghanistan	Y	N	Y	N
2.	UNMIBH	Y	Y	N	N
3.	EUPM	Y	Y	N	N
4.	ONUB	Y	Y	N	N
5.	UNOCI	N	Y	N	N
6.	MONUC	N	N	N	Y
7.	EUPOL Kinshasa	N	Y	Y	N
8.	EUPOL RD Congo	N	Y	N	N
9.	EUPOL Proxima	N	Y	N	N
10.	EUPAT	N	Y	N	N
11.	MIPONUH	N	N	N	N
12.	MINUSTAH	N	N	N	N
13.	UNMIK	Y	Y	N	N
14.	UNMIL	Y	Y	N	N
15.	**EUPOL COPPS**	**Y**	**Y**	**Y**	**Y**
16.	UNOMSIL	Y	Y	N	N
17.	UNAMSIL	Y	N	N	N
18.	UNMIS	Y	Y	Y	N
19.	**UNAMID**	**Y**	**Y**	**Y**	**Y**
20.	EU AMIS	N	Y	N	N
21.	UNTAET	N	N	N	N
22.	UNMISET	N	N	N	N
23.	UNMIT	N	N	Y	Y

Source: Author.

All the EU missions have at least one of the variables, but 4 of the 15 UN missions did not include any of the variables in their mandates.

The Mission

One of the major debates about the involvement of civilian police in peacekeeping is the time that it takes for police to deploy. It usually takes police more time to deploy than the military. Table 17.8.A shows that more than half the 23 missions were deployed within one month of the mandate being adopted. Of the 15 UN missions, 9 are included in this category, which is surprising considering that the slowness debate centers on the UN deployment of police. Although table 17.8.A identifies the stage of police deployment, it does not pinpoint when the missions achieved their authorized strength. This issue was discussed within each individual case study in chapters 3–16.

The second point is that the mandates of six missions identified themselves as being follow-on missions. In each of the cases, the police staff rolled over from the completed mission into the new mission. This circumstance accounts for the large number of missions in which the police component deployed quickly.

Table 17.8. Stage of Police Deployment, Original Authorized Strength, and Increase in Numbers of Police Officers after Mission Mandate

A. Stage at which Police Were Deployed after Adoption of Mission Mandate

Stage of Police Deployment	Total Missions	UN Missions	EU Missions
Date not indicated	5	4	1
Within 1 month	14	9	5
Between 1 and 2 months	1	1	0
Between 2 and 3 months	2	1	1
Between 5 and 6 months	1	0	1

B. Original Authorized Strength of Civilian Police Officers

Number of Police Officers	Total Missions	UN Missions	EU Missions
Fewer than 10	1	1	0
Between 10 and 50	5	1	4
Between 50 and 100	3	2	1
Between 100 and 200	1	0	1
Between 200 and 500	2	0	2
Between 600 and 900	1	1	0
Between 1,200 and 1,400	5	5	0
Between 1,400 and 2,000	1	1	0
Between 2,000 and 2,200	1	1	0
Between 3,600 and 3,800	1	1	0
Greater than 4,500	2	2	0

C. Missions that Increased the Number of Police Officers during the Mandate

	Total Missions	UN Missions	EU Missions
Not indicated	13	7	6
Did increase the number of police deployed	10	8	2

Source: Author.

Combining the stage of police deployment and authorized strength of a mission demonstrates that both the UN and the EU are logistically and administratively efficient in getting uniforms on the ground.

Table 17.8.B presents the size of each mission. Fewer than 500 civilian police officers were included in half the missions, while approximately 45 percent of the missions comprised more than 1,200 officers. The larger missions were all deployed by the UN, the largest being UNAMID at 4,675 officers. The UN also deployed the smallest mission: UNOMSIL with five officers.

The EU deployed mainly smaller missions, although the largest, EUPM with 862 officers, is of a substantial size. The smallest EU mission was EU AMIS with 16 officers.

The complicating factor is the disconnect between the authorized strength, the actual number of police in situ, and the point when authorized strength is reached. In a number of missions, the authorized strength was never actually attained, and in others, an increase in strength was authorized and adopted before the previously authorized strength was attained or when the mandate was renewed. Table 17.8.C shows that in more than half the

Table 17.9. Classification of Police Officers' Country of Origin, plus Military's Mandated Role

A. Classification of Country where Deployed Police Officers Originated

Origin	Total Missions	UN Missions	EU Missions
Not indicated	3	1	2
Mainly developed	4	0	4
Developed and developing	14	12	2
Mainly developing	2	2	0

B. The Military's Mandated Role

Military Role	Total Missions	UN Missions	EU Missions
Not applicable	10	3	7
Provide security to mission or local population or both	5	4	1
Monitor ceasefire or peace agreement or both	4	4	0
Undertake local military reform	2	2	0
DDR	2	2	0

Source: Author.

missions, it could not be determined whether the authorized strength was increased during the mandate. The UN performed slightly better than did the EU in this regard.

The two EU missions that had increases in their authorized strength were EUPM and EUPOL Afghanistan. The eight UN missions that had increases in their authorized strength were MINUSTAH, MONUC, UNAMID, UNAMSIL, UNMIL, UNMIK, UNMIS, and UNOCI. Increases in the authorized strength of UN missions was generally due to a change in the security situation or a specific reason such as the introduction of a special training program during the time leading up to local elections. The reason for the increases in two EU missions could not be identified.

The origin of the deployed civilian police is often another point of contention within missions. Approximately half (12) the UN missions consisted of a mixture of police officers from both developed and developing nations. Four of the EU missions comprised police officers only from developed nations. Two missions contained police officers from countries that had applied to join the EU. Table 17.9.A shows that two UN missions were composed principally of police officers from developing nations.

The role of the military usually forms the major part of any mission's mandate. Usually the military provides high-level security for the mission and is tasked with enforcing the ceasefire or peace agreement. In the 23 mission case studies, 9 did not include the military, and another mission operated separately from the military. Those 10 missions are indicated as "not applicable" in table 17.9.B. That table also includes the missions in which the military would have had an influence on the mission environment or on the success or failure of the police component within the mission. In most missions, the military's role—alone or in combination with local police—was to provide security or to monitor specific political agreements.

Local Police Capacity

One of the major tasks outlined in mission mandates was the reintegration or disbanding of the existing local military and police force. Table 17.10 shows that in less than half the missions, the option of reintegration or disbanding was either not indicated or not applicable. However, in most missions where reintegration was indicated, both the local military and police were reintegrated.

Reintegration may be a policy more frequently adopted by the UN than by the EU. However, a larger number of UN missions were undertaken in Africa following civil wars, while the majority of EU missions were police-only missions that supported the local police.

To assist with the implementation of the missions' principal achievement identified in the mandate, 17 missions developed a police mission component reform, capacity development, or project plan. Table 17.11.A demonstrates that in more than half the UN missions, a reform, capacity

Table 17.10. Reintegration of Local Police and Military

Category	Total Missions	UN Missions	EU Missions
Not indicated	6	4	2
Not applicable	4	0	4
Military only were reintegrated	2	2	0
Police only were reintegrated	1	0	1
Military and police were reintegrated	8	7	1
Military and police were disbanded	2	2	0

Source: Author.

development, or project plan was developed with regard to the reorganization of the local police and that approximately half the EU missions had developed a plan.

However, only nine of these plans were developed in consultation with either the national government or the local police. In the majority of cases, it could not be determined whether any form of consultation had taken place. In both the UN and EU missions, about one-third had developed some form of specific project plan (see table 17.11.B.).

Table 17.11.C shows that approximately half the missions' police component reform, capacity development, and project plans contained a principal aim or objective. Despite the general wording of all the plans, the UN aims and objectives appear to provide more operational direction.

Although 16 missions developed some form of reform, capacity development, or project plan, only 7 of the 23 missions that were identified as having a plan included benchmarks and performance measures and implemented action plans. Only one EU mission (EUPOL COPPS), presented in table 17.11.D, included performance measures and action plans within its project plan.

Nearly all the EU missions and approximately one-third of the UN missions failed to include a time frame within their reform plan or program. However, one EU mission (EUPOL COPPS) did outline a three-year time

Table 17.11. Information about Mission Police Components

A. Mission Police Component that Developed a Reform, Capacity Development, or Project Plan

	Total Missions	UN Missions	EU Missions
Not indicated	7	3	4
Missions that developed a plan	16	12	4

B. Mission Police Component that Included Local Participation in Developing the Reform, Capacity Development, or Project Plan

	Total Missions	UN Missions	EU Missions
Not indicated	14	8	6
Yes	9	7	2

C. Principal Aim or Objective of the Mission Police Component Reform, Capacity Development, or Project Plan

Aim or Objective	Total Missions	UN Missions	EU Missions
Not indicated	13	7	6
Improve local police	4	2	2
Develop local police	3	3	0
Reform local police	2	2	0
Develop capacity of local police	1	1	0

D. Mission Police Component Reform, Capacity Development, or Project Plan that Included Performance Measures or Framework

	Total Missions	UN Missions	EU Missions
Not indicated	16	9	7
Yes	2	1	1
Benchmarks and action plans	5	5	0

Source: Author.

Table 17.12. Time Frame for Implementing the Mission Police Component Reform, Capacity Development, or Project Plan

Time Frame	Total Missions	UN Missions	EU Missions
Not indicated	14	7	7
2 years	2	2	0
3 years	1	0	1
4 years	1	1	0
5 years	2	2	0
Term not specified	1	1	0
Varied depending on phase or conditions	2	2	0

Source: Author.

frame for the implementation of its change program. Two of the UN missions (UNMIL and UNTAET) did not specify a time frame because the length of the program depended on the achievement of phases or conditions.

There did not appear to be an acceptable time to implement a police reform, capacity development, or project plan across the missions that did have a time frame. As presented in table 17.12, the time frame in missions that did specify a period varied from two to five years.

The following tables present the methods and tactics adopted by the missions to implement the transformation of the local police.

The model adopted by individual missions to reform the local police or develop capacity varied. Of the 23 missions, 18 were identified as having adopted a model to implement local police reform or capacity development. "Mentoring, monitoring, training, and advising" was the most common model adopted by the missions. Table 17.13.A shows that although this description is vague and encapsulates a number of individual aspects, it was applied operationally and was used for all levels of the local police from constable to senior executive. The two UN missions (UNMIBH and UNMIL) that adopted the "comprehensive model" had developed very specific and

Table 17.13. Change Models and Change Methods Used by Mission Police Components, plus Comprehensive Reforms

A. Model Used by the Mission Police Component in Local Police Reform or Capacity Development

Change Model	Total Missions	UN Missions	EU Missions
Not indicated	5	1	4
Mentoring, monitoring, training, and advising	9	6	3
Training and capacity development	1	0	1
At the station level	1	1	0
Training only	3	3	0
Vetting, training, and certification	2	2	0
Comprehensive model	2	2	0

B. Principal Change Management Method Used by the Mission Police Component in Implementing the Reform, Capacity Development, or Project Plan

Change Method	Total Missions	UN Missions	EU Missions
Not identified	2	0	2
Mentoring, monitoring, and training	3	2	1
Coordinated or in phases or both	8	7	1
Advice and support	2	1	1
Embedding with local police	3	1	2
Geographically based	2	2	0
Training only	3	2	1

C. Mission Police Component Reform, Capacity Development, or Project Plans that Were Part of a Comprehensive Reform of the Criminal Justice System

	Total Missions	UN Missions	EU Missions
Not indicated	17	12	5
Yes	4	3	1
No	2	0	2

Source: Author.

detailed change programs, which included the phases and benchmarks to be achieved.

Although only 16 missions developed reform, capacity development, or project plans, 21 missions described the methods through which they would undertake the transformation of the local police. Using coordinated stages or phases in which the local police officers were required to achieve a specific benchmark before moving on to the next stage was the most common method used in the change management program. Those methods are presented in table 17.13.B.

One of the major failings when developing institutional capacity was that the reform was conducted in isolation from other government agencies. Only four missions (EUPOL COPPS, UNMIBH, UNMISET, and UNMIT) included the reform of the local police within a coordinated or comprehensive reform of the total criminal justice system. The two EU missions (EUPM and EUPOL Afghanistan), indicated as "no" in table 17.13.C, specified in their respective mandates that the mission was tasked with police reform. The EUPM mission, however, noted that the mission also included the reform of the border police and the state investigation and protective agency. The EUPOL Afghanistan mandate noted that the mission would "support justice through improving the Afghan Police."

Policing Approach

To implement the mandated tasks and the change model, institutions embedded the police component in the local police in approximately half the missions. Embedding was achieved geographically by deploying officers and advisers to stations across the country and by sharing offices at different levels from constable to senior executive. The sole EU mission, EUPOL Afghanistan (shown in table 17.14.A), implemented a structure that was parallel to that used by the local police.

One method of sharing good practices and observing change within the local police is by joint patrol. As table 17.14.B demonstrates, only five of the missions undertook joint patrols, and two missions (UNMIK and EUPOL Afghanistan) specified that they would not undertake such patrols. It was not possible to uncover whether joint patrols had been undertaken in 16 of the missions. However, some missions may have undertaken those patrols, but it was not specified within the mandate or noted in the mission reports.

The mission reports cited two reasons for the introduction of new legislation to assist in reforming the indigenous police. The first was because the law of the country had depreciated to a state (a) that law did not exist anymore or (b) that corruption within government was at such a level that the country was undemocratic. The second reason for the introduction of the legislation was to enable or assist the activities of the police component of the mission.

In nearly all 23 missions, legislation was introduced because of the first reason outlined in the previous paragraph (see table 17.14.C). However, mission-enabling legislation was introduced in only five missions (EUPM, MONUC, ONUB, UNMIS, and UNMIT). In each case, enabling legislation was introduced because of (a) the lack of cooperation of local governments, (b) the absence of executive provisions, or (c) the security situation in some countries. The deployment of UNMIT to Timor-Leste as a result of the security crisis in August 2006 is one such example.

To assist in the transformation of the local police, institutions introduced Western models of policing in approximately half the missions. Table 17.14.D presents the two Western models included in the mission mandates. Most EU missions failed to use a policing model, while almost half the UN missions reported that they had introduced either community policing, civilian policing, or democratic and community policing. However, none of 11 missions defined what community policing, civilian policing, or democratic policing was; how it was to be introduced; or what it was to achieve.

It appears that the term "democratic policing" was used in earlier missions to describe the police reform approach and was combined with or replaced community policing in the more modern missions. Democratic policing was used to describe police reform in 1998 on UNOMSIL, and in 1999 on UNAMSIL, and was used together with community policing on UNMIBH (1995), UNTAET (1999), and UNMIS (2005). The remaining missions that identified a police reform or capacity development program all used the terms "community policing" or "community policing" and "civilian policing."

Table 17.14. Additional Information about Police Components

A. Missions in which Police Component Was Embedded with Local Police

	Total Missions	UN Missions	EU Missions
Not indicated	11	7	4
Yes	11	8	3
Parallel structure	1	0	1

B. Missions in which Police Component Undertook Joint Patrols with Local Police

	Total Missions	UN Missions	EU Missions
Not indicated	16	9	7
Yes	5	5	0
No	2	1	1

C. Missions that Introduced New Legislation to Assist Police Component Activities

	Total Missions	UN Missions	EU Missions
Not indicated	18	11	7
Yes	5	4	1

D. Form of Policing Model Introduced by Police Component to Implement Reform or Capacity Development Program

	Total Missions	UN Missions	EU Missions
Not indicated	12	5	7
Community policing or civilian policing or both	6	5	1
Democratic policing	2	2	0
Democratic and community policing	3	3	0

Source: Author.

Program Evaluation

To complete the performance measurement feedback loop, the analysis reviewed the mission reports to iden-

Table 17.15. Evaluation and Assessment of Missions

A. Missions that Were Evaluated or Assessed

	Total Missions	UN Missions	EU Missions
Not indicated	16	10	6
Yes	7	5	2

B. Method of Evaluating or Assessing Missions

Form of Assessment	Total Missions	UN Missions	EU Missions
Internal assessment	5	3	2
External assessment	2	2	0

Source: Author.

tify whether the missions had been evaluated or assessed and whether any objectives had been achieved (see table 17.15.A). Evaluation or assessment was identified as not having occurred in 16 missions, and of the 7 that were evaluated or assessed, 5 were UN missions (UMIBH, UNMIL, UNMIS, UNMISET, and UNMIT) and 2 were EU missions (EUPOL COPPS and EUPOL Kinshasa).

As highlighted in table 17.15.B, only seven mission evaluations or assessments were completed. Of those seven missions, only two, both of which were UN missions (UNMIS and UNMIT), were assessed by an external organization. However, both of the external reviews were undertaken by teams comprising mission members and external consultants.

Only 10 missions reported a problem with implementing the mission mandate. Of the remaining 13 missions that did not report an implementation problem, 7 were UN missions and 6 were EU missions. Only two EU missions identified a problem with implementing their mandates. EUPM was going to take longer than planned, and EUPOL Afghanistan had problems with corruption of local officials.

The most commonly identified problem with implementing the UN mission mandates was local police capacity, which is presented in table 17.16. This problem

Table 17.16. Principal Problem Identified by Police Component in Implementing Mandate

	Total Missions	UN Missions	EU Missions
Not indicated	13	7	6
Implementation taking longer than planned	2	1	1
Corruption	1	0	1
Local police capability	4	4	0
Logistics	1	1	0
Politics	2	2	0

Source: Author.

was identified in four African missions: ONUB, UNMIL, UNOCI, and UNOMSIL. All those countries suffered horrific conflicts, and most centered on the civil population and government institutions such as the police. Identifying the reason for the local police capacity being an issue in those four missions and not in the remaining 19 missions requires further in-depth research.

The final three tables present different aspects of the evaluation or assessment of the mission. The number of missions identified as achieving the specific police component of the mission is indicated in table 17.17.A. Four EU missions and only three UN missions did not report whether they had achieved their mandates. Neither the UN nor the EU missions reported that their missions had failed to achieve their mandates. Sixteen missions were found to have achieved their mandate under three different categories. Three UN and three EU missions were found to have achieved their mandate, and one each of the UN and EU missions were found to have partially achieved their mandates. Eight of the UN missions were noted as having made progress toward achieving their mandates.

Only nine missions were acknowledged by their respective councils as successful, and one of those missions was noted as only "conditionally" successful. In half the EU missions and two-thirds of the UN missions, success could not be determined from council or mission reports.

Table 17.17. Components That Achieved Mandates or Were Identified as Successful, plus Method to Determine Success

A. Mission Police Component Identified as Achieving Its Mandate

	Total Missions	UN Missions	EU Missions
Not indicated	7	3	4
Yes	6	3	3
Partially	2	1	1
Made progress	8	8	0

B. Mission Police Component Identified by United Nations or European Union as Successful

	Total Missions	UN Missions	EU Missions
Not indicated	14	10	4
Yes	8	5	3
Conditionally	1	0	1

C. Method Used to Determine Success of Mission

	Total Missions	UN Missions	EU Missions
Not indicated	10	6	4
Security Council/ European Union Council	8	5	3
Assessment team	3	2	1
Mission assessment	2	2	0

Source: Author.

Again, it was not indicated in either the UN or EU reports whether the mission was unsuccessful (see table 17.17.B).

Three methods, shown in table 17.17.C, were used to assess the success of an individual mission. The most frequent method for determining a mission's success was through the respective council. This approach would have been based on the monthly report from the mission's planning or administration team. However, in three missions, success was based on the result of an independent assessment team deployed from New York or Brus-

Table 17.18. Current Police Peacekeeping Model, 1999 to 2007

Police Mission Planning	
Model Component	**Component Requirement**
Mission duration	Short term (2 to 3 years) for majority of missions
Mission form	Combined with military
Mission function	Support or reform of local police
Predeployment plan	Not always developed or police not involved
Reform specified in mandate	Either mentoring, monitoring, or specific to the mission
Principal achievement	Implementation of a specific agreement or plan
Principal task	Reform of local police
Further direction	Not indicated
Strategic plan	Developed on some missions
Strategic aim	Usually not included, but some missions stated aim as assisting or developing local police
Strategic objective(s)	Not developed
Performance measures	Not developed
The Mission	
Deployment stage	Usually within one month of mandate's being adopted
Increased police numbers during mission	An increase of some missions' police numbers
Police officer country of origin	Usually from developed or developing countries
Military's role	Usually provide security for the mission police component
Local Police Capacity	
Local police reintegrated	A few missions
Police reform plan developed	Most missions
Local participation involved in planning	No
Aim of reform plan	Not indicated in reform plan
Reform plan performance measures	Not indicated in reform plan
Reform time frame	Usually short (less than 5 years)
Reform model	Mentoring, monitoring, training, and advising
Reform change management method	Coordinated or in phases
Police reform part of government reform	Not indicated
Policing Approach	
Embedded with local police	Most missions
Undertook joint patrols	Very few missions
Introduced new legislation	Very few missions
Police model introduced	Usually not identified; if identified, community, civilian, or democratic policing
Program Evaluation	
Method used to evaluate mission	Very few missions that were evaluated, or evaluations that were undertaken by deploying institution
Achieved mission mandate	Some missions that acknowledged success or stated simply "mandate was achieved"

Source: Author.

sels, and two missions based their success on an internal mission assessment, which, in both cases, was composed of teams including mission police advisers and independent local and international staff members.

The final area examined was mission safety, in particular, the number of civilian police officer fatalities. The UN suffered fatalities in 13 of its missions, and the remaining 2 missions (UNMIK and UNOMSIL) did not state whether they had suffered any fatalities. The EU did not state whether any of its eight missions had suffered any fatalities.

The Current Police Peacekeeping Model

The application of the 39 questions has enabled the 23 case studies to be analyzed individually by the deployment institution and in aggregate. The application of the questions has identified gaps in the information obtained from the UN and the EU missions. This approach has also highlighted trends across the missions and identified the police peacekeeping model used from 1999 to 2007, which was based on the 39 questions and is presented in table 17.18.

The model highlights a number of deficiencies in the 23 case study missions, especially with regard to the crucial areas of predeployment planning, strategic direction of the mission, performance measures, local participation in planning, and mission evaluation.

All 23 missions were based on an adopted mandate, but very few developed a strategic plan or predeployment plan that was based on the mandate. The EU was better in this regard than was the UN. This lack of planning is where the problems encountered on a mission begin, especially in deciding what direction the mission should take, how to measure performance and achievements, and when the mission is completed.

The completion of a mission strategic plan would provide the basis for mission planners and management to develop specific, measurable objectives and for the development of a local police reform plan.

Conclusion

The purpose of the 39 questions is not to determine whether an individual mission was successful or whether a mission was successful in comparison to another. The purpose of the questions was to provide a framework for developing a new civilian police peacekeeping model that incorporates the lessons learned from the 23 case studies.

This step has been completed by constructing the police peacekeeping model that was used from 1999 to 2007 and that was from the individual analysis of the 23 missions and the application of the 39-question template. The next chapter discusses the process of aggregating the lessons learned so reviewers can develop a new civilian police peacekeeping model.

Chapter 18

Identification of a New Police Peacekeeping Model

Introduction

The process for developing a model for police reform in postconflict and transitioning countries is based on the analysis of the 23 case studies of the United Nations (UN) and European Union (EU) missions that commenced or were completed between 1999 and 2007. The analysis of the lessons learned from those missions is presented in three sections: professional approach to police peacekeeping, foundation of a new police peacekeeping model, and new police peacekeeping model. The latter two sections use the five major peacekeeping mission aspects headings, which were presented in table 1.5, as those sections discuss and develop the new model.

The seven-part framework used throughout each case study in part II chapter 3 (background to the mission, mandate of the mission, mission deployment environment, actions of the mission [output], mission implementation [model], mission achievements [outcomes], and ways in which the mission was evaluated) and the five-part analysis outlined in chapter 17 (police mission planning, the mission, local police capacity, policing approach, and program evaluation) were used as the basis for developing the proposed model.

Two prominent variables from a planning perspective were found that influence the likelihood of a mission's success. The first variable is the reason that the UN or the EU became involved and established the mission. Those foundational reasons affect each mission's operations, structure, and objectives. The second variable, which is heavily influenced by the first variable, is the mandate of the mission. The mandate becomes the mission's prime planning, resourcing, and deploying document.

Although the mission mandate needs to be clear, it also needs the support of the influential powers within the UN or the EU, and it needs to be accepted by the nation receiving the intervention. "An ambiguous or incomplete mandate can indeed make a straightforward mission difficult, or a difficult mission impossible, but the clearest mandate in the world cannot make an impossible mission more feasible" (Durch, 1993, p. 26).

However, a mandate that is less than clear may have its benefits. A nonspecific mandate allows the mission some flexibility in interpreting the details of the mandate and allows flexibility in applying the operational components of the mission. An imprecise mandate can also have an advantageous political dimension by allowing states to support the mandate without endorsing specific actions taken under the mandate (Durch, 1993).

The reform of the security sector is one aspect of the mandate that needs to be clearly defined and specific because any reform of the military and security service agencies will affect the proposed reform of the local police. The reform of policing systems will be caught up in the wider discussion about providing national security, but any mission must include a time frame in which it will achieve its mandated objectives. The sustainable capacity development of the local police may take decades to achieve, and this possibility needs to be considered when identifying the roles and the domains of individual components of the security sector.

In review of the literature, a civilian police component of a peacekeeping or intervention mission has five distinct phases:

1. Stabilization of the environment
2. Re-creation of local institutions of governance (Dobbins et al., 2005)
3. Sustainable development of local institutions
4. Responsibility for the delivery of police services handed to the local police as soon as possible (Joulwan and Schoonmaker, 1998)
5. Completion and departure of the mission

From the analysis of the 23 missions in this research, it appears that the UN and the EU have been reasonably successful in achieving the first two of those distinct phases. However, in many cases, the institutions have not been successful in achieving the third phase. According to Lewis and Marks (1999), six interrelated guiding principles should be considered in reforming local police if a mission is to achieve the third phase:

1. The mission needs to focus on elements critical to democratic policing.
2. Western policing models should not be replicated merely because they work in democratic nations.
3. Postconflict police reform requires local cultural sensitivity.
4. Advanced technologies are unlikely to improve indigenous police service delivery.
5. Police are an important aspect of the political life of any society.
6. Many parties have a vested interest in local police reform, and any one of those parties could subvert any aspect of the reform.

Two final points should be highlighted in this discussion. Policy makers and academics have sought to define police reform, but there is no single, widely shared understanding of the concept (Call, 2003). The lack of definition about what police reform means creates a situation in which there is no understanding about the direction reform should take, what should be achieved, how the program is to be achieved, or how the program should be measured and evaluated. The problem with using the word "reform" in the postconflict context is that by its very nature, it presumes that whatever indigenous police organization currently exists is inadequate and requires modification (Call, 2003; Hills, 2009).

According to Call (2003), there are five philosophical modes of police reform. Those modes are based on the "differentiation between alternative perspectives" (p. 2) and form the foundation of the approach involved in the reform. The five modes are as follows (Call, 2003, pp. 2–3):

1. Human rights perspective
2. Peacekeeping or military perspective
3. Law enforcement perspective
4. Economic-development perspective
5. Democratization perspective

Although the modes can be individually defined, in practice, they are not mutually exclusive; moreover, most reform programs incorporate more than one mode.

The second major consideration in postconflict indigenous police reform is determining what type of service delivery model should be implemented. Are Western models of policing appropriate for countries that do not share similar cultural orientations (Bayley and Perito, 2010)? The problem is that even Western nations do not have many policing models from which they can draw so they can restructure the police in a postconflict nation. Such models should begin by focusing on elements critical to democratic policing (Greener, 2009). However, reformers presume that the population of a postconflict nation values Western democratic forms of policing, and as Tonry (2007) notes, any evidence of a successful introduction of Western policing models in postconflict nations is inconclusive.

The use of Western policing models in reforming indigenous postconflict police may mean that reformers need to consider the issues more deeply and possibly to reassess democratic policing priorities (Goldsmith, 2009), values, structures, and strategies. The complexity and the size of modern police reform missions can, according to Greener (2009), "mean too much focus on the material aspects of policing versus the all-important practice of policing" (p. 116). The complexity of a mission is caused by the multifaceted components within the reform program. This complexity affects not only police advisers, but also several other development agencies. The more reflective the approach to reform is, the more emphasis is placed on the skills of the mission planners and the police advisers on the ground. Police advisers must be able to adapt their experiences to the postconflict environment and must be able to consider sustainable structures that are more suitable to the context.

Professional Approach to Police Peacekeeping

The approaches that underpin current peacekeeping missions were developed in response to the lessons learned from the operations in Bosnia, Rwanda, and Somalia (Bellamy, Williams, and Griffin, 2009) and were documented in the August 2000 *Report of the Panel on United Nations Peace Operations* (the "Brahimi Report"). The report noted that the problems in the civilian policing component of peacekeeping missions were both quantitative and qualitative. For example, not enough civilian police officers were deployed, and of those deployed, most were not appropriately trained.

The Brahimi Report identified a gap between the theory and practice of peacekeeping, principally because the current peacekeeping missions were based on a series of ad hoc responses to specific problems with previous missions. The report noted that future missions should be based on robust principles, and it specifies three broad components on which future peacekeeping missions should be based (adapted from Bellamy et al., 2009, pp. 172–73):

1. Each mission "should be robust and able to move with ease between traditional peacekeeping and peace enforcement."

2. Each mission should be given the resources to achieve its mandate.

3. The purpose of a mission is to establish democratic societies.

The evolving role of missions "on the ground" has proved a challenge for the councils of the UN and the EU and is further compounded by ever more complex mandates being assigned to the police component of the missions. For example, the United Nations Mission in Bosnia and Herzegovina (UNMIBH) successfully adopted the three broad components identified in the Brahimi Report into the mission's role in providing support and direction to the International Police Task Force (IPTF). The role of the UNMIBH evolved over time to include the training of local police in addition to mentoring and monitoring. In 1998, justice reform was added to the mission (Durch, 2006).

One of the major changes that are in the mission mandates and that influence the philosophy of the civilian police approach is the inclusion of civilian police in security sector reform (SSR). This inclusion places more emphasis on personal and public security than on the usual civilian police role of community-oriented investigations and of law and order. Although the issue of the rule of law is often included in SSR, SSR pertains to the protection from and prevention of political violence (Brzoska, 2006), and its principal tenet is the creation of new security sector institutions and the disarmament, demobilization, and reintegration of indigenous armed forces and militants.

Those fundamental changes are the result of the continual evolution of missions, which means that the UN and the EU not only must plan for missions on a case-by-case basis, but also must determine the civilian policing model to be used and to assess the time and resources needed to reach the desired end state (Bailey, Maguire, and Pouliot, 2000). A more comprehensive approach should be considered because the reform of indigenous civilian police is not a short-term undertaking. Neither does one model of policing fit all postconflict situations nor is one model able to be implemented everywhere.

There has been a lack of agreement and coordination about the model of policing that should be implemented when planning the civilian police component of the mission. Both performance benchmarks that measure the implementation of the reform program and a list of skills required to achieve the implementation are also lacking. The uncoordinated approach has resulted in police officers from different countries with different operating styles attempting to develop and implement training and technical assistance programs with no strategic framework or goal to be achieved (Thomas and Spataro, 2000; Marenin, 2005).

The lack of a systematic approach to indigenous police reform creates a vacuum in the knowledge of civilian police advisers. Those advisers may be unaware of what they can achieve in their role and of what other agencies are capable of achieving in the reform program.

Foundation of a New Police Peacekeeping Model

The reform of police agencies and policing methods is a continuous process. As a result, the police need to ensure that their organizations are adaptive to the evolving environment of which they are a part. However, in the postconflict situation, civilian police may never have existed, or the indigenous police organization may have collapsed or may no longer exist.

The principal issues of police reform in transitioning and postconflict nations are the demilitarization of police organizations and the future relationships of the police with the military and security intelligence organizations. Western liberal democracies view the military and civil police as having two separate roles. The reasons for the existence of the military and of the civilian police are very different. The police commitment to service, the rule of law, and the protection of human rights will be weakened if they remain part of the military (Bayley, 1995; Bayley and Shearing, 2001; Neild, 2001; 2002). Therefore, the reform of civilian police needs to be considered separately from the reorganization and the restructuring of military and intelligence services.

Police Mission Planning

Any proposed civilian police reform program should provide the framework for the organization to function in both a managerial and administrative capacity. The reform program should also provide the capacity for adaptation and should ensure that a culture is created that values service, accountability, and integrity. To provide this framework, the proposed reform program should

be based on these five strategic principles (adapted from Marenin, 2005):

1. Understand the nature of policing.
2. Understand the local context.
3. Ensure the reform program is flexible and adaptive to the sequencing of events because reform is not linear.
4. Focus on creating and sustaining a process of change and innovation, not structures.
5. Think in both the short and long term.

The adoption of those five strategic reform principles is based on understanding the limitations of the indigenous police agency that receives the support. The reform principles rely on the consistent provision of key aspects of the reform program and on allowances being made for the fact that each reform program will be different (Thomas and Spataro, 2000). As Bailey et al. (2000) note, each peacekeeping mission is unique, and mission planners should not only describe the resources required for the mission, but also consider carefully the context in which the mission is being deployed.

The Mission

Without adequate planning and mission preparation, deployed civilian police are often functionally ineffective (Broer and Emery, 2002). The military planning process begins by stating the objective (Durch, 2006). However, as the experiences in Afghanistan and Iraq demonstrate, any plan should include provisions for peace as well as for war. This planning implies that in the case of the civilian police reform component of a peacekeeping mission, the planning for the reform program should be based on the identified end state of the indigenous police agency. This approach eliminates any ambiguity in the strategic objective and provides a backdrop for developing the phases of the program and benchmarks to be achieved.

The plan should be based on a realistic assessment of the length of the police deployment (Durch, 2006) and should include the proposed indigenous police structure, composition, and philosophy. Identifying those elements would then enable the development and design of a change management project. The implementation process will ensure the building of an effective police agency.

Local Police Capacity

Police reform is more than a technical or mechanical process. Not only does it include philosophical, change, and strategic management elements, but also it is heavily influenced by organizational culture and politics. Reform programs should not be based on piecemeal training of personnel but should be undertaken in the context of long-term sustainable development and institutional strengthening (Call, 2003).

The most fundamental requirement of police reform is that it is grounded in the local context in which it will be implemented (Marenin, 2005). The mandate of the police component of the mission needs to consider the issue of traditional mechanisms and how they affect local law enforcement (Mobekk, 2005). Any reform program will need to be event and country specific and to comprise a sequence of phases, milestones, and objectives.

According to Scheye (2002), postconflict police reform comprises three elements:

1. The individual: developing professional police officers
2. The institution: establishing an accountable, transparent, and rights-respecting law enforcement institution
3. The environment: integrating that institution within the larger justice sector

The three-element reform process and the stepped implementation of phases enable planners to reappraise and reevaluate each completed phase and to make any required adjustments to future phase methodology or resources. The reform program should include the design of a locally consulted and phased implementation strategy. This strategy will comprise a number of program-specific aspects and will include an evaluation or feedback loop.

Reformers should have an understanding of policing and law enforcement systems and of why police behave as they do. They also need to take a long-term view because an effective reform program may take longer than 10 years. The length of the reform program depends on how quickly indigenous police can be established and can display the capacity to function effectively.

According to Hills (2009), the problem with police reform is that it is not based on any underpinning theory and that the effectiveness of reformed police is assumed rather than proven. The issue is exacerbated by the use of Western reform models and principles and the fact that "there is little or no international interest in understanding the function, role, and culture of indigenous police" (Hills, 2009, p. 56). For those reasons, the performance of indigenous police is measured "in so far as it contributes to Western [rather than indigenous] notions of good policing" (Hills, 2009, p. 64).

Policing Approach

1. Community-Oriented Policing

Since the late 1990s, the preferred approach when undertaking postconflict reform is to ensure that the indigenous police agencies resemble police organizations in Western democracies. The favored police model used in postconflict reform has been a form of community-based or community-oriented policing (COP) (South Eastern and Eastern Europe Clearinghouse for the Control of Small Arms and Light Weapons, 2003). The popularity of COP is probably due to its wide use in Western nations and its adaptability to a number of contexts.

COP is also ideally suited for most transitional and postconflict states because it often very closely resembles traditional justice and historic policing approaches. Furthermore, with COP's emphasis on problem solving, partnerships, accountability, and local ownership, most indigenous police agencies understand its basic concepts.

However, there are five major current problems when depending on COP as the principal police reform model in transitioning and postconflict nations:

1. Previous initiatives for civilian police reform have concentrated on developing operational frontline staff members or senior managers, whereas COP—as with the majority of change management programs—places an emphasis on midlevel managers. As

Marenin (2005) notes, midlevel managers are the link between the top and the bottom of the organization and are crucial in implementing sustainable change.

2. There is no agreed definition of COP, which results in a number of different versions of COP being implemented within a reform program, depending on the country of origin of the officers in the mission's civilian police component.

3. COP, in the postconflict context, is based on unsubstantiated assumptions and, according to Hills (2009, p. 72), "is applied in societies where the prospects for long-term change are slim."

4. COP's relationship with the mission's wider SSR program has not been researched, and it is not currently understood if the two are compatible.

5. Because COP is a Western policing model, it is uncertain if COP is appropriate or can be implemented in a transitioning or postconflict nation.

2. Police and Security Sector Reform

At the international and national level, SSR provides a useful framework for developing and coordinating proposed reform programs. However, previous SSR initiatives have been based on rebuilding security forces rather than on understanding how those forces function in transitional and developing states (Hendrickson and Karkoszka, 2005).

If the reform of the indigenous police is to be achieved through the use of currently understood and accepted democratic models, then the police reform program should be disassociated from SSR (Holm and Eide, 2000) and from the term "security." The reform of the indigenous civilian police would then be more appropriately combined with a comprehensive reform of the justice sector (police, courts, prisons, and probation).

Program Evaluation

Researchers and policy makers may have only a perfunctory knowledge and understanding of the achievements of the civilian police in previous peacekeeping missions. This minimal understanding is because most research and literature have concentrated on the military aspect of peacekeeping, and deploying institutions have been too

slow in developing "tools for assessing the effectiveness of their policies" (Hendrickson and Karkoszka, 2005, p. 32). The result of the tardiness in developing mission assessment tools is due to political reasons and the unavailability of skills to the institutions.

Measuring civilian police reform programs or specific initiatives within a program is difficult (Dinnen, McLeod, and Peake, 2008). Previous performance measurement of civilian police reform programs appears to have been ad hoc and has depended heavily on the counting of outputs; for instance, the number of police officers trained or the number of new police stations opened. Although numerically based indicators such as the number of training courses delivered are useful for appraising the output of individual civilian police advisers, they do not evaluate the quality of the achievement and whether the delivery of the courses is achieving the strategic objectives or the specification in the mission mandate. Furthermore, such indicators do not describe the effect or the outcome of the activity (Dinnen et al., 2008).

A New Police Peacekeeping Model

Most civilian police components of the 23 missions included in this research have concentrated on training indigenous police officers to the detriment of institutional, sustainable capacity development and strengthening. The UN and the EU civilian police reform program should include training the indigenous police because it is an important element. However, the training needs to include comprehensive, culturally based, and sustainable restructuring, reorganizing, and process review elements.

This comprehensive approach will require not only skills in policing, but also skills in governance and public sector management. Because of the complexity of this police reform approach, collaboration from other skilled actors is required for success. Attempting to introduce change or reform to a police agency is difficult because such agencies are "notoriously conservative and resilient institution[s]" (Hills, 2009, p. 212) whether they are Western or indigenous. Viewing police reform in isolation from other justice sector agencies will undermine the program's effectiveness. Further skills will assist with the entrenched and resilient nature of the police culture and consequent problems of reform. As Ioannides (2007, p. 372, as quoted in Hills, 2009) notes, police reform has become a "piecemeal, incremental, administrative, and technical exercise" (p. 212).

According to Bayley and Perito (2010, p. 128), if police reform stops "at the training and equipping of indigenous security forces, [reform is] unlikely to succeed." Civilian police reform programs do not operate in an environmental vacuum but are influenced by the transitioning or postconflict nation's level of economic development and its political strength and ability. This context means that reform programs need to be more comprehensive and to include the creation of a politically and economically stable environment that will allow the program to be implemented. The establishment of such an environment that will allow for the commencement of a nation to rebuild following conflict can be achieved only by the deployment of international civilian police to fill the vacuum until the indigenous police are capable of providing the appropriate level of security.

The purpose and role of the civilian police component of the mission must be identified before commencing the police reform program. The depth of the reform program will depend on the capacity of the indigenous police and their levels of education and literacy. If local police are unable to grasp the important fundamentals of the reform within agreed time frames, the capacity development will not be sustainable and the time period of the program will need to be extended. Extending a police reform program too long creates a climate of dependency on the intervening police. Table 18.1 presents the average years of schooling that adults had in 2010 in the 13 countries that have been included in this research and highlights the challenges faced by police reformers.

Police Mission Planning

Initial planning for the civilian police component of the mission should commence before the respective institutional council approves the mandate. On approval of the mandate, the planning should commence in earnest. The plan should be comprehensive and should itemize a road map of the proposed civilian police mission and the indigenous police reform program. The plan should highlight

Table 18.1. Average Years of Schooling for Adults for Specific Countries in 2010

	Country	Years
1.	Afghanistan	1.7
2.	Bosnia and Herzegovina	<9.0
3.	Burundi	<3.0
4.	Côte d'Ivoire	<3.0
5.	Democratic Republic of the Congo	<3.0
6.	Former Yugoslav Republic of Macedonia	<9.0
7.	Haiti	2.8
8.	Kosovo	9.0
9.	Liberia	2.5
10.	Palestinian Territories	N/K
11.	Sierra Leone	2.4
12.	Sudan and Darfur	2.1
13.	Timor-Leste	<5.0

Source: Nationmaster.com, 2011.
Note: N/K = not known.

the civilian police component's proposed achievements, its aims, or its mission statement. Moreover, the plan should include the following:

- An environmental scan and the strategy for what follows after the reform program is completed
- The compilation of the matrix of three levels: (a) tactical, (b) operational and strategic or individual, and (c) institutional and environmental
- The inclusion of an implementation process and a change management methodology
- The identification of measureable phases, milestones, time frames, benchmarks, goals, and objectives
- The number of personnel required and lists of personnel skills, resources, and responsibilities
- An evaluation framework, including performance indicators, and an adaptability or refocusing strategy
- A communications strategy

A comprehensive plan will provide a strategic vision for the operation and will provide a basis for all staff

Figure 18.1. Proposed Reform Program Planning Process for the Mission's Civilian Police Component

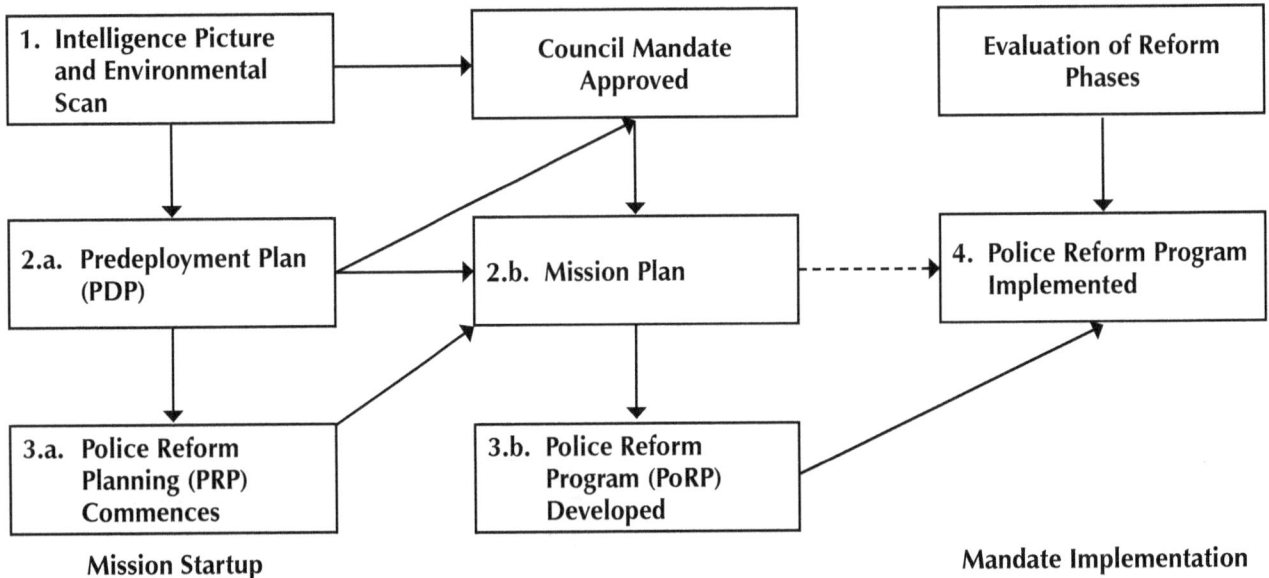

Source: Author.

members to understand the direction of the mission. The plan must be completed before the deployment of personnel because once the mission begins, there will not be time and the staff may not be inclined to undertake the required analysis. However, the final plan must be designed to be flexible in its foundation to allow for unforeseen events in the field and for the phases or projects to be run in parallel. According to Hills (2009), there is little understanding of how the different phases of a reform program relate to one another. This is one of the main reasons that mission planners and evaluators need to critically assess the short-, medium-, and long-term implications of an indigenous program of police reform.

The intelligence picture of the nation and the environmental scan are the two most important predeployment documents. Those documents form the baselines from which the mission and the reform plan are developed, and they also form the basis for determining the initial number of staff members to be deployed. The approved mandate is the third document that will influence the preparation of the mission plan. The mandate needs to

determine the political objectives and parameters and to be clear but not overly restrictive. This specificity will ensure that the likelihood of mission creep or the horizontal expansion of the mission is kept to a minimum (Smith, Holt, and Durch, 2007).

To allow for the differences in each mission, institutions should divide the comprehensive and informed planning approach into three broad stages (adapted from United Nations Peacekeeping Best Practices Section, 2008):

1. Predeployment or mission startup
2. Mandate implementation
3. Mandate completed (mission handover, withdrawal, or liquidation)

Figure 18.1 presents a comprehensive planning process for a reform program for the civilian police component of a mission. The process starts with the drafting of a predeployment plan (PDP), which is based on the intelligence from the conflict and the present situation of the country involved and from an environmental scan of the country. This predeployment plan forms the basis for developing the indigenous police reform plan (PRP). Both the PDP and the PRP form the mission plan and the specific police reform program (PoRP), which will contain comprehensive strategies, objectives, and a performance measurement framework.

This planning process will provide direction for staff members and will provide a framework to coordinate numerous components of the mission and reform program. Figure 18.1 identifies the four stages of the proposed planning process, the broad phases of the mission, and the interrelationships among phases.

The Mission

Although many of the 23 case study missions were considered to have been relatively successful, several clearly illustrate that without adequate predeployment planning and preparation, civilian police reform programs are not comprehensive and are often functionally ineffective. Furthermore, the experiences of earlier missions were repeated in the modern larger-scale missions in this research.

Some of the major problems facing missions center on the deployment of civilian police officers. Missions need to comprise experienced and well-trained officers not only in civilian policing, but also in the environment and culture of the postconflict country. The number of officers, the length of deployment, and the rotation of personnel form the basis of the planning and the design of the mission. Too few officers make it difficult to provide a secure environment and implement a reform program, and too many officers place a serious burden on mission logistics, training, administration, and management.

The provision of security by the deployed civilian police component of a mission is a core function of the peace-building effort (Bellamy et al., 2009). Two levels of security are required in a postconflict environment (Brzoska, 2006). The first level is the prevention of and protection from political violence. The second level is the delivery of security, especially with respect to governance and the rule of law. The establishment of a sense of security will enable the return to normalcy and is achieved by the local police resuming responsibility for law and order with the assistance of the mission civilian police.

Local Police Capacity

A principal issue in determining local police capacity is the decision about whether to keep the existing organization or start from scratch and establish a new organization. A common conclusion in literature (Jones, Wilson, Rathmell, and Riley, 2005; Carothers, 2006; Stromseth, Wippman, and Brooks, 2006; Call, 2007) is that dismantling the old and that creating the new police organizations seem to be more successful than attempting to establish new practices and concepts in existing organizations.

The PRP needs to take into account the capacity of the organization and the ability of the indigenous officers to absorb the proposed changes. This issue is key because a successful implementation of the reform plan requires the vertical and horizontal inclusion and integration of all stakeholders in the process (Marenin, 2005).

The approach taken needs to ensure that indigenous police members, sworn and civilian, at all levels of the organization are either trained or replaced. Programs must be developed specifically for practitioners, supervisors, midlevel managers, senior managers, and executives. Midlevel managers are important to the police reform process because they are usually the administrators and because they connect the organizational command element to street-level operational staff members. Without the support of midlevel managers, reforms are almost guaranteed to fail (Marenin, 2005).

The current midlevel managers will be the organization's future senior and executive management. By investing in training and mentoring at this level, the reform should create sustainable organizational capacity and should provide future leaders for the organization.

The Policing Approach

Most currently, active missions have cited the introduction of community or democratic policing as their major objective. It appears that those concepts have been accepted uncritically into peace operations without an analysis of their potential advantages or limitations in a postconflict context (Mobekk, 2002; Hills, 2009). Although community and democratic policing may be appropriate in the postconflict situation, it should not be used just because it is a popular concept or because it was used in the police advisers' home country.

Community-oriented policing has become the accepted approach by law enforcement in Western countries. However, its benefits and effectiveness are widely debated, and there is little agreement on its empirical definition. Furthermore, community policing can be an elusive concept, and little is known about its applicability in the context of transitioning or postconflict nations. The application of community policing has not been examined in the postconflict context (Mobekk, 2002).

The major problem with defining community policing is that every law enforcement agency has implemented a different model to suit its own specific circumstances and environment. However, it could be argued that adopting the most suitable policing approach is one of community policing's strengths, because many agreed-upon basic principles for community policing are not context specific. For example, the principle that agencies in the community policing model are decentralized and community focused is not specific to a particular context.

Nevertheless, several academics "maintain that [community policing] is not necessarily as effective or positive as claimed" (Mobekk, 2002). Research conducted in Western cities on the effectiveness of community policing in reducing crime or increasing public satisfaction is inconclusive (Bayley, 1994; Brogden, 1999; Bull, 2010; Skogan and Hartnett, 1997; Sherman et al., 1998).

The problem of conceptualizing community policing is exacerbated in the postconflict situation. For example, in the UNTAET mission to Timor-Leste in 1999, 41 different nations attempted to implement 41 different versions of community policing. Such a large number of differing definitions and forms of community policing made the strategy difficult for the mission to implement and for the indigenous police to understand.

The appropriateness of introducing the community policing concept in a postconflict nation must be considered and evaluated, rather than accepting that it is the best solution (Mobekk, 2002). Community policing may not be the best approach in some postconflict countries. Some members of the public in postconflict nations may not be comfortable with law enforcement wanting to be closer to the community. In some areas, such an approach may be interpreted as spying (Mobekk, 2002).

Current community policing or democratic policing approaches developed in Western nations may be seen as an improvement in providing service and protection to the community in postconflict states. However, the actual model must be based on and adapted to the historic and cultural parameters of the postconflict nation. If those constraints are not included in the development of the approach, the implementation of community or democratic policing in the country will be difficult, if not impossible (Bayley and Perito, 2010).

Community policing and democratic policing, in their many forms, are part of a positive system for policing local communities. However, for those approaches to be implemented in a postconflict nation, the accepted model must do the following:

- Contain an agreed definition.
- Be accepted as appropriate for the specific postconflict nation.
- Have substantial local ownership.
- Be implemented in a clearly defined project framework that comprises implementation strategies, policy structures, and phased plans.
- Include a fundamental accountability and transparency framework.
- Be included in the induction or predeployment training of the mission police advisers.
- Be part of a comprehensive law-enforcement-agency-specific and justice-sector reform program.
- Be part of an extensive public information and education campaign.

The introduction and implementation of community policing within a postconflict nation's law enforcement agency can be successful only if a comprehensive change management and reform framework is developed and instituted at the same time. This extensive structure should encompass a detailed training and mentoring program for indigenous police officers, which would form the basis of sustainable capacity development of both individuals and organizations.

The structured approach to implementing a community policing or democratic policing model can also form a part of an SSR program. An SSR program shares a number of basic principles with community policing and democratic policing. For example, both emphasize human rights, transparency, accountability, and democratic norms, and both require extensive coordinated planning, implementation, and evaluation (Bayley and Perito, 2010).

Program Evaluation

The tools to assess postconflict programs of law enforcement reform are limited, and it is often difficult to collect good social and crime data or information in transitioning and postconflict countries. However, the evaluation framework should be developed so that it assesses and measures the reform program outcomes, not just its outputs. This method will result in a more comprehensive evaluation of the reform program and will include the assessment of both qualitative and quantitative performance measures. According to Jones et al. (2005, p. xxi), one of the advantages of using outcome measures is that they "encourage experimentation by local managers." Such experimentation will ensure that the reform program can adapt to unforeseen changes while implementing the program and to any challenges that may arise.

Although Call (2007) notes that no "single yardstick" can be used to measure police reform efforts, any program evaluation framework should be developed in parallel with the initial mission planning and should be based on the mission's strategic goals, objectives, and implementation. Such a comprehensive evaluation approach will require the collection and assessment of data during each phase of implementing the reform plan and will require the creation of input, output, and outcome performance measures and benchmarks.

Regular progress evaluations and assessments of the reform program will provide information for improving practical and operational activities in the field and will provide lessons and best practices for future missions (Smith et al., 2007). The development of best practices is crucial for planning and deciding on future police reform strategies, programs, and activities. Such an adaptive and flexible evaluation should also provide a foundation for developing operational frameworks from which an assessment program for future missions can also be developed.

Summary of a New Police Peacekeeping Model

The components of a police peacekeeping model can be developed from an analysis of the case studies of the 23 missions. The proposed model will address both the practical and political problems identified in the analysis. The model contains five main sections (police mission planning, the mission, local police capacity, policing approach, and program evaluation) and 13 components. Table 18.2 presents the sections and components of the model and the requirements of each of the 13 components.

The proposed new civilian police peacekeeping model (NCPPM), presented in table 18.2, can be adapted to any future civilian police mission and reform program. The NCPPM is comprehensive and is developed to be flexible depending on the environment and situation leading to the intervention.

The NCPPM is not based on one principal policing approach but is primarily focused on the culture of the nation receiving the assistance. The comprehensiveness of the NCPPM will place specific emphasis on the intelligence build-up to the mission, the environmental scan, an enhanced mission planning process, and the implementation of a structure evaluation process.

This more robust model will require changes in the mission mandate development process and in the contents of the document. Mission mandates will need to include high-level and strategic information relating to the five main sections of the NCPPM listed in table 18.2 to enable the model to be developed and implemented.

Conclusion

The analysis in this chapter shows that one size definitely does not fit all in police reform programs in postconflict nations. To ensure successful, sustainable implementation, any indigenous police reform program needs to be based on the makeup of the state and the nature of the conflict that led to the establishment of the peacekeeping mission (Schnabel and Ehrhart, 2005).

The reform program will be affected by a number of factors outside the control of the mission. For example, local acceptance, politics, and "the absorptive capacity of

Table 18.2. Components of a New Police Peacekeeping Model

Police Mission Planning	
Model Component	**Component Requirement**
Premission planning	• Includes predeployment plan (PDP) • Is prepared "by police for police" • Is prepared in consultation with the wider mission (mission plan) and indigenous government or police • Includes concept of operations and strategic plan (vision, aim, objectives) • Includes a performance measurement framework • Considers contingencies • Includes exit plan • Provides sustainable plan
Personnel	• Proposes training requirements of civilian police advisers • Determines skills and competencies appropriate for mission
Mission mandate	• Is realistic and achievable with allocated resources • Is comprehensive but not detailed and inflexible • Provides high-level description of mission direction
The Mission	
Deployment	• Provides for timely deployment of civilian police • Determines appropriate number of civilian police for situation • Contains appropriate mix of developed- and underdeveloped-origin civil police officer advisers
Security	• Stabilizes the environment • Restores order • Engages in "reassurance" policing and patrols • Establishes rule of law
Local Police Capacity	
Training	• Occurs at all levels within the organization (recruit, officer, supervisor, middle management, and executive) • Uses appropriate, culturally based curriculum • Links with culturally based policing approach • Employs appropriately qualified police trainers
Mentoring and monitoring	• Includes qualified, embedded advisers • Contains a maximum 1:5 ratio of civilian police advisers to indigenous police • Uses advisers who are at equivalent or higher rank than indigenous officer • Is developed as part of the strategic plan with performance measures (mentoring program) • Is based on individual development plan

existing institutions will all affect the success of the pro-gramme" (Jones et al., 2005, p. 214).

Two fundamental issues are pivotal to the success of any police reform program. Further research is required to recommend ways that those issues could be included in any future peacekeeping mission or police postconflict reform program. The first fundamental issue is the development of doctrine and strategies for the police reform component of a peacekeeping mission. This doctrine would form the basis for planning for, recruiting, and deploying police officers and for measuring the success of the implementation of the program in the field.

Table 18.2. (cont.) Components of a New Police Peacekeeping Model

Policing Approach	
Model Component	**Component Requirement**
Reform program plan	• Is based on thorough evaluation of indigenous police organization • Includes detailed police reform plan (PRP) and indigenous police reform program • Is implemented in measurable, sustainable phases • Is designed to be flexible to meet unforeseen issues • Has phased implementation plan with the PRP (contains performance measures) • Incorporates a change management model • Is based on sustainable capacity development (individual and organization) • Includes strategic direction, objectives, and performance measurement framework • First Phase includes dismantling existing indigenous civilian police organization and reintegrating officers after vetting, certifying, and training • Second Phase includes developing a new civilian police organization
All-of-government	• Includes relationships and links with other government reform programs • Takes comprehensive justice sector approach including police, courts, prisons, and probation
Policing approach	• Is appropriately culturally based • Takes appropriate crime approach, e.g., Eck Problem-Solving Triangle • Could be modified Western approach, e.g., community-oriented policing
Modernization plan	• Uses phased and measured approach to technology introduction • Contains intelligence framework
Program Evaluation	
Program assessment	• Is assessed at completion of each stage • Is assessed against reform program plan and implementation plan objectives and measures • Feeds back into reform program plan • Uses a quarterly mission review to ensure that program objectives are being achieved
Program evaluation	• Involves complete independent mission and reform program evaluation

The second fundamental issue concerns the structure of the mission. Historically, except for police-only missions, both the UN and the EU have structured their missions so that the civilian police component is ranked next, and often is answerable to, the military mission commander. This structure could be interpreted as the postconflict nation still being in a state of hostility (Greener, 2009). Alternatives to this approach are (a) to have future missions led by the police as was the case in the Regional Assistance Mission to Solomon Islands or (b) to hand the mission over to civilian police at a predetermined stage. The change in the structure of the mission and the increased emphasis on policing would alter "the overall trajectory" (Greener, 2009, p. 128) of the mission and the police reform program.

Chapter 19

Conclusion and Implications

The focus of this book is to examine the role that civilian police play in the postconflict context, especially with regard to reforming indigenous police. Despite the importance of the inclusion of civilian police within postconflict peacekeeping missions, the United Nations (UN) and the European Union (EU) do not appear to appreciate or understand the basics of policing or how police operations are undertaken. The lack of understanding has been exacerbated by UN and EU member states' reluctance to commit police personnel to peacekeeping missions.

This situation has resulted in quantitative and qualitative shortfalls in the civilian police peacekeeping mission component. The shortfalls are quantitative in the customary small number of civilian police deployed to complete the comprehensive mission goals and qualitative in that those officers often do not have the skills and analytical frameworks needed to undertake the strategic components of indigenous police reform as part of the mission.

The civilian police component of a peacekeeping mission is, indeed, an important part of the international postconflict intervention. If members of the civilian police are to provide security for themselves and the public and to undertake the indigenous police reform program, they need the personnel and tools to do so. This book has developed a new model for civilian police reform by using data from an analysis of 23 UN and EU peacekeeping missions that either commenced or were completed between 1999 and 2007 and in which the principal task

of the mission's civilian police component was to reform the local police.

The examination of the 23 missions is based on three empirical questions: (a) What are the appropriate roles for civilian police in intervention or postconflict missions? (b) What are the appropriate policing service delivery and the reform or capacity development models for civilian police to use in intervention and postconflict environments? (c) What is an appropriate performance management methodology for missions dealing with civilian police postconflict? This chapter summarizes the answers to those questions as it highlights the implications of the role of civilian police in peacekeeping and as it provides assistance to decision makers and policy makers in planning and implementing future assistance missions.

The 23 missions were analyzed using the seven headings outlined in the introductory chapter. The seven headings provided a framework to elicit and summarize the information gathered from each individual case study, and they formed the basis for developing the 39-question template referred to in chapter 17. A model was developed by examining the concepts of the 23 missions and the answers to the 39-question template and by reviewing the identified components of the mission. This process enabled a new model for civilian police reform to be proposed in chapter 18.

The proposed new civilian police peacekeeping model (NCPPM) is a dynamic, flexible police reform framework that takes into account the culture of the nation being assisted. The NCPPM relies heavily on a gathering of intelligence before the mission, an environmental scan of the country, and an enhanced mission planning process. According to Call (2008, p. 380), interveners that overemphasize state capacity over state design tend to implement reform programs that consist of training and advising. Such a tendency enhances the "human and material capacity of state ministries and agencies" while taking "for granted the prevailing design of state institutions." Accepting the existing functions of an indigenous civilian police organization will "diminish the chances of a culturally or socially ill-fitting model" (Call, 2008, p. 380) that is being promoted by reformers. The proposed model will reduce the tendency of both academics and practitioners to approach police reform as a technical exercise devoid of local history, culture, and political risk.

The analyses of the case studies suggest three findings regarding indigenous civilian police reform. First, the comprehensiveness of an approach that may be adopted in reform programs will be constrained by historical precedent. Second, indigenous political leaders control the design and the implementation of the reform program. Third, the reform process is as important as the program outcomes and achievements.

The case studies provide vivid presentations of lost opportunities and examples of different reform approaches that did not establish sustainable development of the indigenous police. Three main conclusions stand out from the research and serve to organize this chapter:

1. The reform of indigenous police is not simply a matter of implementing Western policing models or training officers in Western police practices. Efforts to consolidate Western policing practices in postconflict societies—no matter how well intentioned—can be harmful in a number of ways, especially if the local culture is not taken into consideration.

2. Legitimate indigenous civilian police remain crucial for the sustainability of security.

3. Reestablishing indigenous civilian police organizations is a deeply political process that creates winners and losers (Call, 2008). This conclusion has implica-

tions for two aspects of police reform: (a) assisting indigenous police when implementing democratic procedures and (b) ensuring organizational capacity.

Those three conclusions frame the main challenges in managing the complex process of establishing sustainable security and in rebuilding local police organizations.

One of the most lasting impressions left by the research of the case studies is that the efforts to reform indigenous police are fraught with problems that leave local organizations weak and vulnerable to collapse and corruption. The reformation of indigenous police organizations that have followed conflicts has been disappointing on all levels (Dobbins et al., 2005; Hills, 2009; Jett, 1999; Stromseth, Wippman, and Brooks, 2006). The result has been caused not by a lack of effort by all involved, but because the reform program has been generally "based on simplistic assumptions about the relationship between formal legal institutions and durable cultural change" (Stromseth et al., 2006, p. 369). As highlighted throughout this book, both the UN and the EU have tended to ignore the fundamentals of accepted practices of police reform (e.g., consultation and the inclusion of a strategic vision). As a result, many postconflict programs of civilian police reform have concentrated primarily on training police and on refurbishing or opening new police stations. Concentrating on those forms of technical assistance cannot alone produce police reform (Stromseth et al., 2006).

Analysis of the 23 missions uncovered a number of shortcomings with premission planning, program management, performance measurement, and mission evaluation. There was no definition of success or failure in any of the documentation of the 23 missions nor did the documentation determine how success or failure would be measured. Some authors suggest that the measure of success or failure of a mission should be described in the mission mandate (Diehl, 1993; Jones, Wilson, Rathmell, and Riley, 2005), but it would be impossible to evaluate the 23 case study missions included in this book on that basis because no performance frameworks or measures that could be used to assess the missions were outlined in any of the documentation. Furthermore, relying on the fulfillment of a mission mandate disregards the principal purpose of a peacekeeping mission and limits the comparison of such missions. Those shortcomings differ from Jett's observations that "[t]he success or failure of a peacekeeping operation can be preordained even before the arrival of the blue helmets on the scene of the conflict" (Jett, 1999).

The question of preordained success or failure hinges on two factors: (a) the intervening institution's capability and procedures and (b) the basis and reasons for the conflict. An intervening institution can quickly become bound by bureaucratic process and procedures and by a lack of technical capability. Most missions are understaffed and are usually sized and deployed on the basis of weak intelligence, best case assumptions, and insignificant planning. The quality of police personnel is often uneven and of mixed competence, and those personnel are usually totally reliant on the practices of their home country.

The first step to improve the situation is to acknowledge that the current approach used to reform civilian police in postconflict nations is not reaching its full potential: a new approach to civilian police reform is needed. This research has enabled a new, comprehensive, strategic, and culturally based model to be developed. A broader approach should be taken when planning and developing the missions' implementation framework and the performance measurement processes. Operational, political, cultural, and environmental issues—which are critical to the success of narrower, more focused reforms—should be taken into account (Stromseth et al., 2006).

Measuring an individual mission's success or failure is problematic because of the multiplicity of the conditions and challenges on the ground that both mission planners and practitioners face. The very diversity and ad hoc nature of police missions increases the difficulty in implementing programs of indigenous police reform (Hills, 2009). For example, the requirements and needs of the indigenous police reform program in Afghanistan are similar in some ways but different in other ways from those identified in Timor-Leste. This problem is exacerbated by the vagueness of mission mandates and by the multiple goals of modern, multidimensional peacekeeping missions.

According to Gunnar Billinger (2002, p. 498), mandates "are political compromises which are often of a general nature" and are designed to cover situations that are difficult to predict. Gunner Billinger also notes that most mandates are designed principally for the military component of a peace mission. The vagueness and military-oriented design of mission mandates create a vacuum for the civilian police component of a peacekeeping mission and raise the question of whether the current mandate development process should be redesigned to specifically include the civilian police component.

However, mission mandates are strategic, high-level documents, and it is appropriate that they provide direction rather than individual, mission-component performance goals, objectives, and targets. The current approach enables mandates to be compared rather than the missions per se, but the mandates need to be expanded to include the vision and the direction required to enable the police component to undertake and complete its mission.

The current mission adoption frameworks of the UN and EU councils allow a mission to specify the tasks and the guidelines for the civilian police as long as they are within the mandate. This research accepts that the current approach is appropriate but recommends that a set procedure and process for developing predeployment, operational, and reform plans and performance measures are implemented.

One option to strengthen the current mandate and civilian police deployment process is to develop a specific planning process for the police component of the mission. Figure 19.1, which is a limited version of figure 18.1, presents a proposed planning process for the civilian police component of the mission program. This proposed process would ensure that a comprehensive picture of the environment and the issues facing police in the postconflict nation are obtained and that this information informs the mission mandate, the predeployment plan, and the mission plan. Such an approach will make police planners aware of the objectives when developing a mission and will ensure that the appropriate technical skills and resources are identified to design a phased measurable reform program. Both Timor-Leste (UNTAET and UNMISET) and Bosnia and Herzegovina (UNMIBH) illustrate the dangers of launching civilian police reform programs without sufficient planning and strategic direction.

The proposed planning process would also provide a framework for the development of guidelines or doctrine when police reform is undertaken in postconflict situations and would minimize the recurring problems that are created by international intervention and that were

Figure 19.1. Proposed Planning Process for the Civilian Police Component of the Mission Program

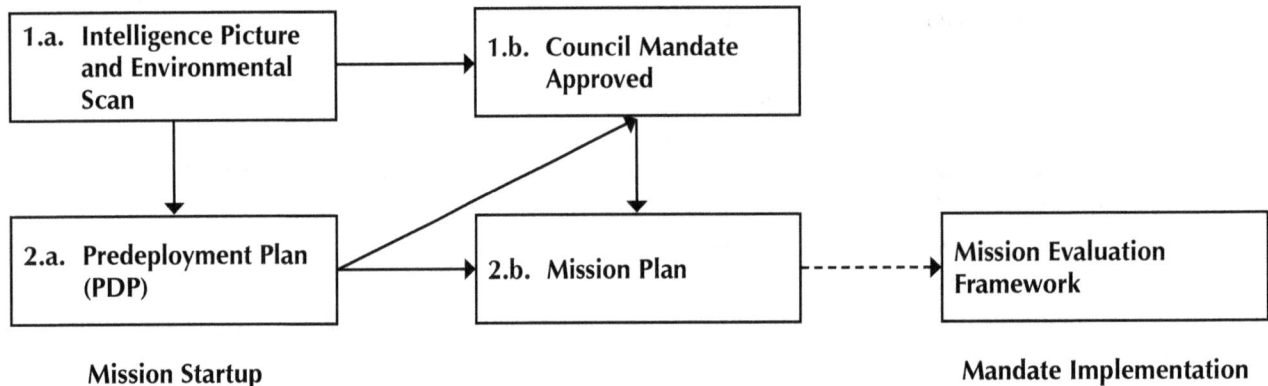

Mission Startup   Mandate Implementation

Source: Author.

uncovered in the 23 case studies. The recurring problems (adapted from Call, 2008, p. 375–76) include these:

- Intervening civilian police mission components ignore or dismiss the preexisting indigenous police organization's authority, prior achievements, and capability.
- Those components do not prioritize elements of the reform program.
- They do not appreciate that transitional or short-term measures have negative side effects.
- They do not recognize that intervention and assistance missions can leave the indigenous police organization weak.

This book has sought to critically examine the role of civilian police in peacekeeping and the police's approach to reforming indigenous police organizations. Past scholarship about peacekeeping has tended to ignore members of the civilian police and their capability within missions. Moreover, where scholarship has mentioned members of the civilian police, the complexity and difficulty of their role has been understated.

The findings of this book do not offer any straightforward answers to the challenges of reforming indigenous civilian police organizations in postconflict nations. However, deploying institutions and academics need to accept that the emphasis of peacekeeping missions has changed and that the profile and the role of civilian police need to increase to a military equivalent.

The proposed model developed by this research is one step in that direction. Although each mission is a response to a different situation in a cultural, political, and practical sense, the new model for civilian police reform takes this condition into account and offers a flexible and generic framework that appears to be applicable to a wide variety of postconflict situations. The new model also allows both institutions and practitioners to think about police reform more holistically and is one aspect in providing a foundation for the sustainable capacity development of the postconflict nation.

Appendix A

List of 23 Case Study Missions, Short Title, Country of Intervention, and Start and Finish Dates

	Mission Full Title	Short Title	Country	Mission Dates*
1	European Union Police Mission to Afghanistan	EUPOL Afghanistan	Afghanistan	30/05/07 to present
2	United Nations Mission in Bosnia and Herzegovina	UNMIBH	Bosnia and Herzegovina	21/12/95 to 31/12/02
3	European Union Police Mission to Bosnia and Herzegovina	EUPM	Bosnia and Herzegovina	01/01/03 to present
4	United Nations Operation in Burundi	ONUB	Burundi	21/05/04 to 31/12/06
5	United Nations Operation in Côte d'Ivoire	UNOCI	Cote d'Ivoire	27/02/04 to present
6	United Nations Mission in the Democratic Republic of the Congo	MONUC	Democratic Republic of the Congo	24/02/99 to 30/06/10
7	European Union Police Mission in Kinshasa	EUPOL Kinshasa	Democratic Republic of the Congo	09/12/04 to 30/06/07
8	European Union Police Mission in the Democratic Republic of the Congo	EUPOL RD Congo	Democratic Republic of the Congo	12/06/07 to present
9	European Union Police Mission to the Former Yugoslav Republic of Macedonia	EUPOL Proxima	Former Yugoslav Republic of Macedonia (FYROM)	29/09/03 to 14/12/05
10	European Union Police Advisory Team in the Former Yugoslav Republic of Macedonia	EUPAT	Former Yugoslav Republic of Macedonia (FYROM)	24/11/05 to 14/06/06
11	United Nations Police Mission in Haiti	MIPONUH	Haiti	20/11/97 to 15/03/00
12	United Nations Stabilization Mission in Haiti	MINUSTAH	Haiti	30/04/04 to present

	Mission Full Title	Short Title	Country	Mission Dates*
13	United Nations Interim Administration Mission in Kosovo	UNMIK	Kosovo	10/06/99 to present
14	United Nations Mission in Liberia	UNMIL	Liberia	19/09/03 to present
15	European Union Police Co-ordinating Office for Palestinian Police Support	EUPOL COPPS	Palestinian Territories	18/06/05 to present
16	United Nations Observers Mission in Sierra Leone	UNOMSIL	Sierra Leone	13/07/98 to 22/10/99
17	United Nations Mission in Sierra Leone	UNAMSIL	Sierra Leone	22/10/99 to 31/12/05
18	United Nations Mission in Sudan	UNMIS	Sudan	24/03/05 to present
19	United Nations and African Union Mission in Darfur	UNAMID	Sudan	31/07/07 to present
20	European Union Support to the African Union Mission to Sudan and Darfur	EU AMIS	Sudan	20/07/05 to 31/12/07
21	United Nations Mission of Support in East Timor	UNMISET	Timor-Leste	20/05/02 to 20/05/05
22	United Nations Office in Timor-Leste	UNOTIL	Timor-Leste	20/05/05 to 20/08/06
23	United Nations Mission in Timor-Leste	UNMIT	Timor-Leste	25/08/06 to present

Present = As of 15 June 2010.

References

African Press Organization. (2009, April 27). *Security situation in Darfur* (Darfur/UNAMID Daily Media Brief). Retrieved from http://appablog.wordpress.com/2009/04/27/darfur-unamid-daily-media-brief-22.

Appiah-Mensah, S. (2006). The African mission in Sudan: Darfur dilemmas. *African Security Review, 15*(1), 2–19.

Ashdown, J. J. D. (2003, January 15). *HR/EUSR speech at the EUPM inaugural ceremony.* Office of the High Representative, European Union Police Mission Headquarters, Sarajevo, Bosnia and Herzegovina.

AusAID. (2004). *Capacity development: Principles and practices.* Canberra, Australia: Australian Government.

Bailey, M., Maguire, R., and Pouliot, J. O. G. (2000). Haiti: Military-police partnership for public security. In R. Oakley, M. Dziedzic, and E. Goldberg (Eds.), *Policing the new world disorder: Peace operations and public security* (pp. 215–252). Washington, DC: National Defense University Press.

Bajraktari, Y., Boutellis, A., Gunja, F., Harris, D., Kapsis, J., Kaye, E., and Rhee, J. (2006). *The PRIME system: Measuring the success of post-conflict police reform.* New York, NY: United Nations.

Bayley, D. (1985). *Patterns of policing.* New Brunswick, NJ: Rutgers University Press.

Bayley, D. (1994). *Police for the future.* Oxford, U.K.: Oxford University Press.

Bayley, D. (1995). A foreign policy for democratic policing. *Policing and society, 5*(2), 79–94.

Bayley, D. (2006). *Changing the guard: Developing democratic police abroad.* New York, NY: Oxford University Press.

Bayley, D., and Perito, R. (2010). *The police in war: Fighting, insurgency, terrorism, and violent crime.* Boulder, CO: Lynne Rienner.

Bayley, D., and Shearing, C. (2001). *The new structure of policing.* Washington, DC: National Institute of Justice.

BBC News. (1999, November 10) World: Europe; UN gives figure for Kosovo dead. Retrieved from http://news.bbc.co.uk/2/hi/europe/514828.stm.

Behrens, M. (2006). *Midterm-review of the EU joint action supporting the African Union mission in Sudan.* Retrieved from http://martinbehrens.pbworks.com/f/EU+Joint+Action+Supporting+AMIS+II+-+Mid-term+review%E2%80%A6.pdf.

Bellamy, A., Williams, P., and Griffin, S. (2009). *Understanding peacekeeping.* Malden, MA: Polity Press.

Botes, J., and Mitchell, C. (1995). Constraints on third party flexibility. *Annals of the American Academy of Political and Social Science, 542,* 168–184.

Brahimi Report. (2000). *Report of the Panel on United Nations Peace Operations.* Retrieved from http://www.un.org/peace/reports/peace_operations/.

Bratt, D. (1996). Assessing the success of UN peacekeeping operations. *International Peacekeeping, 3*(4), 64–81.

Broer, H., and Emery, M. (2002). Civilian police in UN peacekeeping operations. In R. Oakley, M. Dziedzic, and E. Goldberg (Eds.), *Policing the new world disorder: Peace operations and public security* (pp. 365–398). Washington, DC: National Defense University Press.

Brogden, M. (1999). Community policing as cherry pie. In R. Mawby (Ed.), *Policing across the world: Issues for the twenty-first century.* London, U.K.: UCL Press.

Bruno, L. (2007, July 25). *Formed police unit tasks: INPROL consolidated response* (07-006). Retrieved from http://inprol.org/sites/default/files/publications/2011/cr07006.pdf.

Brzoska, M. (2006). Introduction: Criteria for evaluating post-conflict reconstruction and security sector reform in peace support operations. *International Peacekeeping, 13*(1), 1–13.

Bull, M. (2010). Working with others to build cooperation, confidence, and trust. *Policing, 4*(3), 282–290.

Call, C. (1999). *From soldiers to cops: War transitions and the demilitarization of policing in Latin America and the Caribbean* (Doctoral dissertation). Stanford University, Stanford, CA.

Call, C. (2003). *Challenges in police reform: Promoting effectiveness and accountability.* New York, NY: International Peace Academy.

Call, C. (2007). *Constructing justice and security after war.* Washington, DC: United States Institute of Peace.

Call, C. (2008). *Building states to build peace.* Boulder, CO: Lynne Rienner.

Canadian International Development Agency. (2000). *Capacity development: Occasional series.* Gatineau, QB: Canadian International Development Agency.

Carothers, T. (2006). *Promoting the rule of law abroad: In search for knowledge.* Washington, DC: Carnegie Endowment for International Peace.

Chesterman, S. (2004). *You, the people: The United Nations, transitional administrations, and state-building.* Oxford, U.K.: Oxford University Press.

Common Security and Defence Policy European Union. (2010, February). *EU police mission in Afghanistan* (Communication Afghanistan/17). Brussels, Belgium: Author.

Council of the European Union. (2002). *Council Joint Action 210* (CJA 2002/210/CFSP). Brussels, Belgium: Author.

Council of the European Union. (2003). *Council Joint Action 681* (CJA 2003/681/CFSP). Brussels, Belgium: Author.

Council of the European Union. (2004a). *Council Joint Action 789* (CJA 2004/789/CFSP). Brussels, Belgium: Author.

Council of the European Union. (2004b). *Council Joint Action 847* (CJA 2004/847/CFSP). Brussels, Belgium: Author.

Council of the European Union. (2005a, November 14). *Council establishes EU police mission in the Palestinian territories* (14402/05, Presse 295). Brussels, Belgium: Author.

Council of the European Union. (2005b). *Council Joint Action 556* (CJA 2005/556/CFSP). Brussels, Belgium: Author.

Council of the European Union. (2005c). *Council Joint Action 557* (CJA 2005/557/CFSP). Brussels, Belgium: Author.

Council of the European Union. (2005d). *Council Joint Action 797* (CJA 2005/797/CFSP). Brussels, Belgium: Author.

Council of the European Union. (2005e). *Council Joint Action 824* (CJA 2005/824/CFSP). Brussels, Belgium: Author.

Council of the European Union. (2005f). *Council Joint Action 826* (CJA 2005/826/CFSP). Brussels, Belgium: Author.

Council of the European Union. (2006a, December 8). *Council extends the mandate of the EU police mission in Kinshasa (EUPOL Kinshasa)* (16525/06, Presse 358), Brussels, Belgium: Author.

Council of the European Union. (2006b). *Council Joint Action 913* (CJA 2006/913/CFSP). Brussels, Belgium: Author.

Council of the European Union. (2006c, October 17). *2755th General Affairs Council meeting.* Luxembourg City, Luxembourg: Author.

Council of the European Union. (2007a, December 10). *Council conclusions on Afghanistan: 2839th General Affairs Council meeting.* Brussels, Belgium: Author.

Council of the European Union. (2007b). *Council Joint Action 369* (CJA 2007/369/CFSP). Brussels, Belgium: Author.

Council of the European Union. (2007c). *Council Joint Action 405* (CJA 2007/405/CFSP). Brussels, Belgium: Author.

Council of the European Union. (2007d). *Council Joint Action 749* (CJA 2007/749/CFSP). Brussels, Belgium: Author.

Council of the European Union. (2007e, June 15). *EU police mission in Afghanistan starts* (10939/07, Presse 140). Brussels, Belgium: Author.

Council of the European Union. (2008a, May 26). *Council conclusions on Afghanistan: 2870th External Relations Council Meeting.* Brussels, Belgium: Author.

Council of the European Union. (2008b). *Council Joint Action 485* (CJA 2008/485/CFSP). Brussels, Belgium: Author.

Council of the European Union. (2008c). *Council Joint Action 958* (CJA 2008/958/CFSP). Brussels, Belgium: Author.

Council of the European Union. (2009a). *Council Joint Action 769* (CJA 2007/769/CFSP). Brussels, Belgium: Author.

Council of the European Union. (2009b). *EU Police Mission in Afghanistan* (S086/09). The Hague, Netherlands: Author.

Council of European Union. (2009c, November 17). *Extract from council conclusions on ESDP, Brussels* (Press Release). Retrieved from http://www.consilium.europa.eu/eeas/security-defence/eu-operations/completed-eu-operations/eupm/press-releases?lang=en.

Council of the European Union. (2009d, October 27). *Strengthening EU action in Afghanistan and Pakistan: 2971st External Council Meeting.* Luxembourg City, Luxembourg: Author.

Department of Peacekeeping Operations. (2010). *Formed police units in United Nations peacekeeping operations* (Reference 2009.32). New York, NY: United Nations.

Diehl, P. (1993). *International peacekeeping*. Baltimore, MD: John Hopkins University Press.

Dinnen, S., McLeod, A., and Peake, G. (2008). Police-building in weak states: Australian approaches in Papua New Guinea and Solomon Islands. In G. Peak, E. Scheye, and A. Hills (Eds.), *Managing insecurity: Field experiences of security sector reform* (pp. 1–22). New York, NY: Routledge.

Dobbins, J., Jones, S., Crane, K., Rathmell, A., Steele, B., Teltschik, R., and Timilsin, A. (2005). *The UN's role in nation building: From the Congo to Iraq*. Santa Monica: RAND.

Druckman, D., and Stern, P. (1997). Evaluating peacekeeping missions. *Mershon International Studies Review, 41*(1), pp. 151–165.

Durch, W. (1993). *The evolution of UN peacekeeping: Case studies and comparative analysis*. London, U.K.: Macmillan.

Durch, W. (2006). *Twenty-first-century peace operations*. Washington, DC: United States Institute of Peace.

Durch, W. J., Holt, V. K., Earle, C. R., and Shanahan, M. K. (2003). *The Brahimi report and the future of UN peace operations*. Washington, DC: Henry L. Stimson Center.

Dwan, R. (Ed.). (2002). *Executive policing: Enforcing the law in peace operations* (Stockholm International Peace Research Institute Research Report 16). Oxford, U.K.: Oxford University Press.

Eck, J. (2006). When is a bologna sandwich better than sex? A defense of small-n case study evaluations. *Journal of Experimental Criminology, 2*(3), 345–362.

European Mission in Afghanistan. (2008). "EUPOL Head of Mission Completes His Tour of Duty." Press release of April 2008 to be published on September 25, 2008. Kabul: EUPOL Press and Public Information Office.

European Union. (2002, February 18). *Minutes to the 2409th council meeting*. Brussels, Belgium: General Affairs.

European Union. (2009a, September). *EU police mission for the DRC (EUPOL RD Congo)* (European Security and Defence Policy RDC/06). Brussels, Belgium: Author.

European Union. (2009b, March). *EU police mission for the Palestinian territories* (European Security and Defence Policy COPPS/12). Brussels, Belgium: Author.

European Union. (2010a, January). *EU police mission for the Palestinian territories.* (European Security and Defence Policy COPPS/15). Brussels, Belgium: Author.

European Union. (2010b, March). *European Police Mission in Bosnia and Herzegovina* (EUPM) (Common Security and Defence Policy EUPM/10). Brussels, Belgium: Author.

European Union Co-ordinating Office for Palestinian Police Support. (2006). *European Union Co-ordinating Office for Palestinian Police Support (EU COPPS) and Palestinian Civil Police Development Programme 2005–2008: Fact sheet*. Ramallah, West Bank: European Union Co-ordinating Office for Palestinian Police Support.

European Union Co-ordinating Office for Palestinian Police Support. (2008, December 15). *EUPOL COPPS Present, past, and future*. Ramallah, West Bank: European Union Co-ordinating Office for Palestinian Police Support.

European Union Co-ordinating Office for Palestinian Police Support. (2009). *EUPOL COPPS and the Jericho Police Training School*. Ramallah, West Bank: European Union Co-ordinating Office for Palestinian Police Support, Ramallah.

European Union Co-ordinating Office for Palestinian Police Support. (2010). *Background (EUPOL COPPS)*. Retrieved from http://www.consilium.europa.eu/showpage.aspx?id=974&lang=en.

European Union Council Secretariat. (2003, December 8). *Termination of the EU-led military operation Concordia (fYROM): Launch of the EU police mission Proxima (fYROM)* (Press Briefing). Brussels, Belgium: European Union Council Secretariat.

European Union Council Secretariat. (2005a, October). *Darfur: Consolidated EU package in support of AMIS II* (Factsheet AMIS II/02). Brussels, Belgium: European Union Council Secretariat.

European Union Council Secretariat. (2005b, December). *EU police advisory team (EUPAT) in the former Yugoslav Republic of Macedonia* (Factsheet EUPAT/00). Brussels, Belgium: European Union Council Secretariat.

European Union Council Secretariat. (2005c, April 28). *The European Union's engagement towards stability and security in the Democratic Republic of Congo (DRC)* (Background RDC/000). Brussels, Belgium: European Union Council Secretariat.

European Union Council Secretariat. (2005d, May 23). *The European Union's engagement towards stability and security in the Democratic Republic of Congo (DRC)* (Background RDC/000). Brussels, Belgium: European Union Council Secretariat.

European Union Council Secretariat. (2006, March). *Darfur: Consolidated EU package in support of AMIS II* (Factsheet AMIS II/03). Brussels, Belgium: European Union Council Secretariat.

European Union Council Secretariat (2008, January) *EU support to the African Union Mission in Darfur: AMIS* (AMIS Factsheet, II/08).

European Union Police Mission for the DRC (2006, June) *DRC Elections 2006: EU Support for the DRC during the election process* (Background RDC/02/EN).

European Union Police Mission in Afghanistan. (2008, September 25). *EUPOL head of mission completes his tour of duty* (Press Release 4/2008). Kabul, Afghanistan: Author.

European Union Police Mission in Kinshasa (EUPOL). (2006, October). *The first European police mission in Africa* (Press Document). Retrieved from http://www.consilium.europa.eu/showpage.aspx?id=788&lang=en.

European Union Police Mission Proxima. (2003, December 15). *Fact sheet.* Retrieved from http://www.consilium.europa.eu/uedocs/cmsUpload/ProximaBrochure.pdf.

Fetherston, A. (1994). *Towards a theory of United Nations peacekeeping.* New York, NY: St. Martin's Press.

Franke, B. (2009). The European Union supporting actions to the African Union Missions in Sudan (AMIS) and Somalia (AMISOM). In G. Grevi, D. Helly, and D. Keohane (Eds.), *European security and defence policy: The first 10 years (1999–2009)* (pp. 255–264). Condé-sur-Noireau, France: European Union Institute for Security Studies.

Garland, D. (1996). The limits of the sovereign state: Strategies of crime control in contemporary society. *British Journal of Criminology, 36*(4), 445–471.

Geberwold, B. (2007). *Africa and fortress Europe: Threats and opportunities.* Aldershot, U.K.: Ashgate.

George, A. (1979). Case studies and theory development: The method of structured, focused comparison. In P. Lauren (Ed.), *Diplomacy: New approaches in history, theory, and policy* (pp. 43–68). New York, NY: Free Press.

Goldsmith, A. (2009). It wasn't like normal policing: Voices of Australian police peace-keepers in Operation Serene, Timor-Leste 2006. In P. Grabosky (Ed.), *Community policing and peacekeeping* (pp. 119–133). Boca Raton, FL: CRC Press.

Greener, B. (2009). *The new international policing.* Basingstoke, U.K.: Macmillan.

Grevi, G., Helly, D. and Keohane, D. (2009), *European security and defence policy: The first 10 years (1999–2009).* Condé-sur-Noireau, France: European Union Institute for Security Studies.

Griffiths, C., Dandurand, Y., and Chin, V. (2005) *Development assistance and police reform: Programming opportunities and lessons learned. Canadian Review of Policing Research,* 1. Retrieved from http://crpr.icaap.org/index.php/crpr/article/view/32/40.

Gunnar Billinger, N. (2002). Report of the Special Swedish Commission on International Police Activities. In R. Oakley, M. Dziedzic, and E. Goldberg (Eds.), *Policing the new world disorder: Peace operations and public security* (pp. 459–535). Washington, DC: National Defense University Press.

Harris, F. (2005). *The role of capacity-building in police reform.* Pristina, Kosovo: Department of Police Education and Development, Organisation for Security and Cooperation in Europe Mission in Kosovo.

Hendrickson, D., and Karkoszka, A. (2005). Security sector reform and donor policies. In A. Schnabel and H.-G. Ehrhard (Eds.), *Security sector reform and post-conflict peacebuilding* (pp. 19–44). Tokyo, Japan: United Nations Press.

Hills, A. (2009). *Policing post-conflict cities.* London: Zed Books.

Holm, T. T., and Eide, E. B. (2000). Introduction. In T. T. Holm and E. B. Eide (Eds.), *Peacebuilding and Police Reform* (pp. 1–8). London, U.K.: Frank Cass.

Ioannides, I. (2007). *The European Union and learning from support for post-conflict police reform: A critical analysis of Macedonia (2001–2005)* (Doctoral dissertation). University of Bradford, Bradford, U.K.

Ioannides, I. (2009). The EU Police Mission (EUPOL Proxima) and the European Union Police Advisory Team (EUPAT) in the former Yugoslav Republic of Macedonia. In G. Grevi, D. Helly, and D. Keohane (Eds.), *European security and defence policy: The first 10 years (1999–2009)* (pp. 187–199). Condé-sur-Noireau, France: European Union Institute for Security Studies.

Jakobsen, P. (2006). *Nordic approaches to peace operations: A new model in the making?* Abingdon, U.K.: Routledge.

Jett, D. (1999). *Why peacekeeping fails.* New York, NY: St. Martin's Press.

Jones, S., Wilson, J., Rathmell, A., and Riley, J. (2005). *Establishing law and order after conflict.* Santa Monica, CA: RAND.

Joulwan, G., and Schoonmaker, C. (1998). *Civilian-military cooperation in the prevention of deadly conflict: Implementing agreements in Bosnia and beyond.* New York, NY: Carnegie.

Lewis, W. (1994). Peacekeeping: Whither U.S. Policy? In D. Quinn (Ed.), *Peace support operations and the U.S. military* (p. 185). Washington, DC: National Defense University Press.

Lewis, W., and Marks, E. (1999). Overview. In J. Burack, W. Lewis, and E. Marks (Eds.), *Civilian police and multinational peacekeeping: A workshop series—A role for democratic policing* (pp. 1–2). Washington, DC: National Institute of Justice.

Linden, R., Last, D., and Murphy, C. (2007). Obstacles on the road to peace and justice: The role of civilian police in peacekeeping. In A. Goldsmith and J. Sheptycki (Eds.), *Crafting transnational policing: Police capacity-building and global policing reforms* (pp. 149–176). Portland, OR: Hart.

Mani, R. (2000). Contextualizing police reform: Security, the rule of law and post-conflict peacebuilding. In T. T. Holm and E. B. Eide (Eds.), *Peacebuilding and police reform* (pp. 9–26). Abingdon, U.K.: Frank Cass.

Marenin, O. (2005). Restoring policing systems in conflict torn nations: Process, problems, prospects (Occasional Paper 7). Geneva, Switzerland: Geneva Centre for Democratic Control of Armed Forces.

McFarlane, J., and Maley, W. (2001). Civilian police in UN peace operations: Some lessons from recent Australian experience. In R. Thakur and A. Schnabel (Eds.), *United Nations peacekeeping operations: Ad hoc missions, permanent engagement* (pp. 182–212). Tokyo, Japan: United Nations University.

McLeod, A. (2009). Police capacity development in the Pacific: The challenge of local context. *Policing and Society*, 19(2), 147–160.

Merlingen, M., and Ostrauskaite, R. (2006). *European Union peacebuilding and policing.* London, U.K.: Routledge.

Mobekk, E. (2002). Policing from below: Community policing as an objective in peace operations. In R. Dwan (Ed.), *Executive policing: Enforcing law in peace operations* (Stockholm International Peace Research Institute Research Report 16) (pp. 53–66). Oxford, U.K.: Oxford University Press.

Mobekk, E. (2005). *Identifying lessons in United Nations international policing missions* (Policy Paper 9). Geneva, Switzerland: Geneva Centre for Democratic Control of Armed Forces.

Morgan, P. (1998). *Capacity and capacity development.* Ottawa, Canada: Canadian International Development Agency.

Murtaugh, C. (2010). *United Nations peacekeeping mandates* (International Network to Promote the Rule of Law Consolidated Response 10-005). Retrieved from http://inprol.org/publications/united-nations-peacekeeping-mandates.

NationMaster.com (2011, February 8). *Average years of schooling of adults.* Retrieved from http://www.nationmaster.com/graph/edu_ave_yea_of_sch_of_adu-education-average-years-schooling-adults.

Neild, R. (2001). Democratic police reforms in war-torn societies. *Conflict, Security, and Development*, 1(1), 21–43.

Neild, R. (2002). *Sustaining reform: Democratic policing in Central America* (Citizen Security Monitor Briefing). Washington, DC: Washington Office on Latin America.

North Atlantic Treaty Organization (NATO). (2010a). *History of the NATO-led Stabilisation Force (SFOR) in Bosnia and Herzegovina.* Retrieved from http://www.nato.int/sfor/docu/d981116a.htm.

North Atlantic Treaty Organization (NATO). (2010b). *NATO's role in Kosovo.* Retrieved from http://www.nato.int/cps/en/natolive/topics_48818.htm.

North Atlantic Treaty Organization (NATO). (2010c). *NATO's role in relation to the conflict in Kosovo.* Retrieved from http://www.nato.int/kosovo/history.htm.

Oakley, R., Dziedzic, M., and Goldberg, E. (Eds). (1998). *Policing the new world's disorder: Peace operations and public security.* Washington, DC: National Defense University Press.

O'Neill, W. (2005). *Police reform in post-conflict societies: What we know and what we still need to know.* New York, NY: International Peace Academy.

Organisation for Economic Co-operation and Development. (2007). *DAC handbook on security system reform: Supporting security and justice.* Paris, France: OECD Publishing.

Palestine Ministry of Interior. (2008). *Palestinian civil police: Funding request.* Ramallah, West Bank: Author.

Peace Implementation Council. (2002, February 28). *Communiqué by the PIC Steering Board.* Brussels, Belgium: Author.

Pino, N., and Wiatrowski, M. (2006). *Democratic policing in transitional developing countries.* Aldershot, U.K.: Ashgate.

Ratner, S. (1995). *The new UN peacekeeping: Building peace in lands of conflict after the Cold War.* New York, NY: St. Martin's Press.

Rausch, C. (2002). The assumption of authority in Kosovo and East Timor: Legal and practical implications. In R. Dwan (Ed.), *Executive policing: Enforcing law in peace operations* (Stockholm International Peace Research Institute Research Report 16), (pp. 11–32). Oxford, U.K.: Oxford University Press.

Rogel, C. (2003). Kosovo: Where it all began. *International Journal of Politics, Culture, and Society*, 17(1), 167–182.

Scheye, E. (2002). Transitions to local authority. In R. Dwan (Ed.), *Executive policing: Enforcing law in peace operations* (Stockholm International Peace Research Institute Research Report 16), (pp. 102–123). Oxford, U.K.: Oxford University Press.

Schmidl, E. (1998). Police functions in peace operations: An historical overview. In R. Oakley, M. Dziedzic, and E. Goldberg (Eds.), *Policing the new world order: Peace operations and public security* (pp. 19–40). Washington, DC: National Defense University Press.

Schnabel, A., and Ehrhart, H.-G. (2005). Post-conflict societies and the military: Challenges and problems of security sector reform. In A. Schnabel and H.-G. Ehrhart (Eds.), *Security sector reform and post-conflict peacebuilding.* (pp. 1–16). Tokyo, Japan: United Nations Press.

Serbian Academy of Sciences and Arts (SANU). (1986, September 24). *Serbian Academy of Sciences and Arts Memorandum*. Belgrade: Author. Retrieved from http://www.trepca.net/english/2006/serbian_memorandum_1986/serbia_memorandum_1986.html.

Sherman, L., Gottfredson, D., MacKenzie, D., Eck, J., Reuter, P., and Bushway, S. (1998). *Preventing crime: What works, what doesn't, what's promising*. Washington, DC: National Institute of Justice.

Skogan, W., and Hartnett, S. (1997). *Community policing, Chicago style*. Oxford, U.K.: Oxford University Press.

Smith, J., Holt, V., and Durch, W. (2007). *Enhancing United Nations capacity to support post-conflict policing and rule of law* (Report 63). Washington, DC: Stimson Center.

Solana, J. (2002a, March 1). The EU after the United Nations' International Police Task Force IDTF: A good day for European integration. Retrieved from http://www.consilium.europa.eu/uedocs/cmsUpload/A%20good%20day%20for%20European%20integration.pdf.

Solana, J. (2002b, December 3). Letter from the high representative, Javier Solana, to Amnesty International. Retrieved from http://www.consilium.europa.eu/uedocs/cmsUpload/Letter%20HR%20Amnesty%20International.pdf.

Solana, J. (2003, January 15). Remarks by Javier Solana, EU high representative for the common foreign and security policy, at the opening ceremony of the EU Police Mission in Bosnia and Herzegovina (EUPM). Retrieved from http://www.consilium.europa.eu/uedocs/cmsUpload/opening%20ceremony.pdf.

South Eastern and Eastern Europe Clearinghouse for the Control of Small Arms and Light Weapons (SEESAC). (2003). *Philosophy and principles of community-based policing*. Belgrade, Serbia: South Eastern Europe Clearinghouse for the Control of Small Arms and Light Weapons.

Stromseth, J., Wippman, D., and Brooks, R. (2006). *Can might make rights? Building the rule of law after military interventions*. Washington, DC: Cambridge University Press.

Thomas, L., and Spataro, S. (2000). Peacekeeping and policing in Somalia. In R. Oakley, M. Dziedzic, and E. Goldberg (Eds.), *Policing the new world disorder: Peace operations and public security* (pp. 175–214). Washington, DC: National Defense University Press.

Tonry, M. (2007). Preface. In T. Tyler (Ed.), *Legitimacy and criminal justice: International perspectives* (pp. 3–8). New York, NY: Russell Sage Foundation.

United Nations. (1993). *Security Council Resolution 867* (S/RES/867). Retrieved from http://www.un.org/Docs/scres/1993/scres93.htm.

United Nations. (1994). *Security Council Resolution 940* (S/RES/940). Retrieved from http://www.un.org/Docs/scres/1994/scres94.htm.

United Nations. (1995a). *Security Council Resolution 1031* (S/RES/1031). Retrieved from http://www.un.org/Docs/scres/1995/scres95.htm.

United Nations. (1995b). *Security Council Resolution 1035* (S/RES/1035). Retrieved from http://www.un.org/Docs/scres/1995/scres95.htm.

United Nations. (1995c). *Security Council Resolution 975* (S/RES/975). Retrieved from http://www.un.org/Docs/scres/1995/scres95.htm.

United Nations. (1996a, March 29). *Report of the secretary-general pursuant to Resolution 1035* (S/1996/210). Retrieved from http://www.nato.int/ifor/un/u960329b.htm.

United Nations. (1996b, June 18). *Report of the secretary-general pursuant to Resolution 1035* (S/1996/460). Retrieved from http://www.nato.int/ifor/un/u960621a.htm.

United Nations. (1996c, December 9). *Report of the secretary-general pursuant to Resolution 1035* (S/1996/1017). Retrieved from http://www.nato.int/ifor/un/u961209a.htm.

United Nations. (1996d). *Security Council Resolution 1063* (S/RES/1063). Retrieved from http://www.un.org/Docs/scres/1996/scres96.htm.

United Nations. (1996e). *Security Council Resolution 1088* (S/RES/1088). Retrieved from http://www.un.org/Docs/scres/1996/scres96.htm.

United Nations. (1997a, June 16) *Report of the secretary-general on the United Nations mission in Bosnia and Herzegovina* (S/1997/468).

United Nations. (1997b, September 8). *Report of the secretary-general on the United Nations mission in Bosnia and Herzegovina* (S/1997/694).

United Nations. (1997c, November 20). *Addendum to report of the secretary-general on the United Nations transition mission in Haiti,* (S/1997/832/Add. 1).

United Nations. (1997d, December 10). *Report of the secretary-general on the United Nations mission in Bosnia and Herzegovina* (S/1997/966). Retrieved from http://www.nato.int/ifor/un/u971210a.htm.

United Nations. (1997e). *Security Council Resolution 1103* (S/RES/1103). Retrieved from http://www.un.org/Docs/scres/1997/scres97.htm.

United Nations. (1997f). *Security Council Resolution 1107* (S/RES/1107). Retrieved from http://www.un.org/Docs/scres/1997/scres97.htm.

United Nations. (1997g). *Security Council Resolution 1123* (S/RES/1123). Retrieved from http://www.un.org/Docs/scres/1997/scres97.htm.

United Nations. (1997h). *Security Council Resolution 1141* (S/RES/1141). Retrieved from http://www.un.org/Docs/scres/1997/scres97.htm.

United Nations. (1997i). *Security Council Resolution 1144* (S/RES/1144). Retrieved from http://www.un.org/Docs/scres/1997/scres97.htm.

United Nations. (1998a, February 20). *Report of the secretary-general on the United Nations civilian police mission in Haiti* (S/1998/144). Retrieved from http://www.un.org/Docs/sc/reports/1998/sgrep98.htm.

United Nations. (1998b, March 12). *Report of the secretary-general on the United Nations mission in Bosnia and Herzegovina* (S/1998/227). Retrieved from http://www.nato.int/ifor/un/1998/u980312a.htm.

United Nations. (1998c, March 17). *Fourth report of the secretary-general on the situation in Sierra Leone* (S/1998/249). Retrieved from http://www.un.org/Docs/sc/reports/1998/sgrep98.htm.

United Nations. (1998d, June 9). *Fifth report of the secretary-general on the situation in Sierra Leone* (S/1998/486). Retrieved from http://www.un.org/Docs/sc/reports/1998/sgrep98.htm.

United Nations. (1998e, June 10) *Report of the secretary-general on the United Nations mission in Bosnia and Herzegovina* (S/1998/491). Retrieved from http://www.un.org/Docs/sc/reports/1998/sgrep98.htm.

United Nations. (1998f, August 12). *First progress report of the secretary-general on the situation in Sierra Leone* (S/1998/750). Retrieved from http://www.un.org/Docs/sc/reports/1998/sgrep98.htm.

United Nations. (1998g, August 24). *Report of the secretary-general on the United Nations civilian police mission in Haiti* (S/1998/796). Retrieved from http://www.un.org/Docs/sc/reports/1998/sgrep98.htm.

United Nations. (1998h, September 16). *Report of the secretary-general on the United Nations mission in Bosnia and Herzegovina* (S/1998/862). Retrieved from http://www.un.org/Docs/sc/reports/1998/sgrep98.htm.

United Nations. (1998i, October 16). *Second progress report of the secretary-general on the situation in Sierra Leone* (S/1998/960). Retrieved from http://www.un.org/Docs/sc/reports/1998/sgrep98.htm.

United Nations. (1998j, November 11). *Report of the secretary-general on the United Nations civilian police mission in Haiti* (S/1998/1064). Retrieved from http://www.un.org/Docs/sc/reports/1998/sgrep98.htm.

United Nations. (1998k). *Security Council Resolution 1168* (S/RES/1168). Retrieved from http://www.un.org/Docs/scres/1998/scres98.htm.

United Nations. (1998l). *Security Council Resolution 1176* (S/RES/1176). Retrieved from http://www.un.org/Docs/scres/1998/scres98.htm.

United Nations. (1998m). *Security Council Resolution 1181* (S/RES/1181). Retrieved from http://www.un.org/Docs/scres/1998/scres98.htm.

United Nations. (1998n). *Security Council Resolution 1184* (S/RES/1184). Retrieved from http://www.un.org/Docs/scres/1998/scres98.htm.

United Nations. (1998o). *Security Council Resolution 1212* (S/RES/1212). Retrieved from http://www.un.org/Docs/scres/1998/scres98.htm.

United Nations. (1999a, February 19) *Report of the secretary-general on the United Nations civilian police mission in Haiti* (S/1999/181).

United Nations. (1999b, March 4). *Fifth report of the secretary-general on the United Nations observer mission in Sierra Leone* (S/1999/237). Retrieved from http://www.un.org/Docs/sc/reports/1999/sgrep99.htm.

United Nations. (1999c, June 4). *Sixth report of the secretary-general on the United Nations observer mission in Sierra Leone* (S/1999/645). Retrieved from http://www.un.org/Docs/sc/reports/1999/sgrep99.htm.

United Nations. (1999d, June 11). *Report of the secretary-general on the United Nations mission in Bosnia and Herzegovina* (S/1999/670). Retrieved from http://www.un.org/Docs/sc/reports/1999/sgrep99.htm.

United Nations. (1999e, July 12). *Report of the secretary-general on the United Nations interim administration mission in Kosovo* (S/1999/779). Retrieved from http://www.un.org/Docs/sc/reports/1999/sgrep99.htm.

United Nations. (1999f, September 16). *Report of the secretary-general on the United Nations interim administration mission in Kosovo* (S/1999/987). Retrieved from http://www.un.org/Docs/sc/reports/1999/sgrep99.htm.

United Nations. (1999g, September 17). *Report of the secretary-general on the United Nations mission in Bosnia and Herzegovina* (S/1999/989). Retrieved from http://www.un.org/Docs/sc/reports/1999/sgrep99.htm.

United Nations. (1999h). *Security Council Resolution 1244* (S/RES/1244). Retrieved from http://www.un.org/Docs/scres/1999/sc99.htm.

United Nations. (1999i). *Security Council Resolution 1246* (S/RES/1246). Retrieved from http://www.un.org/Docs/scres/1999/sc99.htm.

United Nations. (1999j). *Security Council Resolution 1250* (S/RES/1250). Retrieved from http://www.un.org/Docs/scres/1999/sc99.htm.

United Nations. (1999k). *Security Council Resolution 1257* (S/RES/1257). Retrieved from http://www.un.org/Docs/scres/1999/sc99.htm.

United Nations. (1999l). *Security Council Resolution 1260* (S/RES/1260). Retrieved from http://www.un.org/Docs/scres/1999/sc99.htm.

United Nations. (1999m). *Security Council Resolution 1262* (S/RES/1262). Retrieved from http://www.un.org/Docs/scres/1999/sc99.htm.

United Nations. (1999n). *Security Council Resolution 1264* (S/RES/1264). Retrieved from http://www.un.org/Docs/scres/1999/sc99.htm.

United Nations. (1999o). *Security Council Resolution 1270* (S/RES/1270). Retrieved from http://www.un.org/Docs/scres/1999/sc99.htm.

United Nations. (1999p). *Security Council Resolution 1272* (S/RES/1272). Retrieved from http://www.un.org/Docs/scres/1999/sc99.htm.

United Nations. (1999q). *Security Council Resolution 1279* (S/RES/1279). Retrieved from http://www.un.org/Docs/scres/1999/sc99.htm.

United Nations. (1999r). *Security Council Resolution 1291* (S/RES/1291). Retrieved from http://www.un.org/Docs/scres/1999/sc99.htm.

United Nations. (2000a, January 26). *Report of the secretary-general on the United Nations transitional administration in East Timor* (S/2000/53). Retrieved from http://www.un.org/Docs/sc/reports/2000/sgrep00.htm/.

United Nations. (2000b, March 3). *Report of the secretary-general on the United Nations interim administration mission in Kosovo* (S/2000/177). Retrieved from http://www.un.org/Docs/sc/reports/2000/sgrep00.htm/.

United Nations. (2000c, March 7). *Third report on the United Nations mission in Sierra Leone* (S/2000/186). Retrieved from http://www.un.org/Docs/sc/reports/2000/sgrep00.htm/.

United Nations. (2000d, June 6). *Report of the secretary-general on the United Nations interim administration mission in Kosovo* (S/2000/538). Retrieved from http://www.un.org/Docs/sc/reports/2000/sgrep00.htm/.

United Nations. (2000e, July 31). *Fifth report on the United Nations mission in Sierra Leone* (S/2000/751). Retrieved from http://www.un.org/Docs/sc/reports/2000/sgrep00.htm/.

United Nations. (2000f, August 24). *Sixth report on the United Nations mission in Sierra Leone* (S/2000/832). Retrieved from http://www.un.org/Docs/sc/reports/2000/sgrep00.htm/.

United Nations. (2000g, September 18). *Report of the secretary-general on the United Nations interim administration mission in Kosovo* (S/2000/878). Retrieved from http://www.un.org/Docs/sc/reports/2000/sgrep00.htm/.

United Nations. (2000h, October 31). *Seventh report on the United Nations mission in Sierra Leone* (S/2000/1055).

United Nations. (2000i, December 15). *Report of the secretary-general on the United Nations interim administration mission in Kosovo* (S/2000/1196). Retrieved from http://www.un.org/Docs/sc/reports/2000/sgrep00.htm/.

United Nations. (2000j). *Security Council Resolution 1289* (S/2000/1289). Retrieved from http://www.un.org/Docs/scres/2000/sc2000.htm.

United Nations. (2000k). *Security Council Resolution 1291* (S/2000/1291). Retrieved from http://www.un.org/Docs/scres/2000/sc2000.htm.

United Nations. (2001a, January 16). *Report of the secretary-general on the United Nations transitional administration in East Timor* (S/2001/42). Retrieved from http://www.un.org/Docs/sc/reports/2001/sgrep01.htm.

United Nations. (2001b, February 27). *Fourth quarterly report of the executive chairman of the United Nations Monitoring, Verification, and Inspection Commission under paragraph 12 of Security Council Resolution 1284 (1999)* (S/2001/177). Retrieved from http://www.un.org/Depts/unmovic/documents/S-2000-177.PDF.

United Nations. (2001c, March 14). *Ninth report on the United Nations mission in Sierra Leone* (S/2001/228). Retrieved from http://www.un.org/Docs/sc/reports/2001/sgrep01.htm.

United Nations. (2001d, June 7). *Report of the secretary-general on the United Nations interim administration mission in Kosovo* (S/2001/565). Retrieved from http://www.un.org/Docs/sc/reports/2001/sgrep01.htm.

United Nations. (2001e, June 7). *Report of the secretary-general on the United Nations mission in Bosnia and Herzegovina* (S/2001/571). Retrieved from http://www.un.org/Docs/sc/reports/2001/sgrep01.htm.

United Nations. (2001f, June 25). *Tenth report on the United Nations mission in Sierra Leone* (S/2001/627). Retrieved from http://www.un.org/Docs/sc/reports/2001/sgrep01.htm.

United Nations. (2001g, September 7). *Eleventh report on the United Nations mission in Sierra Leone* (S/2001/857). Retrieved from http://www.un.org/Docs/sc/reports/2001/sgrep01.htm.

United Nations. (2001h, October 18). *Report of the secretary-general on the United Nations transitional administration in East Timor* (S/2001/983). Retrieved from http://www.un.org/Docs/sc/reports/2001/sgrep01.htm.

United Nations. (2001i, November 29). *Report of the secretary-general on the United Nations mission in Bosnia and Herzegovina* (S/1999/1132). Retrieved from http://www.un.org/Docs/sc/reports/2001/sgrep01.htm.

United Nations. (2001j, December 13). *Twelfth report on the United Nations mission in Sierra Leone* (S/2001/1195). Retrieved from http://www.un.org/Docs/sc/reports/2001/sgrep01.htm.

United Nations. (2001k). *Security Council Resolution 1338* (S/RES/1338). Retrieved from http://www.un.org/Docs/scres/2001/sc2001.htm.

United Nations. (2001l). *Security Council Resolution 1346* (S/RES/1346). Retrieved from http://www.un.org/Docs/scres/2001/sc2001.htm.

United Nations. (2001m). *Security Council Resolution 1355* (S/RES/1355). Retrieved from http://www.un.org/Docs/scres/2001/sc2001.htm.

United Nations. (2001n). *Eighth report of the secretary-general on the United Nations organization mission in the Republic of the Congo.* Retrieved from http://www.un.org/Docs/sc/reports/2001/sgrep01.htm.

United Nations. (2002a, January 15). *Report of the secretary-general on the United Nations interim administration mission in Kosovo* (S/2002/62). Retrieved from http://www.un.org/Docs/sc/reports/2002/sgrep02.htm.

United Nations. (2002b, January 17). *Report of the secretary-general on the United Nations transitional administration in East Timor* (S/2002/80). Retrieved from http://www.un.org/Docs/sc/reports/2002/sgrep02.htm.

United Nations. (2002c, March 14). *Thirteenth report on the United Nations mission in Sierra Leone* (S/2002/267). Retrieved from http://www.un.org/Docs/sc/reports/2002/sgrep02.htm.

United Nations. (2002d, April 17). *Report of the secretary-general on the United Nations transitional administration in East Timor* (S/2002/432). Retrieved from http://www.un.org/Docs/sc/reports/2002/sgrep02.htm.

United Nations. (2002e, April 22). *Report of the secretary-general on the United Nations interim administration mission in Kosovo* (S/2002/436). Retrieved from http://www.un.org/Docs/sc/reports/2002/sgrep02.htm.

United Nations. (2002f, June 5). *Report of the secretary-general on the United Nations mission in Bosnia and Herzegovina* (S/2002/618). Retrieved from http://www.un.org/Docs/sc/reports/2002/sgrep02.htm.

United Nations. (2002g, June 19). *Fourteenth report on the United Nations mission in Sierra Leone* (S/2002/679). Retrieved from http://www.un.org/Docs/sc/reports/2002/sgrep02.htm.

United Nations. (2002h, September 5). *Fifteenth report on the United Nations mission in Sierra Leone* (S/2002/987). Retrieved from http://www.un.org/Docs/sc/reports/2002/sgrep02.htm.

United Nations. (2002i, September 10). *Special report of the secretary-general on the United Nations Organization mission in the Democratic Republic of the Congo* (S/2002/1005). Retrieved from http://www.un.org/Docs/sc/reports/2002/sgrep02.htm.

United Nations. (2002j, November 6). *Report of the secretary-general on the United Nations transitional administration in East Timor* (S/2002/1223). Retrieved from http://www.un.org/Docs/sc/reports/2002/sgrep02.htm.

United Nations. (2002k, December 2). *Report of the secretary-general on the United Nations mission in Bosnia and Herzegovina* (S/2002/1314). Retrieved from http://www.un.org/Docs/sc/reports/2002/sgrep02.htm.

United Nations. (2002l). *Security Council Resolution 1410* (S/RES/1410). Retrieved from http://www.un.org/Docs/scres/2002/sc2002.htm.

United Nations. (2002m). *Security Council Resolution 1417* (S/RES/1417). Retrieved from http://www.un.org/Docs/scres/2002/sc2002.htm.

United Nations. (2002n). *Security Council Resolution 1423* (S/RES/1423). Retrieved from http://www.un.org/Docs/scres/2002/sc2002.htm.

United Nations. (2002o). *Security Council Resolution 1436* (S/RES/1436). Retrieved from http://www.un.org/Docs/scres/2002/sc2002.htm.

United Nations. (2003a, March 3). *Special report of the secretary-general on the United Nations mission of support in East Timor* (S/2003/243). Retrieved from http://www.un.org/Docs/sc/sgrep03.html.

United Nations. (2003b, March 17). *Seventeenth report on the United Nations mission in Sierra Leone* (S/2003/321). Retrieved from http://www.un.org/Docs/sc/sgrep03.html.

United Nations. (2003c, September 11). *Report of the secretary-general to the Security Council on Liberia* (S/2003/875). Retrieved from http://www.un.org/Docs/sc/sgrep03.html.

United Nations. (2003d, April 3). *Letter dated 3 April 2003 from the permanent representative of the United Kingdom of Great Britain and Northern Ireland to the United Nations addressed to the president of the Security Council* (S/2003/379). Retrieved from http://www.laohamutuk.org/reports/UN/UNDocs/2003/S2003_379.pdf.

United Nations. (2003e, April 14). *Report of the secretary-general on the United Nations Interim Administration Mission in Kosovo* (S/2003/421). Retrieved from http://www.un.org/Docs/sc/sgrep03.html.

United Nations. (2003f, April 21). *Report of the secretary-general on the United Nations mission of support in East Timor* (S/2003/449). Retrieved from http://www.un.org/Docs/sc/sgrep03.html.

United Nations. (2003g, May 27). *Second special report of the secretary-general on the United Nations Organization mission in the Democratic Republic of the Congo* (S/2003/566). Retrieved from http://www.un.org/Docs/sc/sgrep03.html.

United Nations. (2003h, June 23). *Eighteenth report on the United Nations mission in Sierra Leone* (S/2003/663). Retrieved from http://www.un.org/Docs/sc/sgrep03.html.

United Nations. (2003i, September 5). *Nineteenth report on the United Nations mission in Sierra Leone* (S/2003/863). Retrieved from http://www.un.org/Docs/sc/sgrep03.html.

United Nations. (2003k, September 12). *Letter dated 12 September 2003 from the secretary-general addressed to the president of the Security Council* (S/2003/879). Retrieved from http://www.undemocracy.com/S-2003-879.

United Nations. (2003l, October 6). *Report of the secretary-general on the United Nations mission of support in East Timor* (S/2003/944). Retrieved from http://www.un.org/Docs/sc/sgrep03.html.

United Nations. (2003m, October 15). *Report of the secretary-general on the United Nations interim administration mission in Kosovo* (S/2003/996). Retrieved from http://www.un.org/Docs/sc/sgrep03.html.

United Nations. (2003n, December 15). *First progress report of the secretary-general on the United Nations mission in Liberia* (S/2003/1175). Retrieved from http://www.un.org/Docs/sc/sgrep03.html.

United Nations. (2003o, December 23). *Twentieth report on the United Nations mission in Sierra Leone* (S/2003/1201). Retrieved from http://www.un.org/Docs/sc/sgrep03.html.

United Nations. (2003p). *Security Council Resolution 1473* (S/RES/1473). Retrieved from http://www.un.org/Docs/sc/unsc_resolutions03.html.

United Nations. (2003q). *Security Council Resolution 1480* (S/RES/1480). Retrieved from http://www.un.org/Docs/sc/unsc_resolutions03.html.

United Nations. (2003r). *Security Council Resolution 1509* (S/RES/1509). Retrieved from http://www.un.org/Docs/sc/unsc_resolutions03.html.

United Nations. (2003s). *Security Council Resolution 1479* (S/RES/1479). Retrieved from http://www.un.org/Docs/sc/unsc_resolutions03.html.

United Nations. (2004a, January 6). *Report of the secretary-general on the United Nations mission in Côte d'Ivoire submitted pursuant to Security Council Resolution 1514* (S/2004/3). Retrieved from http://www.un.org/Docs/sc/sgrep04.html.

United Nations. (2004b, January 26). *Report of the secretary-general on the United Nations interim administration mission in Kosovo* (S/2004/71). Retrieved from http://www.un.org/Docs/sc/sgrep04.html.

United Nations. (2004c, February 13). *Special report of the secretary-general on the United Nations mission of support in East Timor* (S/2004/117). Retrieved from http://www.un.org/Docs/sc/sgrep04.html.

United Nations. (2004d, March 12) Letter from the representative of Belgium to the president of the Security Council (S/2004/201).

United Nations. (2004e). *Report of the secretary-general on Burundi* (S/2004/210). Retrieved from http://www.un.org/Docs/sc/sgrep04.html.

United Nations. (2004f, March 19). *Twenty-first report on the United Nations mission in Sierra Leone* (S/2004/228). Retrieved from http://www.un.org/Docs/sc/sgrep04.html.

United Nations. (2004g, March 22). *Second progress report of the secretary-general on the United Nations mission in Liberia* (S/2004/229). Retrieved from http://www.un.org/Docs/sc/sgrep04.html.

United Nations. (2004h, April 16). *Report of the secretary-general on Haiti* (S/2004/300). Retrieved from http://www.un.org/Docs/sc/sgrep04.html.

United Nations. (2004i, April 29). *Report of the secretary-general on the United Nations mission of support in East Timor* (S/2004/333). Retrieved from http://www.un.org/Docs/sc/sgrep04.html.

United Nations. (2004j, May 26). *Third progress report of the secretary-general on the United Nations mission in Liberia* (S/2004/430). Retrieved from http://www.un.org/Docs/sc/sgrep04.html.

United Nations. (2004k, June 2). *First report of the secretary-general on the United Nations operation in Côte d'Ivoire* (S/2004/443). Retrieved from http://www.un.org/Docs/sc/sgrep04.html.

United Nations. (2004l, July 6). *Twenty-second report on the United Nations mission in Sierra Leone* (S/2004/536). Retrieved from http://www.un.org/Docs/sc/sgrep04.html.

United Nations. (2004m, July 30). *Report of the secretary-general on the United Nations interim administration mission in Kosovo* (S/2004/613). Retrieved from http://www.un.org/Docs/sc/sgrep04.html.

United Nations. (2004n, August 16). *Third special report of the secretary-general on the United Nations Organization mission in the Democratic Republic of the Congo* (S/2004/650). Retrieved from http://www.un.org/Docs/sc/sgrep04.html.

United Nations. (2004o, August 25). *First report of the secretary-general on the United Nations operation in Burundi* (S/2004/682). Retrieved from http://www.un.org/Docs/sc/sgrep04.html.

United Nations. (2004p, August 27). *Second report of the secretary-general on the United Nations operation in Côte d'Ivoire* (S/2004/697). Retrieved from http://www.un.org/Docs/sc/sgrep04.html.

United Nations. (2004q, August 30). *Interim report of the secretary-general on the United Nations stabilization mission in Haiti* (S/2004/698). Retrieved from http://www.un.org/Docs/sc/sgrep04.html.

United Nations. (2004r, August 30). *Report of the secretary-general pursuant to paragraphs 6 and 13 to 16 of Security Council Resolution 1556* (S/2004/703). Retrieved from http://www.un.org/Docs/sc/sgrep04.html.

United Nations. (2004s, September 10). *Third progress report of the secretary-general on the United Nations mission in Liberia* (S/2004/725). Retrieved from http://www.un.org/Docs/sc/sgrep04.html

United Nations. (2004t, November 9). *Progress report of the secretary-general on the United Nations mission of support in East Timor* (for the period from 14 August to 9 November 2004) (S/2004/888). Retrieved from http://www.un.org/Docs/sc/sgrep04.html.

United Nations. (2004u, November 17). *Report of the secretary-general on the United Nations interim administration mission in Kosovo* (S/2004/907). Retrieved from http://www.un.org/Docs/sc/sgrep04.html.

United Nations. (2004v, November 18). *Report of the secretary-general on the United Nations stabilization mission in Haiti* (S/2004/908). Retrieved from http://www.un.org/Docs/sc/sgrep04.html.

United Nations. (2004w, December 10). *Twenty-fourth report on the United Nations mission in Sierra Leone* (S/2004/965). Retrieved from http://www.un.org/Docs/sc/sgrep04.html.

United Nations. (2004x, December 31). *Sixteenth report of the secretary-general on the United Nations Organization mission in the Democratic Republic of the Congo* (S/2004/1034). Retrieved from http://www.un.org/Docs/sc/sgrep04.html.

United Nations. (2004y). *Security Council Resolution 1528* (S/RES/1528). Retrieved from http://www.un.org/Docs/sc/unsc_resolutions04.html.

United Nations. (2004z). *Security Council Resolution 1537* (S/RES/1537). Retrieved from http://www.un.org/Docs/sc/unsc_resolutions04.html.

United Nations. (2004aa). *Security Council Resolution 1542* (S/RES/1542). Retrieved from http://www.un.org/Docs/sc/unsc_resolutions04.html.

United Nations. (2004ab). *Security Council Resolution 1543* (S/RES/1543). Retrieved from http://www.un.org/Docs/sc/unsc_resolutions04.html.

United Nations. (2004ac). *Security Council Resolution 1545* (S/RES/1545). Retrieved from http://www.un.org/Docs/sc/unsc_resolutions04.html.

United Nations. (2004ad). *Security Council Resolution 1547* (S/RES/1547). Retrieved from http://www.un.org/Docs/sc/unsc_resolutions04.html.

United Nations. (2004ae). *Security Council Resolution 1562* (S/RES/1562). Retrieved from http://www.un.org/Docs/sc/unsc_resolutions04.html.

United Nations. (2004af). *Security Council Resolution 1565* (S/RES/1565). Retrieved from http://www.un.org/Docs/sc/unsc_resolutions04.html.

United Nations. (2004ag). *Security Council Resolution 1529* (S/RES/1529). Retrieved from http://www.un.org/Docs/sc/unsc_resolutions04.html.

United Nations. (2004ah). *Security Council Resolution 1573* (S/RES/1573). Retrieved from http://www.un.org/Docs/sc/unsc_resolutions04.html.

United Nations. (2004ai). *Security Council Resolution 1556* (S/RES/1556). Retrieved from http://www.un.org/Docs/sc/unsc_resolutions04.html.

United Nations. (2005a, February 11). *Report of the secretary-general and high representative of the common foreign and security policy of the European Union on the activities of the European Union police mission in Bosnia and Herzegovina, covering the period from 1 July to 31 December 2004* (S/2005/66).

United Nations. (2005b, January 27). *Submission of a nomination by national groups* (S/2005/50). Retrieved from http://www.undemocracy.com/S-2005-50.

United Nations. (2005c, January 31). *Report of the secretary-general on the Sudan* (S/2005/57). Retrieved from http://www.un.org/Docs/sc/sgrep05.htm.

United Nations. (2005d, February 14). *Report of the secretary-general on the United Nations interim administration mission in Kosovo* (S/2005/88). Retrieved from http://www.un.org/Docs/sc/sgrep05.htm.

United Nations. (2005e, February 18). *Progress report of the secretary-general on the United Nations mission of support in East Timor* (for the period from 10 November 2004 to 16 February 2005) (S/2005/99). Retrieved from http://www.un.org/Docs/sc/sgrep05.htm.

United Nations. (2005f, February 25). *Report of the secretary-general on the United Nations stabilization mission in Haiti* (S/2005/124). Retrieved from http://www.un.org/Docs/sc/sgrep05.htm.

United Nations. (2005g, March 2). *Report of the secretary-general on inter-mission cooperation and possible cross-border operations between the United Nations mission in Sierra Leone, the United Nations mission in Liberia, and the United Nations operation in Côte d'Ivoire* (S/2005/135). Retrieved from http://www.un.org/Docs/sc/sgrep05.htm.

United Nations. (2005h, March 8). *Third report of the secretary-general on the United Nations operation in Burundi* (S/2005/149). Retrieved from http://www.un.org/Docs/sc/sgrep05.htm.

United Nations. (2005i, March 15). *Seventeenth report of the secretary-general on the United Nations Organization mission in the Democratic Republic of the Congo* (S/2005/167). Retrieved from http://www.un.org/Docs/sc/sgrep05.htm.

United Nations. (2005j, March 17). *Sixth progress report of the secretary-general on the United Nations mission in Liberia* (S/2005/177). Retrieved from http://www.un.org/Docs/sc/sgrep05.htm.

United Nations. (2005k, March 18). *Fourth progress report of the secretary-general on the United Nations operation in Côte d'Ivoire* (S/2005/186). Retrieved from http://www.un.org/Docs/sc/sgrep05.htm.

United Nations. (2005l, April 26). *Twenty-fifth report on the United Nations mission in Sierra Leone* (S/2005/273). Retrieved from http://www.un.org/Docs/sc/sgrep05.htm.

United Nations. (2005m, May 6). *Report of the Security Council mission to Haiti, 13 to 16 April 2005* (S/2005/302). Retrieved from http://www.undemocracy.com/S-2005-302.

United Nations. (2005n, May 13). *Report of the secretary-general on the United Nations stabilization mission in Haiti* (S/2005/313). Retrieved from http://www.un.org/Docs/sc/sgrep05.htm.

United Nations. (2005o, May 26). *Special report of the secretary-general on elections in the Democratic Republic of the Congo* (S/2005/320). Retrieved from http://www.un.org/Docs/sc/sgrep05.htm.

United Nations. (2005p, May 19). *Fourth report of the secretary-general on the United Nations operation in Burundi* (S/2005/328). Retrieved from http://www.un.org/Docs/sc/sgrep05.htm.

United Nations. (2005q, June 9). *Monthly report of the secretary-general on Darfur* (S/2005/378). Retrieved from http://www.un.org/Docs/sc/sgrep05.htm.

United Nations. (2005r, June 17). *Fifth progress report of the secretary-general on the United Nations operation in Côte d'Ivoire* (S/2005/398). Retrieved from http://www.un.org/Docs/sc/sgrep05.htm.

United Nations. (2005s, September 1). *Eighth progress report of the secretary-general on the United Nations mission in Liberia* (S/2005/560). Retrieved from http://www.un.org/Docs/sc/sgrep05.htm.

United Nations. (2005t, September 12). *Report of the secretary-general on the Sudan* (S/2005/579). Retrieved from http://www.un.org/Docs/sc/sgrep05.htm.

United Nations. (2005u, September 14). *Special report of the secretary-general on the United Nations operation in Burundi* (S/2005/586). Retrieved from http://www.un.org/Docs/sc/sgrep05.htm.

United Nations. (2005v, September 20). *Twenty-sixth report on the United Nations mission in Sierra Leone* (S/2005/596). Retrieved from http://www.un.org/Docs/sc/sgrep05.htm.

United Nations. (2005w, October 6). *Report of the secretary-general on the United Nations stabilization mission in Haiti* (S/2005/631). Retrieved from http://www.un.org/Docs/sc/sgrep05.htm.

United Nations. (2005x, November 21). *Fifth report of the secretary-general on the United Nations operation in Burundi* (S/2005/728). Retrieved from http://www.un.org/Docs/sc/sgrep05.htm.

United Nations. (2005y, December 12). *Twenty-seventh report on the United Nations mission in Sierra Leone* (S/2005/777). Retrieved from http://www.un.org/Docs/sc/sgrep05.htm.

United Nations. (2005z, December 21). *Report of the secretary-general on the Sudan* (S/2005/821). Retrieved from http://www.un.org/Docs/sc/sgrep05.htm.

United Nations. (2005aa). *Security Council Resolution 1590* (S/RES/1590). Retrieved from http://www.un.org/Docs/sc/unsc_resolutions05.htm.

United Nations. (2005ab). *Security Council Resolution 1599* (S/RES/1599). Retrieved from http://www.un.org/Docs/sc/unsc_resolutions05.htm.

United Nations. (2005ac). *Security Council Resolution 1608* (S/RES/1608). Retrieved from http://www.un.org/Docs/sc/unsc_resolutions05.htm.

United Nations. (2005ad). *Security Council Resolution 1609* (S/RES/1609). Retrieved from http://www.un.org/Docs/sc/unsc_resolutions05.htm.

United Nations. (2005ae). *Security Council Resolution 1620* (S/RES/1620). Retrieved from http://www.un.org/Docs/sc/unsc_resolutions05.htm.

United Nations. (2006a, January 3). *Seventh progress report of the secretary-general on the United Nations operation in Côte d'Ivoire* (S/2006/2). Retrieved from http://www.un.org/Docs/sc/sgrep06.htm.

United Nations. (2006b, January 25). *Report of the secretary-general on the United Nations interim administration mission in Kosovo* (S/2006/45). Retrieved from http://www.un.org/Docs/sc/sgrep06.htm.

United Nations. (2006c, January 30). *Monthly report of the secretary-general on Darfur* (S/2006/59). Retrieved from http://www.un.org/Docs/sc/sgrep06.htm.

United Nations. (2006d, February 2). *Report of the secretary-general on the United Nations stabilization mission in Haiti* (S/2006/60). Retrieved from http://www.un.org/Docs/sc/sgrep06.htm.

United Nations. (2006e, March 14). *Tenth progress report of the secretary-general on the United Nations mission in Liberia* (S/2006/159). Retrieved from http://www.un.org/Docs/sc/sgrep06.htm.

United Nations. (2006f, March 14). *Report of the secretary-general on the Sudan* (S/2006/160). Retrieved from http://www.un.org/Docs/sc/sgrep06.htm.

United Nations. (2006g, March 14). *Sixth report of the secretary-general on the United Nations operation in Burundi* (S/2006/163). Retrieved from http://www.un.org/Docs/sc/sgrep06.htm.

United Nations. (2006h, April 11). *Seventh progress report of the secretary-general on the United Nations operation in Côte d'Ivoire* (S/2006/222). Retrieved from http://www.un.org/Docs/sc/sgrep06.htm.

United Nations. (2006i, April 20). *End of mandate report of the secretary-general on the United Nations Office in Timor-Leste* (for the period from 14 January to 12 April 2006) (S/2006/251). Retrieved from http://www.un.org/Docs/sc/sgrep06.htm.

United Nations. (2006j, June 5). *Report of the secretary-general on the United Nations interim administration mission in Kosovo* (S/2006/361). Retrieved from http://www.un.org/Docs/sc/sgrep06.htm.

United Nations. (2006k, June 9). *Eleventh progress report of the secretary-general on the United Nations mission in Liberia* (S/2006/376). Retrieved from http://www.un.org/Docs/sc/sgrep06.htm.

United Nations. (2006l, June 13). *Letter dated 13 June 2006 from the secretary-general addressed to the president of the Security Council* (S/2006/383). Retrieved from http://www.undemocracy.com/S-2006-383.

United Nations. (2006m, June 13). *Twenty-first report of the secretary-general on the United Nations organization mission in the Democratic Republic of the Congo* (S/2006/390). Retrieved from http://www.un.org/Docs/sc/sgrep06.htm.

United Nations. (2006n, June 21). *Sixth report of the secretary-general on the United Nations operation in Burundi* (S/2006/429). Retrieved from http://www.un.org/Docs/sc/sgrep06.htm.

United Nations. (2006o, July 17). *Seventh progress report of the secretary-general on the United Nations operation in Côte d'Ivoire* (S/2006/532). Retrieved from http://www.un.org/Docs/sc/sgrep06.htm.

United Nations. (2006p, July 28). *Report of the secretary-general on Darfur* (S/2006/591). Retrieved from http://www.un.org/Docs/sc/sgrep06.htm.

United Nations. (2006q, July 28). *Report of the secretary-general on the United Nations stabilization mission in Haiti* (S/2006/592). Retrieved from http://www.un.org/Docs/sc/sgrep06.htm.

United Nations. (2006r, August 8). *Report of the secretary-general on Timor-Leste pursuant to Security Council Resolution 1690* (S/2006/628). Retrieved from http://www.un.org/Docs/sc/sgrep06.htm.

United Nations. (2006s, September 12). *Report of the secretary-general on the Sudan* (S/2006/728). Retrieved from http://www.un.org/Docs/sc/sgrep06.htm.

United Nations. (2006t, September 12). *Twelfth progress report of the secretary-general on the United Nations mission in Liberia* (S/2006/743). Retrieved from http://www.un.org/Docs/sc/sgrep06.htm.

United Nations. (2006u, September 21). *Twenty-first report of the secretary-general on the United Nations organization mission in the Democratic Republic of the Congo* (S/2006/759). Retrieved from http://www.un.org/Docs/sc/sgrep06.htm.

United Nations. (2006v, September 28). *Letter dated 28 September 2006 from the secretary-general addressed to the president of the Security Council* (S/2006/779). Retrieved from http://www.undemocracy.com/S-2006-779.

United Nations. (2006w, October 17). *Tenth progress report of the secretary-general on the United Nations operation in Côte d'Ivoire* (S/2006/821). Retrieved from http://www.un.org/Docs/sc/sgrep06.htm.

United Nations. (2006x, October 25). *Eighth report of the secretary-general on the United Nations operation in Burundi* (S/2006/842). Retrieved from http://www.un.org/Docs/sc/sgrep06.htm.

United Nations. (2006y, November 20). *Report of the secretary-general on the United Nations interim administration mission in Kosovo* (S/2006/906). Retrieved from http://www.un.org/Docs/sc/sgrep06.htm.

United Nations. (2006z, December 18). *Ninth report of the secretary-general on the United Nations operation in Burundi* (S/2006/994). Retrieved from http://www.un.org/Docs/sc/sgrep06.htm.

United Nations. (2006aa, December 19). *Report of the secretary-general on the United Nations stabilization mission in Haiti* (S/2006/1003). Retrieved from http://www.un.org/Docs/sc/sgrep06.htm.

United Nations. (2006ab). *Security Council Resolution 1694* (S/RES/1694). Retrieved from http://www.un.org/Docs/sc/unsc_resolutions06.htm.

United Nations. (2006ac). *Security Council Resolution 1704* (S/RES/1704). Retrieved from http://www.un.org/Docs/sc/unsc_resolutions06.htm.

United Nations. (2006ad). *Security Council Resolution 1706* (S/RES/1706). Retrieved from http://www.un.org/Docs/sc/unsc_resolutions06.htm.

United Nations. (2006ae). *Security Council Resolution 1709* (S/RES/1709). Retrieved from http://www.un.org/Docs/sc/unsc_resolutions06.htm.

United Nations. (2006af). *Security Council Resolution 1719* (S/RES/1719). Retrieved from http://www.un.org/Docs/sc/unsc_resolutions06.htm.

United Nations. (2006ag). *Security Council Resolution 1721* (S/RES/1721). Retrieved from http://www.un.org/Docs/sc/unsc_resolutions06.htm.

United Nations. (2007a, January 25). *Report of the secretary-general on the Sudan* (S/2007/42). Retrieved from http://www.un.org/Docs/sc/sgrep07.htm.

United Nations. (2007b, February 1). *Report of the secretary-general on the United Nations integrated mission in Timor-Leste* (for the period from 9 August 2006 to 26 January 2007) (S/2007/50). Retrieved from http://www.un.org/Docs/sc/sgrep07.htm.

United Nations. (2007c, February 23). *Monthly report of the secretary-general on Darfur* (S/2007/104). Retrieved from http://www.un.org/Docs/sc/sgrep07.htm.

United Nations. (2007d, March 9). *Report of the secretary-general on the United Nations interim administration mission in Kosovo* (S/2007/134). Retrieved from http://www.un.org/Docs/sc/sgrep07.htm.

United Nations. (2007e, March 15). *Fourteenth progress report of the secretary-general on the United Nations mission in Liberia* (S/2007/151). Retrieved from http://www.un.org/Docs/sc/sgrep07.htm.

United Nations. (2007f, April 13). *Report of the secretary-general on the Sudan* (S/2007/213). Retrieved from http://www.un.org/Docs/sc/sgrep07.htm.

United Nations. (2007g, May 14). *Thirteenth progress report of the secretary-general on the United Nations operation in Côte d'Ivoire* (S/2007/275). Retrieved from http://www.un.org/Docs/sc/sgrep07.htm.

United Nations. (2007h, June 5). *Letter dated 5 June 2007 from the secretary-general to the president of the Security Council* (Report of the secretary-general and the chairperson of the African Union Commission on the hybrid operation in Darfur) (S/2007/307/Rev. 1). Retrieved from http://www.un.org/Docs/sc/unsc_presandsg_letters07.htm.

United Nations. (2007i, June 29). *Report of the secretary-general on the United Nations interim administration mission in Kosovo* (S/2007/395). Retrieved from http://www.un.org/Docs/sc/sgrep07.htm.

United Nations. (2007j, August 8). *Fifteenth progress report of the secretary-general on the United Nations mission in Liberia* (S/2007/479). Retrieved from http://www.un.org/Docs/sc/sgrep07.htm.

United Nations. (2007k, August 20). *Report of the secretary-general on the Sudan* (S/2007/500). Retrieved from http://www.un.org/Docs/sc/sgrep07.htm.

United Nations. (2007l, August 22). *Report of the secretary-general on the United Nations stabilization mission in Haiti* (S/2007/503). Retrieved from http://www.un.org/Docs/sc/sgrep07.htm.

United Nations. (2007m, August 28). *Report of the secretary-general on the United Nations integrated mission in Timor-Leste* (for the period from 27 January to 20 August 2007) (S/2007/513). Retrieved from http://www.un.org/Docs/sc/sgrep07.htm.

United Nations. (2007n, August 30). *Report of the secretary-general on the deployment of the African Union–United Nations hybrid operation in Darfur* (S/2007/517). Retrieved from http://www.un.org/Docs/sc/sgrep07.htm.

United Nations. (2007o, October 1). *Fourteenth progress report of the secretary-general on the United Nations operation in Côte d'Ivoire* (S/2007/593). Retrieved from http://www.un.org/Docs/sc/sgrep07.htm.

United Nations. (2007p, October 8). *Report of the secretary-general on the deployment of the African Union–United Nations hybrid operation in Darfur* (S/2007/596). Retrieved from http://www.un.org/Docs/sc/sgrep07.htm.

United Nations. (2007q, November 14). *Twenty-fourth report of the secretary-general on the United Nations organization mission in the Democratic Republic of the Congo* (S/2007/671). Retrieved from http://www.un.org/Docs/sc/sgrep07.htm.

United Nations. (2007r, December 24). *Report of the secretary-general on the deployment of the African Union–United Nations hybrid operation in Darfur* (S/2007/759). Retrieved from http://www.un.org/Docs/sc/sgrep07.htm.

United Nations. (2007s). *Report of the secretary-general on the United Nations interim administration mission in Kosovo* (S/2007/768). Retrieved from http://www.un.org/Docs/sc/sgrep07.htm.

United Nations. (2007t). *Security Council Resolution 1745* (S/RES/1745). Retrieved from http://www.un.org/Docs/sc/unsc_resolutions07.htm.

United Nations. (2007u). *Security Council Resolution 1756* (S/RES/1756). Retrieved from http://www.un.org/Docs/sc/unsc_resolutions07.htm.

United Nations. (2007v). *Security Council Resolution 1769* (S/RES/1769). Retrieved from http://www.un.org/Docs/sc/unsc_resolutions07.htm.

United Nations. (2007w). *Security Council Resolution 1780* (S/RES/1780). Retrieved from http://www.un.org/Docs/sc/unsc_resolutions07.htm.

United Nations. (2008a, January 17). *Report of the secretary-general on the United Nations integrated mission in Timor-Leste* (for the period from 21 August 2007 to 7 January 2008) (S/2008/26). Retrieved from http://www.un.org/Docs/sc/sgrep08.htm.

United Nations. (2008b, January 3). *Report of the secretary-general on the United Nations interim administration mission in Kosovo* (S/2008/98). Retrieved from http://www.un.org/Docs/sc/sgrep08.htm.

United Nations. (2008c, March 19). *Sixteenth progress report of the secretary-general on the United Nations mission in Liberia* (S/2007/183). Retrieved from http://www.un.org/Docs/sc/sgrep08.htm.

United Nations. (2008d, March 26). *Report of the secretary-general on the United Nations stabilization mission in Haiti* (S/2008/202). Retrieved from http://www.un.org/Docs/sc/sgrep08.htm.

United Nations. (2008e, April 2). *Twenty-fifth report of the secretary-general on the United Nations organization mission in the Democratic Republic of the Congo* (S/2008/218). Retrieved from http://www.un.org/Docs/sc/sgrep08.htm.

United Nations. (2008f, April 14). *Report of the secretary-general on the deployment of the African Union–United Nations hybrid operation in Darfur* (S/2008/249). Retrieved from http://www.un.org/Docs/sc/sgrep08.htm.

United Nations. (2008g, May 9). *Report of the secretary-general on the deployment of the African Union–United Nations hybrid operation in Darfur* (S/2008/304). Retrieved from http://www.un.org/Docs/sc/sgrep08.htm.

United Nations. (2008h, June 12). *Report of the secretary-general on the United Nations interim administration mission in Kosovo* (S/2008/354). Retrieved from http://www.un.org/Docs/sc/sgrep08.htm.

United Nations. (2008i, July 29). *Report of the secretary-general on the United Nations integrated mission in Timor-Leste* (for the period from 8 January to 8 July 2008) (S/2008/501). Retrieved from http://www.un.org/Docs/sc/sgrep08.htm.

United Nations. (2008j, July 31). *Letter dated 30 July 2008 from the president of the Security Council addressed to the secretary-general* (International Tribunal for the Prosecution of Persons Responsible for Serious Violations of International Humanitarian Law Committed in the Territory of the Former Yugoslavia since 1991) (S/2008/508). Retrieved from http://www.un.org/Docs/sc/unsc_presandsg_letters08.htm.

United Nations. (2008k, August 15). *Sixteenth progress report of the secretary-general on the United Nations mission in Liberia* (S/2008/553). Retrieved from http://www.un.org/Docs/sc/sgrep08.htm.

United Nations. (2008l, August 18). *Report of the secretary-general on the deployment of the African Union–United Nations hybrid operation in Darfur* (S/2008/558). Retrieved from http://www.un.org/Docs/sc/sgrep08.htm.

United Nations. (2008m, October 17). *Report of the secretary-general on the deployment of the African Union–United Nations hybrid operation in Darfur* (S/2008/659). Retrieved from http://www.un.org/Docs/sc/sgrep08.htm.

United Nations. (2008n, October 20). *Report of the secretary-general on the Sudan* (S/2008/662). Retrieved from http://www.un.org/Docs/sc/sgrep08.htm.

United Nations. (2008o, December 12). *Report of the secretary-general on the deployment of the African Union–United Nations hybrid operation in Darfur* (S/2008/781). Retrieved from http://www.un.org/Docs/sc/sgrep08.htm.

United Nations. (2008p). *Security Council Resolution 1802* (S/RES/1802). Retrieved from http://www.un.org/Docs/sc/unsc_resolutions08.htm.

United Nations. (2008q). *Security Council Resolution 1856* (S/RES/1856). Retrieved from http://www.un.org/Docs/sc/unsc_resolutions08.htm.

United Nations. (2008r). *United Nations Interim Administration Mission in Kosovo (UNMIK): Kosovo in June 2008.* Retrieved from http://www.un.org/en/peacekeeping/missions/unmik/mandate.shtm.

United Nations. (2009a, February 4). *Report of the secretary-general on the United Nations integrated mission in Timor-Leste* (for the period from 9 July to 20 January 2008) (S/2009/72). Retrieved from http://www.un.org/Docs/sc/sgrep09.htm.

United Nations. (2009b, February 10). *Eighteenth progress report of the secretary-general on the United Nations mission in Liberia* (S/2009/86). Retrieved from http://www.un.org/Docs/sc/sgrep09.htm.

United Nations. (2009c, March 6). *Report of the secretary-general on the United Nations stabilization mission in Haiti* (S/2009/129). Retrieved from http://www.un.org/Docs/sc/sgrep09.htm

United Nations. (2009d, April 3). *Report of the Security Council mission to Haiti* (11 to 14 March 2009) (S/2009/175). Retrieved from http://www.un.org/Docs/sc/missionreports.html.

United Nations. (2009e, April 13). *Twentieth progress report of the secretary-general on the United Nations operation in Côte d'Ivoire* (S/2009/196). Retrieved from http://www.un.org/Docs/sc/sgrep09.htm.

United Nations. (2009f, April 14). *Report of the secretary-general on the deployment of the African Union–United Nations hybrid operation in Darfur* (S/2009/201). Retrieved from http://www.un.org/Docs/sc/sgrep09.htm.

United Nations. (2009g, July 14). *Report of the secretary-general on the United Nations mission in Sudan* (S/2009/357). Retrieved from http://www.un.org/Docs/sc/sgrep09.htm.

United Nations. (2009h, September 1). *Report of the secretary-general on the United Nations stabilization mission in Haiti* (S/2009/439). Retrieved from http://www.un.org/Docs/sc/sgrep09.htm.

United Nations. (2009i, October 2). *Report of the secretary-general on the United Nations Integrated Mission in Timor-Leste* (for the period from 21 January to 23 September 2009) (S/2009/504). Retrieved from http://www.un.org/Docs/sc/sgrep09.htm.

United Nations. (2009j, October 21). *Report of the secretary-general on the United Nations mission in Sudan* (S/2009/545). Retrieved from http://www.un.org/Docs/sc/sgrep09.htm.

United Nations. (2009k, November 16). *Report of the secretary-general on the African Union–United Nations hybrid operation in Darfur* (S/2009/592). Retrieved from http://www.un.org/Docs/sc/sgrep09.htm.

United Nations. (2009l). *Haiti: Mandat.* Retrieved from http://www.un.org/en/peacekeeping/missions/past/unmihmandate.html.

United Nations. (2009m). *United Nations Organisation mission in the Democratic Republic of Congo* (2009) briefing materials. New York, NY: Public Information Division.

United Nations. (2009n). *United Nations transition mission in Haiti.* Retrieved from http://www.un.org/en/peacekeeping/missions/past/untmih.htm.

United Nations. (2009o). *United Nations civilian police mission in Haiti.* Retrieved from http://www.un.org/en/peacekeeping/missions/past/miponuh.htm.

United Nations. (2010a). *Background.* Retrieved from http://www.un.org/en/peacekeeping/missions/past/unmibh/background.html.

United Nations. (2010b). *Côte d'Ivoire: MINUCI—Background.* Retrieved from http://www.un.org/en/peacekeeping/missions/past/minuci/background.html.

United Nations. (2010c). *East Timor: UNMISET—Mandate.* Retrieved from http://www.un.org/en/peacekeeping/missions/past/unmiset/mandate.html.

United Nations. (2010d). *MINUSTAH—Background.* Retrieved from http://www.un.org/en/peacekeeping/missions/minustah/background.shtml.

United Nations. (2010e). *MONUC—Mandate.* Retrieved from http://www.un.org/en/peacekeeping/missions/monuc/mandate.shtml.

United Nations. (2010f, April 5). *Report of the secretary-general on the United Nations mission in Sudan* (S/2010/168). Retrieved from http://www.un.org/Docs/sc/sgrep10.htm.

United Nations. (2010g). *Sierra Leone: UNAMSIL—Background.* Retrieved from http://www.un.org/en/peacekeeping/missions/past/unamsil/background.html.

United Nations. (2010h). *Sierra Leone: UNOMSIL—Background.* Retrieved from http://www.un.org/Depts/DPKO/Missions/unomsil/UnomsilB.htm.

United Nations. (2010i). *UNMIT—Background.* Retrieved from http://www.un.org/en/peacekeeping/missions/unmit/background.shtml.

United Nations. (2010j). *United Nations Interim Administration Mission in Kosovo* (UNMIK). Retrieved from http://www.un.org/peace/kosovo/pages/kosovo12.htm.

United Nations. (2010k). *United Nations Operations in Burundi.* Retrieved from http://www.un.org/en/peacekeeping/missions/past/onub/.

United Nations. (2010l). *UNMIK—Background.* Retrieved from http://www.un.org/peace/kosovo/pages/unmik12.html.

United Nations. (2010m). *UNMIL—Background.* Retrieved from http://www.un.org/en/peacekeeping/missions/unmil/background.shtml.

United Nations. (2010n). *UNMIS—Background.* Retrieved from http://www.un.org/en/peacekeeping/missions/unmis/background.shtml.

United Nations. (2010o). *UNTAET—Background.* Retrieved from http://www.un.org/en/peacekeeping/missions/past/etimor/UntaetM.htm.

United Nations. (2010p). *History of United Nations police.* Retrieved from http://www.un.org/en/peacekeeping/sites/police/history.shtml.

United Nations. (2010q). *Security Council Resolution 1925 (S/RES/1925).* Retrieved from http://www.un.org/Docs/sc/unsc_resolutions10.htm.

United Nations. (2010r). *Security Council Resolution 1916 (S/RES/1916).* Retrieved from http://www.un.org/Docs/sc/unsc_resolutions10.htm.

United Nations Development Programme. (1997). *Capacity development: Technical advisory paper 2.* New York, NY: Management Development and Governance Division, United Nations.

United Nations Mission in Liberia. (2010). *History.* Retrieved from http://unmil.unmissions.org/.

United Nations Peacekeeping Best Practices Section. (2008). *United Nations peacekeeping operations: Principles and guidelines.* New York, NY: Author.

United Nations Security Council. (2001, June 8). *Eighth report of the secretary-general on the United Nations Organization mission in the Democratic Republic of the Congo (S/2001/572).* Retrieved from http://www.undemocracy.com/S-2001-572.

United Nations Security Council. (2003, May 7). *Second special report of the secretary-general on the United Nations Organization mission in the Democratic Republic of the Congo (S/2003/566).* Retrieved from http://www.un.org/Docs/sc/sgrep03.html.

University of Texas Libraries, The University of Texas at Austin. Maps for 13 Countries. Retrieved from http://www.lib.utexas.edu/maps/.

Vircoulon, T. (2009). EUPOL Kinshasa and EUPOL RD Congo. In G. Grevi, D. Helly, and D. Keohane (Eds.), *European security and defence policy: The first 10 years (1999–2009)* (pp. 221–230). Condé-sur-Noireau, France: European Union Institute for Security Studies.

Wiatrowski, M., and Pino, N. (2008). *Policing and intermediate forces during democratic transitions.* Unpublished manuscript. San Marcos, TX: Texas State University–San Marcos.

Wing, K. (2004). Assessing the effectiveness of capacity-building initiatives: Seven issues for the field. *Nonprofit and Voluntary Sector Quarterly, 33*(1), 153–160.

Wulf, D. (2000). *Security sector reform in developing countries: An analysis of the international debate and potentials for implementing reforms and recommendations for technical cooperation.* Bonn, Germany: Deutsche Gesellschaft für Technische Zusammenarbeit.

About the Author

Garth den Heyer, DPubPol, has served with the New Zealand Police for more than 30 years. He holds the rank of inspector and is manager of the National Security Unit.

Dr. den Heyer has extensive experience in police and security sector reform in postconflict nations, including the Solomon Islands; Timor-Leste; Bougainville, Papua New Guinea; and Afghanistan. He has been deployed on a number of occasions for lengthy periods as part of the Regional Assistance Mission to the Solomon Islands, where he advised both the international police deployment and the local police.

In addition to being a senior research fellow at the Police Foundation in Washington, DC, he is a lecturer at Charles Sturt University in Manly, Australia. He holds a master's in science from the University of London; a master's in security and intelligence from Victoria University, Wellington, New Zealand; and a doctorate in public policy from Charles Sturt University.

www.ingramcontent.com/pod-product-compliance
Lightning Source LLC
Chambersburg PA
CBHW081653270326
41933CB00017B/3159